Proceedings of the First European Conference on

TeX FOR SCIENTIFIC DOCUMENTATION

16–17 May 1985, Como, Italy

Edited by
Dario Lucarella
Istituto di Cibernetica
Università degli Studi di Milano, Italy

Addison-Wesley Publishing Company

Reading, Massachusetts • Menlo Park, California
Don Mills, Ontario • Wokingham, England • Amsterdam
Sydney • Singapore • Tokyo • Mexico City • Bogotá
Santiago • San Juan

T$_E$X is a trademark of the American Mathematical Society.

This document was reproduced by Addison-Wesley from camera-ready copy supplied by the authors.

Copyright © 1985 by Addison-Wesley Publishing Company, Inc.

All rights reserved. No part of this publication may be reproduced, stored in a retrieval system, or transmitted, in any form or by any means, electronic, mechanical, photocopying, recording or otherwise, without the prior written permission of the publisher. Printed in the United States of America. Published simultaneously in Canada.

ISBN 0-201-13399-7
ABCDEFGHIJ-AL-898765

Contents

Organizing Committees	1
Preface	3
Typesetting by Authors A. Keller	5
S.D.D.S. : Scientific Document Delivery System G. Canzii, G. Degli Antoni, S. Mussi, G. Rosci	19
Adapting TeX to non-english languages that use latin alphabetic chars S. Romberger, Y. Sundblad	31
The use of TeX in french: hyphenation and typography J. Désarménien	45
The hyphenation of non-english words with TeX W. Appelt	65
TeX and ISO/STPL standard H. Le Van	71
Towards an interactive math mode in TeX J. Andrè, Y. Grundt, V. Quint	83
TeX formulae dictionary D. Lucarella	97
STRATEC and a rationalized keyboard for inputting TeX D. Foata, J. Pansiot, Y. Roy	109
An interactive user-friendly TeX in VM/CMS environment M. Agostini, V. Matano, M. Schaerf, M. Vascotto	121
TeX on riad computers J.S. Bien, H. Kolodziejska	137
Experiments in teaching METAFONT J. André, R. Southall	145
Generalized algorithm for drawing non-parametric splines S. Leitch, F.J. Smith	159

GENERATION OF SOME CHINESE CHARACTERS WITH METAFONT 165
J. Li

IMPLEMENTATION OF METAFONT ON ICL PERQ 175
S. Leitch

THE ROLE OF DEVICE INDEPENDENT OUTPUT 187
I.A. Utting

A LOW COST LASER BEAM PRINTER CONTROLLER 195
L. Cerofolini

GENDRIV A DRIVER GENERATOR FOR LOW COST DEVICES USING BUILT-IN FONTS 201
K. Guntermann

Organizing Committees

Sponsoring Institutions:

CILEA (*Lombard Univ. Consortium for Data Processing*)
CNR (*Italian National Research Council*)
FAST (*Federation of Scientific and Technical Associations*)
Mondadori S.p.A. (*Publishing House*)
UMI (*Italian Mathematical Society*)
Università degli Studi di Milano. Istituto di Cibernetica

Program Committee Members:

S. Bien	Univ. Warsaw (Poland)
L. Cerofolini	Univ. Bologna (Italy)
G. Degli Antoni	Univ. Milano (Italy)
B. Gaulle	CIRCE/CNRS (France)
D.E. Knuth	Stanford University(USA)
B. Løfstedt	RECAU Aarhus (Denmark)
B. Schulze	Univ. Bonn(W. Germany)
C. Vernimb	CEE (Luxemburg)
I. Zabala	Univ. Valencia (Spain)

Organizing Commitee Members:

G.Canzii	Te.Co.Graf.
R. Goucher	American Mathematical Society(USA)
F. Migiarra	Mondadori S.p.A.(Milano)

Conference Chairman:

D. Lucarella   Univ. Milano (Italy)

Preface

This volume collects the papers presented at the European Conference "*TEX for Scientific Documentation*" held at Villa Olmo, Como in May '85. TEX, Trade Mark of the American Mathematical Society, is the well known composition system developed at the Stanford University by Prof. D.E. Knuth.

The aim of the Conference was to provide a state-of-the-art survey of current research activities and the latest applications that are growing around TEX.

The topics covered in the selected papers concern the following fields: Documentation Systems based on TEX, TEX as a tool for the authors, Personalization of TEX for non English languages, Hyphenation, Standardization problems, Facilities for interactive entering and retrieving formulae, METAFONT and font design, Implementation of TEX, METAFONT and Drivers.

This list highlights the central role of the subject and its ability to influence research in related fields of Text Processing and Electronic Publishing.

To acknowledge all contributions to the conference is impossible. I would like to express many thanks to the Sponsoring Institutions, to the Members of Program and Organizing Committees and particularly to Ray Goucher who has actively cooperated in U. S. as well as in Italy in the plain success of the Conference.

Thanks are due to Prof. D.E. Knuth for his agreement on the Conference. During all the sessions we felt his presence through the TEX running in Villa Olmo.

Finally, special thanks are due to Prof. G.Degli Antoni who understood very early the great impact of TEX in the Scientific Communication.

June 1985   D. Lucarella

Typesetting by Authors

Arthur M. Keller
Computer Science Dept.
Stanford University
Stanford, CA 94305, USA

Abstract

We consider some issues of typesetting by authors, especially using the TEX system. There can be differences in how papers are developed or written, and even more so for books. While this approach can significantly improve the preparation of material, it can require additional effort. Especially for books, the author performing his own typesetting should enlist the assistance of a competent designer. The use of TEX offers not only the potential for producing material of the highest quality, but also the possibility of producing unreadable or unæsthetic documents. Elegant typesetting is not a substitute for clear, refined prose.

The preparation of this report was supported in part by the National Science Foundation under grants IST-8201926 and MCS-8300984, and by the System Development Foundation.

TEX for Scientific Documentation   D. Lucarella, Editor
Copyright ©1985 Addison-Wesley Publishing Company, Inc.

1 Overview

Typesetting by authors using TeX has many advantages as well as some disadvantages. Some of these advantages also arise from using a word processor. Additional advantages result from computerized typesetting. There are additional benefits of using TeX. Using TeX yourself entails improvements to book production. Some of these improvements carry over to typesetting your own papers. There are also disadvantages to typesetting your own books and papers. The linkage between TeX and the typesetter affects the use of TeX for preparation of camera-ready copy material. Finally, case histories of books typeset by their authors illustrate the power of TeX.

2 Advantages

TeX shares some of its advantages with word processors. Since the material is developed online, it is easier to modify and refine it. Since changes are that much easier to make, more revision cycles can be performed in a short time period.

Users of TeX also benefit since it is a computerized typesetting system. Most systems allow the inexpensive generation of proof copies which can be reproduced in small quantities for review or for class testing. It is not necessary to rekeyboard the manuscript when it was typed on a word processor and will be typeset on a computerized system. This avoids the numerous errors that rekeyboarding introduces. This reduces the effort of proofreading the galley proofs and correcting these errors. The result is a faster production cycle.

Major advantages are available from using TeX. TeX is output-device independent, as device drivers have been written for a variety of devices producing inexpensive proof copies. Through the use of DVI format, these proof copies can match the format of the final book. TeX facilitates higher quality output. It produces mathematics whose quality matches the highest standards of hand composition. Its hyphenation algorithm is very efficient in time and space utilization and has been used for languages other than English. Breaking paragraphs into lines is done through a dynamic programming technique that efficiently finds an optimal solution for the given constraints. Finally, since TeX is now frozen, there will not be any further changes to TeX that will require modifications to existing documents.

Particularly effective use of TeX can be made by authors typesetting their own books. As an author, it is particularly satisfying to know that when a change is made in the TeX source file, it will appear in the next output run. This is instant gratification. With traditional composition, it is necessary to verify all changes made to the manuscript to ensure that they are incorporated into the typeset version by the publisher. Since the authors have control of the preparation of camera-ready copy, they can incorporate changes into the manuscript to print corrected pages for subsequent printings. Larger scale corrections can be made for subsequent editions.

The use of TEX allows authors to typeset and publish books that would otherwise not be commercially feasible, such as *Mathematics for the Analysis of Algorithms* (Boston: Birkhäuser, 1981) by Daniel H. Greene and Donald E. Knuth.

Authors using TEX themselves can take greater advantage of TEX's flexibility. This permits more effective use of the medium. The form can be harnessed to make the content more accessible. Typefaces can be used for special purposes. For example, the monospace `typewriter font` is often used to represent computer input or output. Layout can also be used effectively. I used a flexible book design in my book, *A First Course in Computer Programming Using Pascal* (New York: McGraw-Hill, 1982), so that program fragments could be broken on pages in semantically appropriate places.

3 TEX and book production

The traditional process of book production involves a series of steps. After all or part of the book is written, the author contacts publishers. The publisher arranges for reviews of the content of the book, both to assist the publisher in making the decision to publish the book and to help the author improve the book after it is accepted. The publisher also arranges for copyediting the manuscript to improve grammar and diction and to detect some errors. The book is then typeset. The author receives galley proofs, which contains the text of the manuscript without figures and before it is divided into pages. The author makes corrections, returns the galley proofs to the publisher, and eventually receives page proofs. These have the manuscript broken into the final pages with space for figures, perhaps with artwork proofs added. The author uses the page proofs to prepare the index. In parallel with the other steps of book production, the artwork is prepared by the publisher based on the specifications of the author. When all this is put together, the book can be printed and bound. The publisher then arranges for marketing and distribution of the book. Hopefully, the book sells, the author gets royalties, and the author is asked to write another edition.

We have already considered the effects of using TEX on writing the book. To recapitulate, the manuscript is easier to modify and refine, the author can print inexpensive proof copies when needed, and mathematics can be coded reasonably in the manuscript.

When contacting publishers, TEX allows the author to distribute proof copy of several polished chapters. The proof copy can look like part of a book. The author can offer to typeset the book to reduce costs and accelerate the production cycle.

The authors can easily print the latest version of the manuscript for content reviews. When changes are suggested, the author can rewrite parts as needed.

TEX can be set to produce double-spaced output for copyediting the manuscript. Since the author incorporates the corrections in the manuscript, he essentially can approve them or change them as appropriate.

Using TEX allows the author to do the typesetting incrementally while writing and refining the manuscript. When it is time to prepare typeset copy, it could merely be a matter of running the final version on the phototypesetter.

Preparing the index is one of the most tedious processes in the preparation of a book. In traditional typesetting, the index entries are gleaned from the page proofs, and then sorted to produce the index. This adds several weeks to the production cycle of a book. With TEX, the author can mark items to be indexed where they are mentioned in the manuscript when it is being written. When the book is typeset, TEX can write a file containing the terms to be indexed and the page numbers on which they appear. With a little more effort, the index can be typeset, in as little as a week after the rest of the book instead of a month later. When subsequent editions are produced, index preparation is that much easier: there is no need to start from the beginning again with the page proofs.

Artwork is an important problem in book production. Some simple line drawings can be typeset using LaTEX, a macro package for TEX. TEX page makeup facilities can be used to do layout by leaving space for artwork to be pasted in. TEX is powerful enough to handle a combination of floating or fixed illustrations. Legends and lettering for artwork can be typeset using TEX and pasted on the artwork.

4 Typesetting papers

There are also advantages to having authors typeset their own papers using TEX. The drafts of papers look like the final form. Mathematical formulæ are always readable in the draft printings. When the paper is published, its appearance is much improved over typewritten output. TEX gives the authors more control over the length of the paper. Major changes can be made to the manuscript, even at the last minute, without incurring high costs.

5 Disadvantages of typesetting your own books

Of course, there also are disadvantages of having the authors do their own typesetting. The authors take on additional responsibilities, which may distract from completing the writing. The authors may not be capable of making all the necessary æsthetic decisions. This problem is ameliorated by having the authors consult a competent designer. Herb Caswell did the design of *The TEXbook* (Reading, Massachusetts: Addison-Wesley, 1984) by Donald E. Knuth. Marshall Hendricks is doing the design of *The LaTEX Manual* (Reading, Massachusetts: Addison-Wesley, in preparation) by Leslie Lamport. I did the design of my own Pascal book, but adapted the designs of existing books to my own purposes. It is also necessary to get an editor who understands the differences involved in author-generated camera-ready copy. It is still necessary to do content reviewing and copyediting of the manuscript. Another potential problem is that authors must be able to run TEX and get proof output. Now that TEX can run on the IBM PC/XT and can produce proof output on such inexpensive devices as the Epson and Okidata, TEX is now easily available to the scientific community. Authors must also have access to a high quality output device, such as a phototypesetter, for producing camera-ready copy. There are already some service bureaus in the United States which provide this service.

With a system as flexible as TEX, it is important to consider the æsthetics of typesetting. Although it is possible to produce the most beautifully typeset documents with TEX, I have seen quite a few documents produced with little regard for æsthetics. Conventions that work well on a typewriter may not extend to typeset work. For example, in the United States we often use 8.5 × 11 inch paper. With the default one inch margins, TEX will give you a 6.5 inch line which is about 39 picas or 16.5 cm. Computer Modern in ten point roman, the default font, has about 15 characters to the inch. This puts almost 100 characters on a line. Not only does this not look very nice, but it is rather hard to read. In last year's course entitled "First Principles of Typographic Design for Document Production," Richard Southall reported that about 65 characters was the maximum legible line length. Incidentally, the English edition of my book appears in an 8.5 × 11 inch trim size, with wide margins. The line width is 30 picas for 65 characters per line. Of course, these are only a few points about document design. A competent designer is aware of many other æsthetic considerations.

6 Disadvantages of typesetting your own papers

There are also disadvantages of typesetting your own papers. The authors may expand more effort because they are also concerned with the appearance of the paper. The authors may spend too much time fine tuning the format at the expense of not sufficiently refining the content. It is important to remember that a beautifully typeset document may appear more polished than it is.

7 Linkage between TEX and typesetter

Some understanding of the linkage between TEX and the output device is important in considering problems such as using fonts that exist on the typesetter but not the proof printer. The TEX font metrics (TFM) contain all the information TEX has about the dimensions of each character in each font and the ligatures and other parameters of each font. The concept of device independent format (DVI) assumes that the desired fonts appear on all the output devices on which the document will be printed. The output device driver converts from DVI format to the language understood by the output device. The actual shape of the character on the font rasters is contained in the generic font (GF) file when created by METAFONT. Particular

How to typeset "the METAFONT logo"

Example 1 Normal output

How to typeset "the   logo"

Example 2 Missing font omitted

How to typeset "the ⊕)∩∫⊔⊗⊗∩

Example 3 Missing font substituted by printer

How to typeset "the METAFONT logo"

Example 4 Missing font substituted in TEX input

How to typeset "the METAFONTlogo"

Example 5 Missing font rasters replaced explicitly

devices may use custom formats of these fonts, such as OC, ANT, AMF, PXL, and FNT formats.

When presented with a request to print characters in an unavailable font, output devices behave in various manners. Example 1 illustrates a sample of text as it should appear. This is to be compared with the examples of output obtained when some fonts are missing. Arthur Samuel's new driver for the IMAGEN 8/300 printer written in WEB will print an error message and omit these characters. Using the TFM files, this driver will determine the desired dimensions of the omitted characters, so that the other characters can be positioned correctly. This approach works satisfactorily for individual special characters, but not when the main text font is missing. See example 2. The Xerox Dover experimental printer will substitute another font, sometimes the best alternative but often the wrong one. See example 3.

The approach of a text processor such as Scribe is to format the document specifically for the device you are printing the document on. This works fine for checking the contents. But since the document will be reformatted for the final output device, it cannot be used to check the formatting. You can have TEX use this approach by specifying that it is to use the fonts available on the proof device. See example 4. Notice the word "logo" is moved to the left compared with the other examples. When it is time to check the formatting, it is important to use the correct metrics for the fonts on the final output device, but it may not be necessary to use the right fonts. In this case, the correct TFM files are used but the output device is explicitly told to use specific substituted font rasters. Peculiar effects will occur at absolute positioning locations, such as after spaces separating words. See example 5.

8   Case histories

We will consider some case histories of books typeset by their authors. When typesetting his Ph.D. thesis, "Mechanisms for broadcast and selective broadcast," Stanford Computer Science Report STAN-CS-82-919 = Stanford Computer Systems Laboratory Technical Report 190 (June 1980), David Wall generated his diagrams with METAFONT, with each diagram as one character in some special font. It was then no problem to incorporate these diagrams into the text using TEX, superimposing lettering as necessary. Some extracts of Dr. Wall's thesis appear in example 6. They are reduced to 77% of the original.

We are trying to show that the graph G_S has no cycles. There is one easy way we might produce a cycle: if a pair of vertices appears on the paths for two of the edges in the tree, and if there are two routes of equal cost between these two vertices, we could pick a different route in each case. The first two lemmas show that nothing this simple will produce a cycle as long as we are using a consistent tie-breaking rule, because we would have to pick the same route both times. As a result, we can only form a cycle from bits and pieces of several paths.

We observe that x precedes y on this path p. For if $x = y$ then this single vertex is on both path q_1 and path q_2, which are represented by edges without a common endpoint. This violates Lemma 4. Similarly, if x follows y then y is on the portion of path p from m to x and so by Lemma 2 it must also be on the portion of path q_1 from m to x. Thus y is on both q_1 and q_2, which again contradicts Lemma 4. So x precedes y.

One Way to Make a Cycle

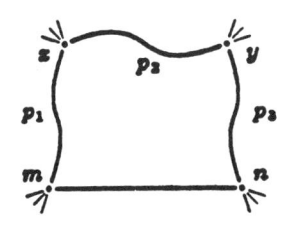

Replacing $\{m, n\}$ with p

Example 6   Unusual use of METAFONT

Richard E. Pattis wrote and typeset *KAREL the ROBOT: A Gentle Introduction to the Art of Programming* (New York: Wiley, 1981). This book teaches a programming language especially designed to be easy to learn. To illustrate the syntax of the language, Mr. Pattis typeset contour diagrams, and one is illustrated in example 7. Karel is a robot who inhabits a rectilinear grid of streets with barriers that block his path and beepers he can pick up and put down. The book is full of diagrams that illustrate this world. Mr. Pattis METAFONTed special symbols to represent the robot and beepers with David Wall's help. The other parts of these worlds are composed of horizontal and vertical rules. This book was produced using the old version of TeX on the Alphatype. One of these diagrams is reproduced in example 8.

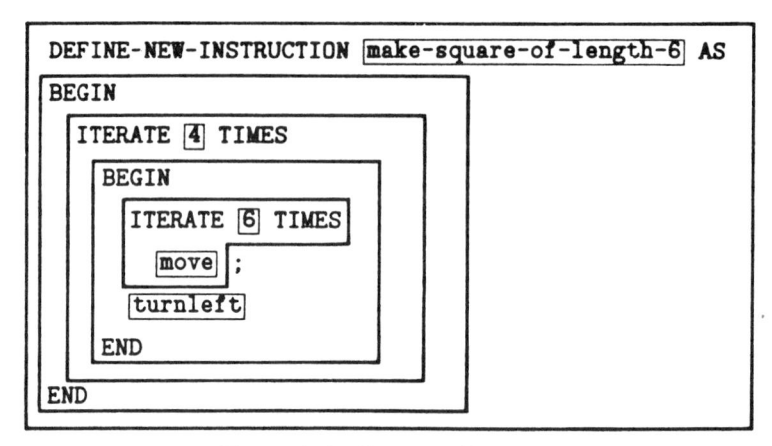

```
DEFINE-NEW-INSTRUCTION  make-square-of-length-6   AS
BEGIN
    ITERATE  4  TIMES
    BEGIN
        ITERATE  6  TIMES
            move  ;
        turnleft
    END
END
```

Example 7 Contour diagram

Scott Kim used TeX to typeset the prose of his book, *Inversions: A Catalog of Calligraphic Cartwheels* (Peterborough, New Hampshire: Byte Books, 1981). He used a non-Metafont typeface, Optima, on Stanford's Alphatype phototypesetter. This book contains numerous illustrations of a unique form of artwork: designs made out of words. These are done by drawing the words using somewhat distorted but still recognizable letters. Some of these read the same rightside up as upside down, others read one thing rightside up and another upside down, still others read one thing in black and another in interstices between the letters. The prose consisted mainly of explanatory material and was done using non-METAFONT typefaces. An example is given in example 9.

Another example is *Mathematics for the Analysis of Algorithms* (Boston: Birkhäuser, 1981) by Daniel H. Greene and Donald E. Knuth. Dr. Knuth reports that this book would not have been commercially feasible were it not typeset by Dr. Greene, largely due to its heavy use of mathematics, illustrated in example 10.

I typeset my own book, *A First Course in Computer Programming Using Pascal* (New York: McGraw-Hill, 1982), using TeX. Since I had direct access to the Alphatype phototypesetter at Stanford, I was able to speed up the process considerably. For example, within a five day period, I completed the last appendices of my Pascal book, sent them from California to New York for copyediting, received the edited manuscript, corrected my online version, produced the camera-ready copy and sent it to the publisher. Such a short length of time from author rough copy to camera-ready copy is unusual for books, but would be too long for newspapers and magazines, which

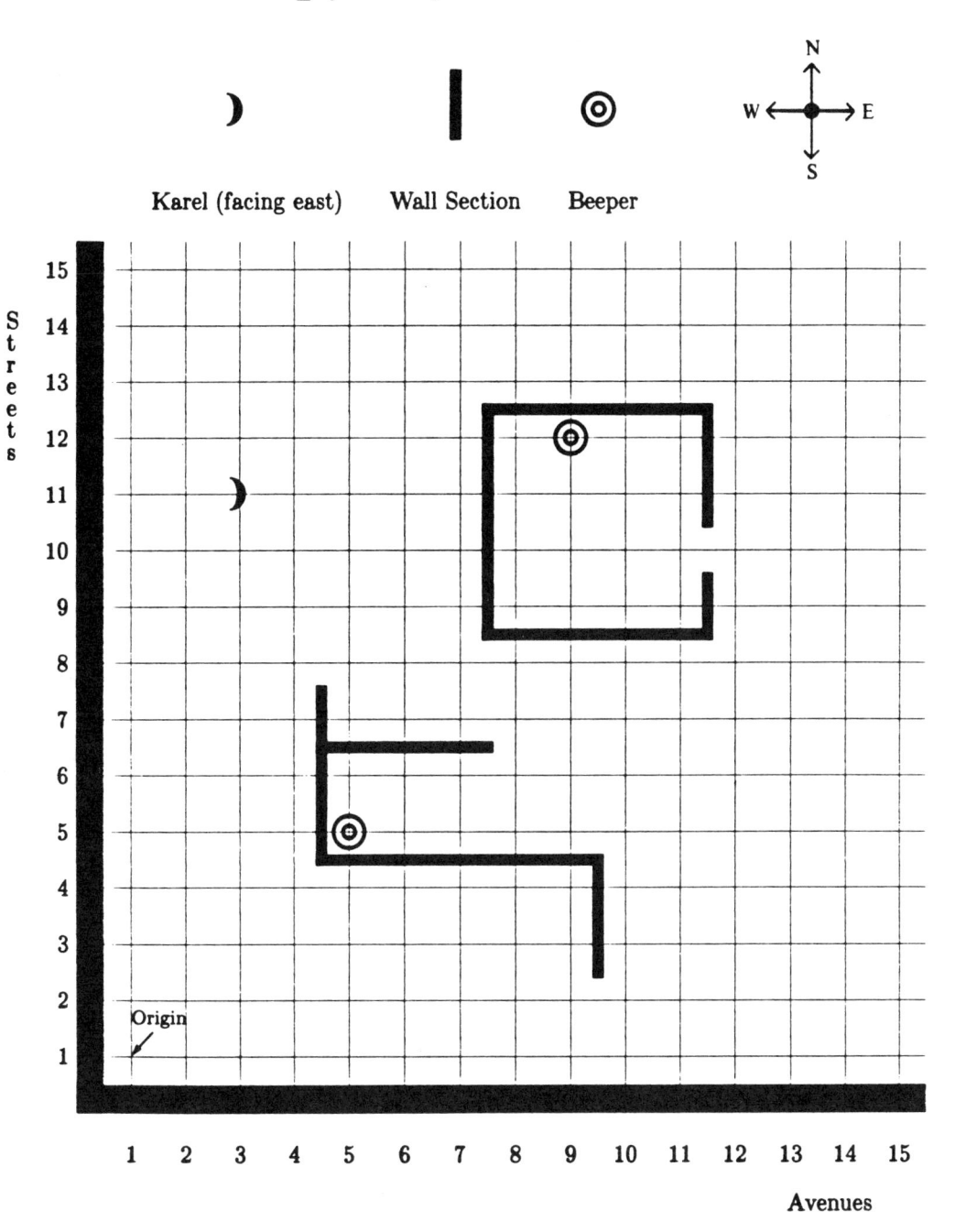

Example 8 Karel's world

→ *Hofstadter* ←

Actually, I dislike the mixing of an uppercase "r" with lowercase letters, but it was the best I could do.

Among my earliest efforts was the company name "Chemway", which I chanced across in a newspaper. Somehow, it flashed into my mind that here was a word that lent itself beautifully to upside-down play, as follows:

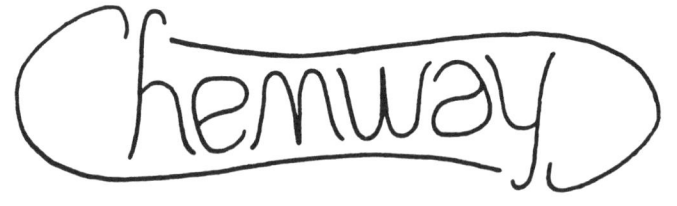

Chemway

Example 9 Non-METAFONT font Optima used with TEX

use custom typesetting systems. Manually drawn artwork in my book had lettering generated by TEX. I separately produced double-size lettering that was added to the artwork. This is illustrated in example 11. Using quarter circles in the old TEX and METAFONT manual font, Michael Plass created macros for typesetting syntax diagrams which was adapted by Jim Boyce for use in my book. An excerpt of the syntax diagram for Pascal is given in example 12.

The first edition (1977) of Gio Wiederhold's book, *Database Design* (New York: McGraw-Hill) was done using a conventional process while the second edition (1983) was typeset in a prototype version of TEX by the author. The third edition will also be typeset by the author in the current version of TEX. Table 1 describes this process.

Table 1 Preparation Schedule, Gio Wiederhold, *Database Design*

Edition Year	first '77	second '83	third ?
How typeset	Traditional	TEX78	TEX82
Writing	5 years	1 year	6 months
Learning TEX or typesetting	1 month	6 months	1 month
Galley proofs and editing	9 months	2 months	?
Production	6 months	2 months	?

Choosing x_n equal to the falling factorial $(n-1)^{\underline{s}}$ makes the sum in equation (2.34) easy to compute:

$$(n-1)^{\underline{s}} = a_n + \frac{12}{n^{\underline{3}}} \sum_{1<k<n} (n-k)(k-1)^{\underline{s+1}}$$

$$= a_n + \frac{12(s+1)!}{n^{\underline{3}}} \sum_{1<k<n} \binom{n-k}{1}\binom{k-1}{s+1} \qquad (2.35)$$

$$= a_n + \frac{12(s+1)!}{n^{\underline{3}}} \binom{n}{s+3};$$

$$a_n = (n-1)^{\underline{s}} - \frac{12}{(s+2)(s+3)}(n-3)^{\underline{s}}. \qquad (2.36)$$

Now we have a family of solutions parameterized by s.

	x_n	a_n
$s = 0$	1	-1
$s = 1$	$(n-1)$	2
$s = 2$	$(n-1)(n-2)$	$\dfrac{2n^2 + 6n - 26}{5}$

Example 10 Examples of mathematical formulæ

There are some things that are possible when typesetting your own work that are not otherwise possible. Because of the long paragraph indentation in *The TEXbook* (Reading, Massachusetts: Addison-Wesley, 1984), it does not look good when the last line of a paragraph is too short. Because Dr. Knuth was typesetting his own book, he was able to rewrite such paragraphs to lengthen this line or eliminate it altogether. The diagram illustrates this problem. Example 13 shows a paragraph with a short line followed by a normal paragraph. Example 14 shows when the last line is lengthened by rewriting the material. Example 15 shows when the last line is removed by decreasing the length of the text, also by rewriting. Dr. Knuth reports that this did improve not only the appearance of the book, but also the presentation as he improved the wording on each iteration.

9 Conclusion

TEX can improve the quality of books and papers, especially when used by the authors. However, the authors must expend more effort, as they are now also concerned with the typesetting. The authors must also beware of traps such as improving the formatting instead of improving the content and failing to get a competent

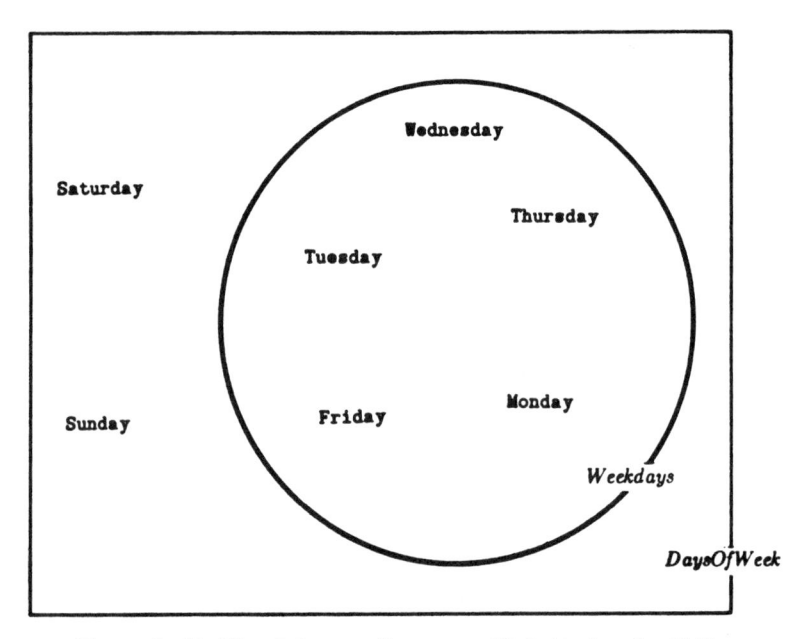

Example 11 Hand-drawn diagram with lettering by TeX

designer, content reviewer, and copyeditor. Because of TeX, we will see more and more books typeset by their authors.

10 Acknowledgements

I would like to thank Dave Fuchs, Don Knuth, Dario Lucarella, Peter Rathmann, Richard Southall, and Gio Wiederhold for their assistance.

The original copy of this paper was produced on an IMAGEN 8/300 printer using TeX and the am series of Computer Modern fonts designed by Dr. Knuth.

11 Bibliography

The Chicago Manual of Style, 13th edition, Chicago: University of Chicago Press, 1982.

Gibaldi, J., and Achtert, W.S., *MLA Handbook for Writers of Research Papers, Theses, and Dissertations*, student edition, New York: Modern Language Association, 1980.

Hartley, J., *Designing Instructional Text*, New York; Nichols, 1978.

Judd, K., *Copyediting: A Practical Guide*, Los Altos, California: William Kaufmann, 1982.

Knuth, D.E., *The TeXbook*, Reading, Massachusetts: Addison-Wesley, 1984.

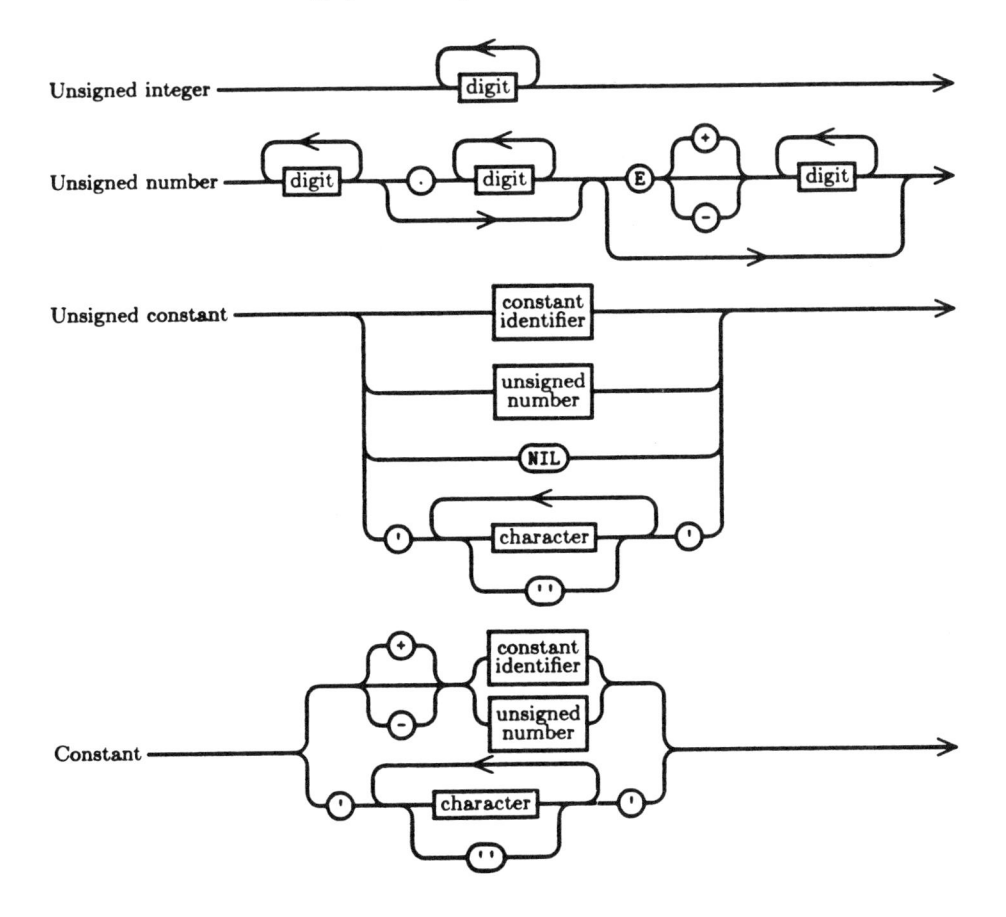

Example 12 Syntax diagrams for Pascal

Knuth, D.E., "TEX incunabula," in *TUGboat*, 5:1, Providence, RI: TEX Users Group, May 1984.

Lamport, L., *LaTeX Manual*, Reading, Massachusetts: Addison-Wesley, in preparation.

McSherry, J.E., *Computer Typesetting, A Guide for Authors, Editors, and Publishers*, Arlington, Virginia: Open-Door, 1984.

Skillin, M.E., Gay, R.M., et al., *Words into Type*, Englewood Cliffs: New Jersey: Prentice-Hall, 1974.

Southall, R., "First principles of typographic design for document production," in *TUGboat*, 5:2, Providence, RI: TEX Users Group, November 1984.

Strunk, W., and White, E.B., *The Elements of Style*, third edition, New York: Macmillan, 1979.

Example 13 Short last line of paragraph

Example 14 Paragraph rewritten to lengthen last line

Example 15 Paragraph rewritten to remove last line

Swanson, E., *Mathematics into Type*, Providence, RI: American Mathematical Society, 1979.

van Leunen, M.C., *A Handbook for Scholars*, New York: Alfred A. Knopf, 1979.

SDDS: Scientific Document Delivery System

G. Canzii [1]

G. Degli Antoni [2]

S. Mussi [3]

G. Rosci [4]

ABSTRACT

This paper presents the SDDS project and the forecasted exploitations in the Italian Scenario. The major objectives of SDDS are examined and the role of TEX is emphasized. A functional view of SDDS is presented describing each functional block that composes the system. Attention is paid to the input functions, where a special purpose package (Easy TEX) has been designed to simplify keying of documents, and to the full text data base, that includes all the functions needed by the users for electronic reading, retrieving, ordering and delivering documents.

Introduction

The SDDS project is carried out by Arnoldo Mondadori Editore S.p.A., CILEA - Consorzio Interuniversitario Lombardo per l'Elaborazione Automatica, the Istituto di Cibernetica dell'Università di Milano and Te.Co.Graf. snc.

The project is partially supported by the Commission of the EEC, among the ten European Projects on Electronic Publishing and Electronic Document Delivery, that constitute the so called DOCDEL programme.

As well known, the concepts of Electronic Publishing and Electronic Document Delivery refer more to a synergistic composition of existing technologies and practices, rather than to newly established ones ([1]).

The major objective of SDDS was indeed to develop a system, where the most advanced techniques for inputting, searching, printing and delivering documents could

---

[1] Te.Co.Graf. snc, Milano

[2] Università degli Studi di Milano

[3] CILEA, Segrate (Milano)

[4] Arnoldo Mondadori Editore S.p.A., Milano

TEX for Scientific Documentation   D. Lucarella, Editor
Copyright ©1985 Addison-Wesley Publishing Company, Inc.

be applied or taken into account for the future. Following these aims, the objective was primarily met adopting TeX, as a powerful kernel to deal with typesetting and printing, and implementing around it suitable facilities, to handle a full text data base and to simplify the input of the documents.

Taking into account the Italian scenario, the SDDS project appears as one of the first experiments, perhaps the first one, to organize a data base where the scientific literature can be easily stored and retrieved, taking advantage on the powerful standard formats, that are set out using TeX.

In the sequel, a general overview of the system is discussed, exploring its motivations, features and functionalities. A description of the implementations that have been done is also given. The exploitations of the system and the forecasted future developments are briefly discussed in the last paragraph.

General Overview

SDDS was originally conceived to cover the documentation needs of the Italian scientific community in a cost effective way; the main capabilities of SDDS ([2]) ([3]) are intended to:

- collect and store electronically the scientific literature from Universities, Research Centers, Industries and professional people;

- support the electronic retrieval, reading, ordering, accounting and billing of the stored documents;

- distribute copies of the stored documents on paper form, on magnetic media and through data communication networks, depending on the user demand.

This wide range of capabilities are, at present, in an advanced stage of development and an experimental usage of SDDS is on the way to be exploited.

SDDS main objectives

Design and implementation of the system are the first, obvious, objectives. The main challenge, we faced with, was to design and to implement a coherent range of interfaces among already available components, that were practically unrelated.

These interfaces refer:

- to the input of the documents (via the package EasyTeX, providing a set of macros for standard formatting, and interfacing several commercial word processors);

- to the output of the documents (implementing drivers for several existing printing devices, developing new low cost devices and implementing hardware interfaces to handle fonts for existing ones);

- to the integration of images, graphics and diagrams with the straight text (using image scanners, graphic fonts, linking pictures to the DVI file);

- to the functions for capturing, storing and retrieving of documents (the full text data base).

Another objective is to check and predict the commercial viability of the services provided by SDDS, taking into account both the present situation and the future trade-off of the Italian environment. Looking at the present situation, the main difficulties arise from the lack of availability of low cost and high speed TLC networks and from the inadequacy of the existing law in coping with this new kind of publishing activity. This often means difficulties to get reading customers and to quickly build up a large data base.

A third objective is to experiment a new partnership on the two traditional sides of the publisher's activity: the side of the authors and the one of the readers. By SDDS, they are able to participate to the publishing process and a valuable reduction on the necessary investments is expected. If the authors can use TeX, in fact, a great part of useless expenses can be avoided, making viable also the production of documents in a very short run. Another side effect of this cooperation is expected with reference to the communication effectiveness that can be achieved, when the author himself is directly involved also in the typographical form setting of his issue. About the electronic delivering, the continuous decline of the implicated costs (communication, printing devices etc.), together with the growing spread of personal computers over the users, encourages expectations that a service like this one will be really cost effective in a near future.

The last objective is to experiment computerized publishing tools that can be gradually introduced in the traditional process too, both to reduce costs and to introduce in it more flexibility than in the present situation.

SDDS Functional View

As already mentioned, SDDS has been designed to organically integrate existing tools and practices in a coherent environment, where several standard interfaces are precisely set.

The interface to input the documents is constituted by the TeX source language, that is also supported by a standard set of macros ([4]). These macros allow the input of a document, obtaining a standard lay-out of:

- the front page;
- the text itself (automatic choosing of fonts, indentations of chapters, sections, paragraphs, footnotes, simple diagrams etc.);
- the reference list;
- the index.

Images, diagrams and graphics are linked to the text using special purpose graphic fonts or commands, like SPECIAL, that are available in TEX82.

Input operations can be performed on a commercial PC, IBM compatible, using a commercial WP. The corresponding ASCII file can be directly loaded in the system via a standard diskette or sent to the Central Processing Center through data communication network.

The input operations of formulæ and text can be greatly improved by using Easy-TEX, avoiding the necessity of a deep knowledge of the TEX source language, on the author side.

When a document has been loaded in the data base, the reading user is allowed to browse it through the catalogues, to check contents, bibliographic data and prices either to find fully qualified documents, or to locate documents relevant to his request. After that, in the same session, the document may be scanned and read on the CRT terminal. This ability reduces the necessity of useless paper copies, when only a small part of the document is requested.

Taking advantage of the intrinsic features of DVI (i.e. independence of the output devices), the system is open to be used with a variety of printing devices, where the quality of the issues only depends on the sophistication and cost of such devices. This is, in our opinion, a very important feature, because this way the high quality can be achieved not only considering the present availability of such equipments but also forecasting future opportunities, when it will be possible to take advantage of always declining commercial prices, often accompanied by improvements of their capabilities.

The last, main functionality lies on the ability, provided to the user, to perform all the above mentioned operations at their own premises through a data communication network. The choice to use only ASCII files, both to enter documents and to transmit them, seems to be at present very effective and advantageous over other techniques, specially when taking into account the transmission speed of presently available networks.

SDDS Main Issues

Summarizing, the main issues that are expected from the practical usage of SDDS in the publishing environment are:

- standardization of the input format, where the friendliness of the usage could be properly balanced with the powerfulness of the tool;

- standardization of the intermediate form of the document, to guarantee that the system is, in some way, open ended, to cope in a cost effective way with new applications and with a possible future adoption of ongoing output devices;

- high typographical quality of the issues, affected only by the economic concerns of the user;

- finally, availability of a tool that can improve the traditional publishing process, as well as it can cope with innovation.

SDDS Functional Blocks

SDDS data base

The SDDS data base (fig. 1) is logically composed of four parts:

- the Document Descriptor File (DDF), which contains a code description (i.e. bibliographic data) of all the documents available to the users.

- the DVI files, which contain the full text of the documents; each document is cut into several delivering units, roughly corresponding to a chapter, that are individually pointed in the entry of DDF describing such a document;

- the ORDERS file, where a new entry is generated each time a user places an order to get a document; each entry contains the user identifier, the document and the ordered chapter identifier; the output form required, the number of copies requested etc.;

- the USERS file where the personal data of the users are arranged.

The access functions to the data base belong to two different classes. The first one, providing online access capabilities, is available to the user, while the second one, providing off-line functions, is available to the system operator and to the data base administrator.

The modules implementing on-line functions (see fig.1) are:

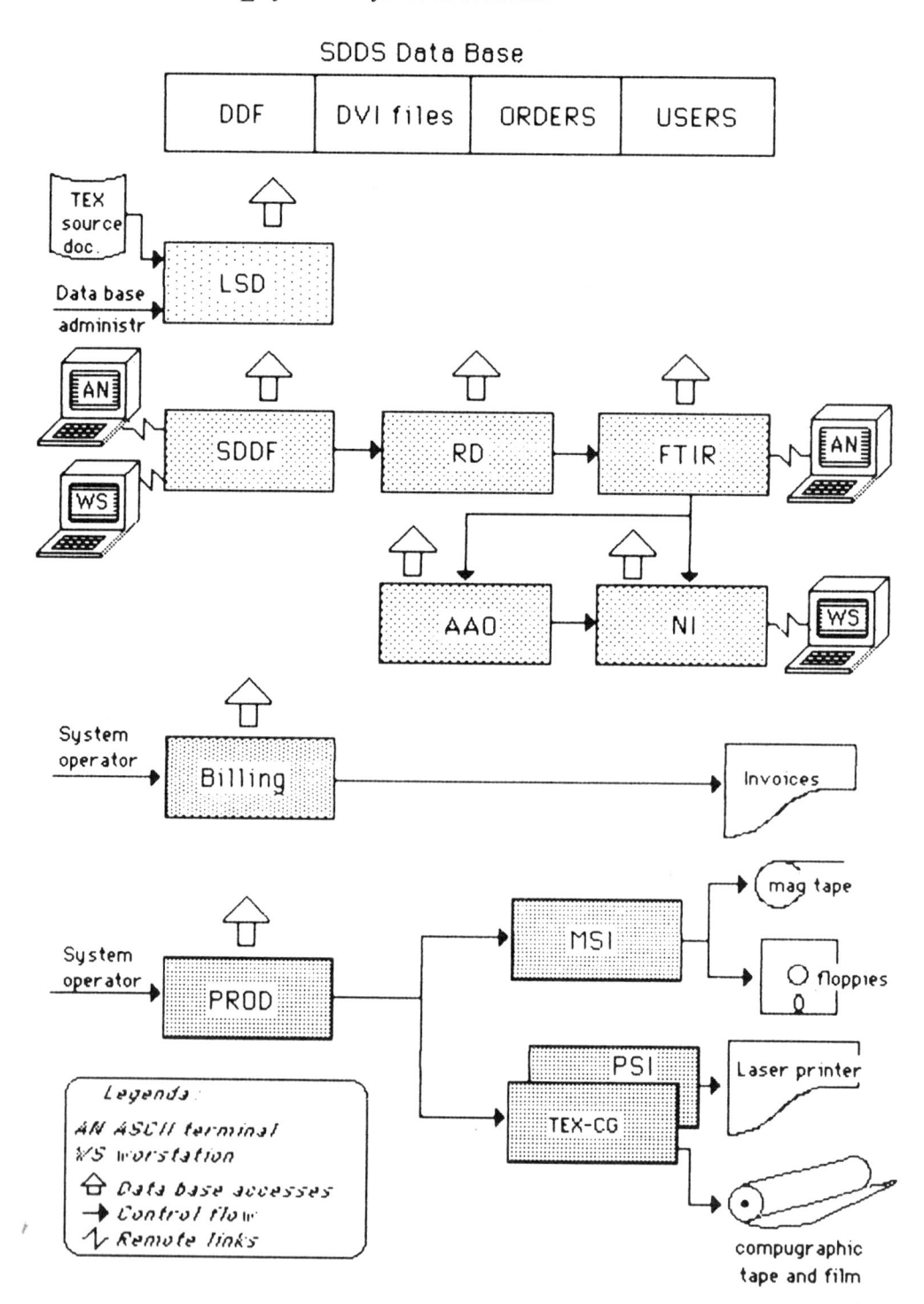

Fig. 1

- SDDF (Searching Document Descriptor File), a sophisticated system for information retrieval, allows the user to search in the DDF, looking for a document; main features of the implemented query language are: practically no limit on the allowed number of search keys, searching with five approximation levels (exact match, word inside, substring inside, minimum distance and pattern matching), searching can be limited on a group of documents where a condition was previously verified, on-line help messages, random access to the document description;

- RD (Reading full text Document) allows the user to read a DVI file on the screen of his own simple ASCII terminal. RD in fact maps the DVI file into an ASCII one, obviously neglecting changes of the typographical fonts and complex formulae eventually included;

- FTIR (Full text Information Retrieval) provides the user with the browsing of the selected document, displaying a window of twenty lines at a time and giving simple searching facilities over the text;

- NI (Network Interface) performs the coding of the DVI file for transmission over the network and handles the physical sending of it;

- AAO (Accepting, Accounting Orders) handles the user orders, checking his authority and generating the corresponding entry in the ORDERS file.

The modules implementing off-line functions (see fig.1) are:

- LSD (Load and Store Documents) which is available to the data base administrator, to input a document in the SDDS data base; this module creates the entry in the DDF and links the entry itself to the DVI files containing the text.

- PROD (PRocessing OrDers) performs the function to satisfy an order placed by an user, retrieving in the ORDERS file the data referring to it and, depending on the specific user request, activating MSI, PSI or TEX-CG. This module is available to the system operator, who normally uses it to periodically process the orders;

- Billing which gets information data from ORDERS and USERS files, to start invoicing to the users; the regular invoice is then sent by mail.

Finally, there are the modules to produce the issues requested by the users, they are:

- MSI (Magnetic Support Interface) which is intended to deliver a copy of the DVI file on magnetic support, like a diskette or tape;

- PSI (PrinterS Interface) which includes the driver to get an output from the DVI file on the laser printer;

- TeX-CG (TeX - CompuGraphic 8600) which provides the output on the phototypesetter Compugraphic 8600; this module integrate both the TeX processor and the driver, because the phototypesetter runs with its own fonts, that are incompatible with those provided for the laser printer.

EasyTeX

As already mentioned, EasyTeX is intended to implement a friendly interface between the author and the TeX world, particularly when a document containing many complex formulæ has to be typed.

The original approach was to implement a simple formula editor, that could only handle formulæ, providing the author with a graphical interface to input them. By this approach, the strings, coding such formulae, had to be inserted in the coded text in a following phase. This fact would require from the user a certain degree of knowledge of the TeX source language, that was considered intolerable with reference to the general requirement about friendliness and easiness of use.

The approach evolved to a more complex one, where the formulæ editor is integrated in an interactive WP. The package, now under development, will integrate several capabilities that span from the mere editing features to the more sophisticated handling of interchangeable fonts and syntactical checks of formulae. EasyTeX has been designed to run on a commercial PC, equipped with hard disk, graphic display and low cost needle printer.

EasyTeX (see fig. 2) is the kernel of such a workstation, integrating all the functions to produce an intermediate file that can be locally printed or, after an automatic translation, sent to the Center to be processed by TeX. This feature allows the user to check locally the draft of his document and to send it to the Center only in the final version. The ability to locally print intermediate files allows the user to employ the workstation alone also for simple in-house publishing applications, at a very low cost.

This workstation can be also equipped to be connected to the Center to retrieve and order documents from the SDDS data base.

Forecasted Usages of SDDS

The first application that is on the way to be realized is to create a large data base, containing the dissertations made by the students of the Faculty of Computer Science of the University of Milan. This choice has been taken because these dissertations

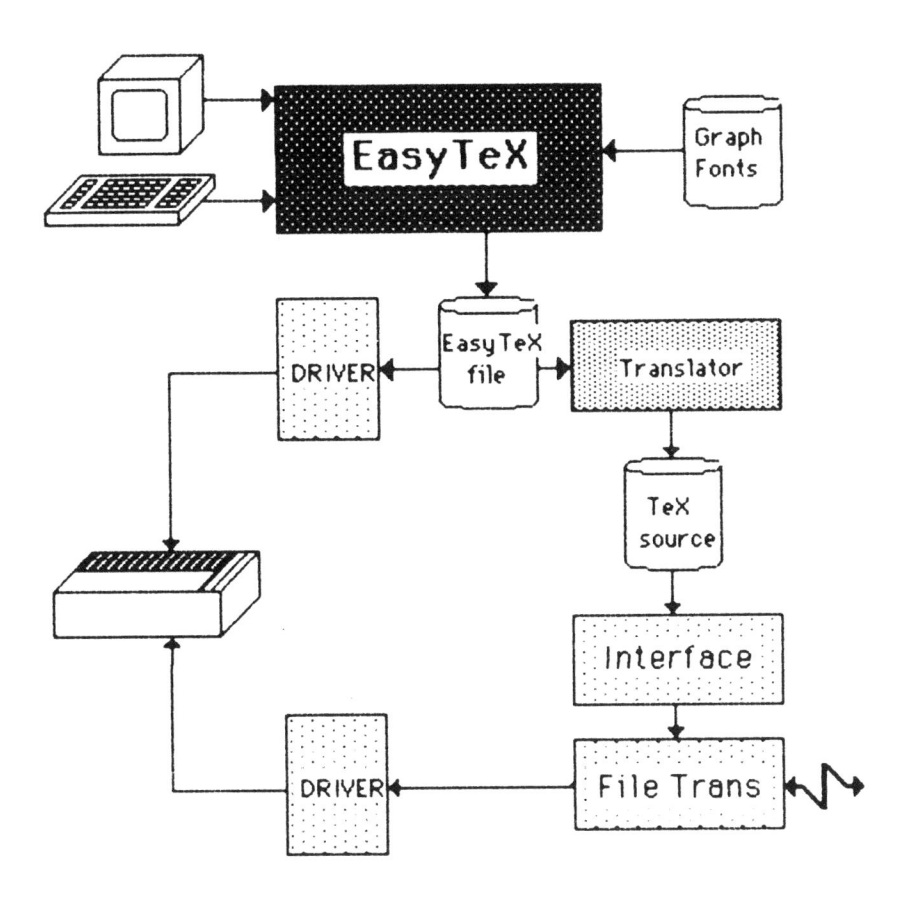

Fig. 2

are often requested outside the University and because this possibility was considered more viable than others. This is due to the fact that a local network connecting terminals to the Center in CILEA is already available in that site and experimenting this new kind of service with people already familiar with computers will reduce implementation costs.

Another application, that will be limited, at the beginning, to private use has been undertaken to offer the Publishing Houses a service for text typesetting and storing in a data bank, like a published issues repository, suitable for following applications.

As already said, the main concern in supplying a public service of electronic publishing and delivering lies on the possible copyright infringements ([5]) ([6]), that can occur, given the poor control that the supplier has on the ability of a malicious customer to do illegal copies of the documents. As it is well known, in fact, the possibility of making copies of a published issue must be strongly controlled to guarantee that the author is not damaged in his fundamental rights, to get his royalty on each copy sold. This is very hard when supplying a service where no control is feasible on the number of copies, entire or partial or "soft", that can be made.

Obviously, there is a way to overcome these difficulties, when you deal with a newly developed issue and you can reach a suitable arrangement with the author (for instance on a forfeit basis), but many troubles arise when an issue has been published, not taking into account this "electronic scenario", because the criteria normally set in the publishing contract, at least in Italy and till now, practically do prevent this usage.

Acknowledgments

The authors want to thank all the people who contributed to the development of the project and especially M.Losano of the Università di Milano, A.Mattasoglio of CILEA, F.Migiarra of Mondadori and D.Lucarella of Istituto di Cibernetica.

Bibliography

[1] F.Mastroddi - *"Integrated Electronic Publishing - Some Pointers to the Future"*

[2] G.Canzii, G.Degli Antoni, D.Lucarella, A.Pilenga - *"A Scientific Document Delivery System"* - Electronic Publishing Review, **1984**, Vol. 4, No. 2

[3] G.Rosci - *"Scientific Document Delivery System"* Conference on Electronic Document Delivery and Electronic Publishing - Luxembourg, June 1984

[4] M.Zocchi - *"Preparazione di Documenti con Formato Predefinito Utilizzando il Sistema di Composizione TEX"* (to be published)

[5] M.Losano - *"Copyright e Memorizzazione"* SDDS internal report 11.84

[6] M.Losano et al. - *"Sistema Contrattuale SDDS"* SDDS internal report 3.85

[7] A.Norman - *"Electronic Document Delivery"* Arthur D. Little, Learned Information, Oxford, **1981**, ISBN 0-904933-29-6

[8] *"Electronic Document Delivery"* Commission of the European Communities, Learned Information, Oxford

[9] T.R.Girill, C.H.Luk - *"A Document Delivery System for On Line Users"* - ACM Communications, Vol. 26, No. 5, May 83

[10] D.E.Knuth - *"The TEXbook"* - Addison-Wesley, **1984**

[11] G.Canzii, D.Lucarella, A.Pilenga - *"TEX at University of Milan"* TUGboat, Vol.3, No.1, American Mathematical Society, March 82

[12] D.E.Knuth, M.F.Plass - *"Breaking Paragraphs into lines"* - Software Practice and Experience, Vol. 11, **1981**

[13] *"ISO. Information Processing Systems - OSI Basic Reference model"* - Draft Proposal ISO-TC 97-SC16-N 890, February 82

[14] D.Lucarella - *"TEX Document Retrieval"* - Protext I Conference and Workshop, Dublin, October 1984

[15] G.Canzii, D.Lucarella, A.Pilenga - *"I Sistemi TEX e METAFONT"* - CLUED, Milano, May 1985

Adapting TeX to Languages that use Latin Alphabetic Characters

Staffan Romberger
Yngve Sundblad
Department of Numerical Analysis and Computing Science
Royal Institute of Technology
S-100 44   STOCKHOLM, Sweden

Abstract: *The adaption of TeX to languages that use the Latin alphabet extended with some national characters and diacritical marks reveals problems that are discussed with examples taken from the Swedish language. Important issues are codes used for input and internal representation, extension of fonts with national letters and diacritical marks, units of measure, denotation of font sizes and hyphenation rules. We present a version of plain TeX with additions for Swedish use, called SweTeX.*
Keywords: *National alphabetic character, accent, diacritical mark, TeX, Metafont, hyphenation, Swedish*

Introduction

Our department has used TeX since 1980, mainly for technical reports and textbooks containing mathematical formulas, but also for shorter documents such as course notes and presentations of our research and education programme to the public. The documents are usually written in Swedish or English or in a mixture of these.

We have not observed any annoying differences between the conventions for writing mathematical formulas used in our country and those embodied in plain TeX. For plain text, however, there are differences. In Swedish there are three national letters, åÅ, äÄ and öÖ, in lower and upper case. These are intrinsic (not just accented letters) and have individual renditions, positions in the alphabet etc. In the standard character code, and hence on the keyboard, Ö, ä and å replace the crucial escape \ and group characters { and } of TeX's input language. To make TeX useful at all

TeX for Scientific Documentation   D. Lucarella, Editor
Copyright ©1985 Addison-Wesley Publishing Company, Inc.

we had to make additions to plain TeX. These additions are under constant development to include also other aspects of Swedish typography, e.g. quotation marks and hyphenation.

These problems are of course not unique for Swedish. Almost every European language uses national letters or accents in addition to the letters A–Z. Adaptions of TeX to French and German are discussed in (Désarménien 1984) and (Schulze 1984). The flexibility and total openness of TeX (as compared to commercial systems) gives the user of a specific language the combined freedom and responsibility to adapt the system to good typography in that language.

The tool TeX does not guarantee good typographic quality. It has to be used and adapted with insight and care. Plain TeX can be seen as an adaption to English typography and it has to be supplemented for other languages. In this paper we discuss general problems with examples from the Swedish language.

A good way to obtain high typographic quality is to design all letters in a language individually and include them in the fonts. The tool that accompanies TeX, **META-FONT**, enables this but has to be used with the same insight and care as TeX. Work is in progress at our department to design ÅÄÖ according to established Swedish conventions for the different fonts distributed with TeX.

Accented and national letters

Virtually all European languages with an alphabet based on the 26 basic Latin letters A–Z also use accents, other diacritical marks, ligatures or specific national letters. A table for 39 living European languages in (ISO 6937, 1983) contains 98 such letters, 192 if both lower and upper case are counted. Typically a specific language uses about 5 of these. In the ISO standard 79 letters are formed from the basic letters and diacritical marks as shown in figure 1.

These letters can either be regarded as consisting of a basic letter and a diacritical mark or be regarded as a specific intrinsic letter. Conventions vary from language to language. For example é, which is used in 23 of the languages including English, French, German and Swedish is usually considered an e with an acute accent. In ë and ï, used in e.g. French, the ¨ is usually considered an accent.

On the other hand, Ö, used in Dutch, Estonian, Finnish, Frisian, German, Hungarian, Icelandic, Lapp, Rhæto-Romanic, Swedish, Turkish and Welsh, is in general considered as a specific letter.

The remaining 15 characters are ligatures, e.g. œ in French and English, ß in German, ĳIJ in Dutch, and specific letters e.g. æÆ and øØ in most Nordic languages, ŀL in Catalan and łL in Polish.

Basic letter	Acute accent	Grave accent	Circumflex accent	Diaeresis or umlaut mark	Tilde	Caron	Breve	Double acute accent	Ring	Dot above	Macron	Cedilla	Ogonek
a A	á Á	à À	â Â	ä Ä	ã Ã		ă Ă		å Å		ā Ā		ą Ą
b B													
c C	ć Ć		ĉ Ĉ			č Č				ċ Ċ		ç Ç	
d D						ď Ď							
e E	é É	è È	ê Ê	ë Ë		ě Ě				ė Ė	ē Ē		ę Ę
f F													
g G	ǵ		ĝ Ĝ				ğ Ğ			ġ Ġ		Ģ	
h H			ĥ Ĥ										
i I	í Í	ì Ì	î Î	ï Ï	ĩ Ĩ					i ī Ī			į Į
j J			ĵ Ĵ										
k K												ķ Ķ	
l L	ĺ Ĺ					ľ Ľ						ļ Ļ	
m M													
n N	ń Ń				ñ Ñ	ň Ň						ņ Ņ	
o O	ó Ó	ò Ò	ô Ô	ö Ö	õ Õ			ő Ő			ō Ō		
p P													
q Q													
r R	ŕ Ŕ					ř Ř						ŗ Ŗ	
s S	ś Ś		ŝ Ŝ			š Š						ş Ş	
t T						ť Ť						ţ Ţ	
u U	ú Ú	ù Ù	û Û	ü Ü	ũ Ũ		ŭ Ŭ	ű Ű	ů Ů		ū Ū		ų Ų
v V													
w W			ŵ Ŵ										
x X													
y Y	ý Ý		ŷ Ŷ	ÿ Ÿ									
z Z	ź Ź					ž Ž				ż Ż			

Figure 1. *Combinations of diacritical marks and basic letters (from ISO 6937)*

With TEX's Computer Modern Roman fonts 83 letter forms similar to the 96 in ISO 6937 can be generated. Missing are the 4 forms with the ogonek diacritical mark, used in Polish and Lithuanian, and 9 of the specific letter forms. The forms that are generated are not completely satisfactory, see the discussion of the Swedish Å below.

National characters in character codes

There are several aspects on character codes in connection with typesetting and TEX. First comes the input language. What is the interpretation of the codes from the keyboard? How are the characters arranged on the keyboard? What does the input text look like on the screen? Next comes the arrangement of characters into fonts. Finally come the questions about storage and transmission of documents. How do we find and agree upon a way to uniquely represent any sequence of characters from different alphabets?

The character representation of TEX is based on ASCII (American Standard Code for Information Interchange) which is a variant of the ISO 7-bit code (ISO 646, 1983). The code contains 128 characters, 94 of which are printing characters and the remaining 34 are used for control.

There is an "International Reference Version" of ISO 646 (IRV) with characters assigned to every position, see the left part of figure 2. The only letters included in IRV are lower and upper case A–Z. The standard prescribes alternatives for two of the positions and ten positions are available "for national or application oriented use". Figure 3 shows the use of these positions in IRV and in Swedish standard.

Adaption of software to other languages would be greatly facilitated if the designers of software would refrain from assigning significant meaning to these characters.

Standard Pascal (ISO 7185, 1983) is a typical example of the opposite. Square brackets, [] , are used around indices and set denotations. They correspond to the Swedish characters Ä and Å. Pascal provides (. and .) as alternatives. Curly brackets, {} , are used around comments. They correspond to the Swedish characters ä and å. Pascal provides (* and *) as alternatives. Hence it is highly unsafe to write comments in Swedish since a comment can be started with a (* but will end at the first å or *). A better convention would be that (* is only matched by *).

Another example is the adaption to national standards of TEX macro packages. Our adaption of plain TEX is described below. LaTEX poses harder problems. Except the special characters of plain TEX LaTEX uses additional special characters, colliding with national characters. Certain format and style files using such special characters are inserted into the source text during composition. We find it still an open question how macro files like LaTEX should be designed and used to facilitate easy adaption to several language environments.

	02	03	04	05	06	07	10	11	12[1)]	13	14	15
00		0	@	P	`	p		°	See 4.3.4	—	Ω	ĸ
01	!	1	A	Q	a	q	¡	±	`	¹	Æ	æ
02	"	2	B	R	b	r	¢	²	´	®	Đ	đ
03	#	3	C	S	c	s	£	³	^	©	ª	ð
04	¤	4	D	T	d	t	$	×	~	™	Ħ	ħ
05	%	5	E	U	e	u	¥	µ	¯	♪	See 4.3.4	ı
06	&	6	F	V	f	v	See 4.3.3	¶	˘	See 4.3.4	Ĳ	ĳ
07	'	7	G	W	g	w	§	·	˙	See 4.3.4	Ŀ	ŀ
08	(	8	H	X	h	x	See 4.3.3	÷	¨	See 4.3.4	Ł	ł
09	)	9	I	Y	i	y	‘	’	See 4.3.4	See 4.3.4	Ø	ø
10	*	:	J	Z	j	z	“	”	˚	See 4.3.4	Œ	œ
11	+	;	K	[	k	{	«	»	¸	See 4.3.4	º	ß
12	,	<	L	\	l	|	←	¼	_	⅛	Þ	þ
13	-	=	M	]	m	}	↑	½	˝	⅜	Ŧ	ŧ
14	.	>	N	^	n	~	→	¾	˛	⅝	Ŋ	ŋ
15	/	?	O	_	o		↓	¿	ˇ	⅞	ŉ	

Figure 2. Printable part of the 8-bit character code from ISO 6937

Adhering to the ISO standard, five national letters in lower and upper case can be accomodated.

From the presentation of national letters above we conclude that 244 codes are

position	IRV graphic character	IRV name	Swedish data input standard graphic character	Swedish data input standard name
64	@	COMMERCIAL AT	@	COMMERCIAL AT
91	[	LEFT SQUARE BRACKET	Ä	CAPITAL LETTER Ä
92	\	BACKSLASH	Ö	CAPITAL LETTER Ö
93	]	RIGHT SQUARE BRACKET	Å	CAPITAL LETTER Å
94	^	CIRCUMFLEX ACCENT	^	CIRCUMFLEX ACCENT
96	`	GRAVE ACCENT	`	GRAVE ACCENT
123	{	LEFT CURLY BRACKET	ä	SMALL LETTER ä
124	|	VERTICAL LINE	ö	SMALL LETTER ö
125	}	RIGHT CURLY BRACKET	å	SMALL LETTER å
126	‾	TILDE, OVERLINE	‾	TILDE, OVERLINE

Figure 3. The character set of IRV and of the Swedish "data input standard"

needed to represent all letters used in one or more of the 39 European languages considered. Clearly not even an 8-bit code is sufficient for this as digits, punctuation marks, control characters, etc., must also be accomodated.

One way to accomodate all the letters in 8 bits is to regard all letters in figure 1 as accented and to represent them by the code for the accent followed by the code for the letter using the codes in figure 2.

Another way is to design two different character sets. The ISO/TC97/SC2 is considering a solution with two sets of 186 printing characters each, one for Western Europe and one for Eastern Europe.

Procedures for code extension by shift and escape codes is treated in (ISO 2022 1982).

Some organizations have established large character sets of their own. Figure 4 shows a character set for Apple equipment, e.g. laser printer and Macintosh (Adobe 1984, Apple supplement). Ideas for the representation of multilingual text are presented in (Becker 1984) and in (Xerox 1984).

Swedish characters in TeX input

Our main requirement when installing TeX was that the keys for åäöÅÄÖ should correspond to typeset åäöÅÄÖ. We invented SweTeX with **/** as escape and **<** and **>** as begin and end group characters and made åäöÅÄÖ active characters defined by the accent mechanism according to the TeXbook (Knuth 1984). This initial version of SweTeX is shown in figure 5 and a typical piece of input in figure 6.

	0	1	2	3	4	5	6	7	8	9	10	11	12	13	14	15
0	NUL	DLE	SP	0	@	P	`	p	Ä	ê	†	∞	¿	–	‡	􀀀
1	SOH	DC1	!	1	A	Q	a	q	Å	ë	°	±	¡	—	·	Ò
2	STX	DC2	"	2	B	R	b	r	Ç	í	¢	≤	¬	"	,	Ú
3	ETX	DC3	#	3	C	S	c	s	É	ì	£	≥	√	"	„	Û
4	EOT	DC4	$	4	D	T	d	t	Ñ	î	§	¥	ƒ	'	‰	Ù
5	ENQ	NAK	%	5	E	U	e	u	Ö	ï	•	µ	≈	'	Â	ı
6	ACK	SYN	&	6	F	V	f	v	Ü	ñ	¶	∂	Δ	+	Ê	ˆ
7	BEL	ETB	'	7	G	W	g	w	á	ó	ß	Σ	«	◊	À	˜
8	BS	CAN	(	8	H	X	h	x	à	ò	®	Π	»	ÿ	Ẽ	¯
9	HT	EM	)	9	I	Y	i	y	â	ô	©	π	…	Ÿ	È	˘
10	LF	SUB	*	:	J	Z	j	z	ä	ö	™	∫	_	/	Í	˙
11	VT	ESC	+	;	K	[	k	{	ã	õ	´	ª	Á	¤	Î	•
12	FF	FS	,	<	L	\	l	|	å	ú	¨	º	Ā	‹	Ï	¸
13	CR	GS	-	=	M	]	m	}	ç	ù	≠	Ω	Õ	›	Ì	˝
14	SO	RS	.	>	N	^	n	~	é	û	Æ	æ	Œ	fi	Ó	˛
15	SI	US	/	?	O	_	o	DEL	è	ü	Ø	ø	œ	fl	Ô	ˇ

Figure 4. The Quick Draw Encoding for Apple Laser Writer and Macintosh

```
Öcatcode 'Ö/=0
/def /ltä<å         /def /gtä>å
/catcode '/<=1      /catcode '/>=2
/catcode '/å=13     /catcode '/ä=13    /catcode '/ö=13
/catcode '/Å=13     /catcode '/Ä=13    /catcode '/Ö=13
/let å=/aa          /def ä</"a>        /def ö</"o>
/let Å=/AA          /def Ä</"A>        /def Ö</"O>
/escapechar='//
```

Figure 5. Swe TEX, additions to plain TEX to be used with Swedish character standard

```
We have not observed any difference between the conventions for
writing mathematical formulas used in our country and those
embodied in plain /TeX. For plain text, however, there are
differences. In Swedish there are three national letters, åÅ, äÄ
and öÖ, in lower and upper case. These are intrinsic (not just
accented letters). In the standard character code, and hence on
the keyboard, Ö, ä and å replace the crucial escape </tt/char92>
and group characters </tt/char123>/ and </tt/char125>/ of /TeX's
input language.
```

Figure 6. A piece of a Swe TEX manuscript

The new escape character appears in messages from TEX thanks to the definition /escapechar='// but the display of begin and end group characters as ä and å confuses most users of SweTEX.

Shape of Swedish letters

Traditional conventions for the form of the Swedish letters can be found in (Lagerström 1927). The ring has the same width as the hairlines and has this width even in bold faces. It is centered above the a or A and detached from the rest of the letter. The level of the center of the ring in å divides the distance between the x-height and the h-height in 2:1. The diameter of the dots is slightly less than the thin vertical stems. The dots in ä, ö, i and j align with the ring in å and the dots in Ä and Ö align with the ring in Å. Inspection of fonts shows that diameter of the ring is about 30% of the H-height.

The problems with ÅÄÖ in Swedish text with imported fonts is not new. Before the 18th century the dominating typeface in Swedish print was gothic. With the Enlightment school of scientists and writers, e.g. Linnæus, came a change to roman fonts, which were imported from France. In figure 7, a Swedish translation of Racine's *Andromache* published in 1723, we see that the printer, in the absence of roman Swedish letters, used gothic. The example is taken from (Nordqvist 1965).

And: Olycxlig Printz! Ach alt för wårdslös om ditt lif!
       Ach alt för säker för de falska Grekers arghet!
       Dråpt i din blomſtrand ungdom, rått uti
       Din båſta ålder, då din mångfalt wundne åhra
       Och hoop af ſegrar dig ſom allramåſt uphögde
       Utöfwer alla Kungar -- ſielfwa Troya
       Nu kunde dig med bitter gråt bexlaga --
Ceph: Skal då Er ſorg bli aldrig åndad?
                                    And: Aldrig,
       Åh aldrig! ney, få långe ſom jag lefwer
       Blir och min ſorg odödlig-- jag år född
       Och utſedd af mitt öde blott til jåmmer--
tilPhœ- Giör anſtalt til Er döde Kungs begrafning,
  nix Pryd honom i des Kunga dråcht och mantel,
       Låt alla tecxen af hans wundne ſegrar
       Med honom utur werlden giöra följe:
       Rees högt det båhl, hvvarpå hans dyra Kropp
       Skal bli til aska, låt des låga braſa up
       Til ſielfwa himlen, och dår möta hans beröm.

Figure 7. Swedish print in "roman" font from 1723

Adaptation of Computer Modern fonts to Swedish characters

The method used in T_EX to construct the letters äöÄÖ is the accent mechanism with an umlaut mark which is included in most fonts but not in all.

The ring is designed to fit lower case å. Upper case Å is constructed by the following definition.

```
/def/AA</setbox0=/hbox<h>/dimen=/ht0/advance/dimen   by-1ex
/rlap</raise.67/dimen/hbox</char'27>>A>
```

This can be interpreted as "raise the ring by 2/3 of the difference between the h-height and the x-height". Figure 8 shows some examples of how the method works in practice.

ÅÄÖÅÄÖ   åäöÅÄÖ   åäöÅÄÖ   åäöÅÄÖ   åäöÅÄÖ   åäöÅÄÖ
amcsc10 amdunh10 amr10   amss10   amti10   amtt10

Figure 8. Examples of Swedish letters generated with plain T_EX (scaled 1440/1000)

Parts of the problems are due to the limited resolution of the laser copier. However, for some fonts different sizes of rings and dot pairs are needed for lower and upper case and it is improper to apply the same placement algorithm to all fonts.

One way to improve the outlook of the Swedish national letters is to redesign the placement algorithm for the ring and dots individually for each font. An example of improvement of amcsc10 compared to figure 8 is shown in figure 9 with the corresponding TEX-definition in figure 10.

$$\text{Å Ä Ö Å Ä Ö}$$
amcsc10

Figure 9. Examples of Swedish letters generated with modified TEX (scaled 1440/1000)

```
/font/f=amcsc10
/def/tensc</f
    /def Å</rlap</kern0em/raise0.6ex/hbox</char23>>A>%
    /def Ä</rlap</kern0.1em/raise0.5ex/hbox</char127>>A>%
    /def Ö</rlap</kern0.13em/raise0.5ex/hbox</char127>>O>%
    /let å=/aa
    /def ä</rlap</kern0em/raise0.25ex/hbox</char127>>a>%
    /def ö</rlap</kern0em/raise0.25ex/hbox</char127>>o>>
```

Figure 10. Modifications of amcsc10 used in figure 9

A definition of this kind gives problems with rounding errors on low resolution devices and with hyphenation as described below.

An other way to improve the national letters is, of course, to design them as individual letters. We have started this design with old **METAFONT** and plan to proceed with the new, "final" **METAFONT** which we have just received.

In the placement of national characters in TEX-fonts the following considerations should be made.
• All TEX-fonts should be alike to promote the exchange of TEX-documents.
• National letters should occupy positions according to their national character code to simplify processing.
• National letters should be placed within positions 0–127 since only characters in these positions can be letters in TEX's meaning.

These requirements are contradictory. The solution chosen in (Désarménien 1984) is to move the upper case Greek letters to positions above 127 and place national letters in the freed positions. In our experiments with SweTeX we have adopted this solution.

An alternate solution chosen in (Schulze 1984) is to represent the national characters as ligatures (e.g. "A for Ä) with the actual characters placed in positions 128–255. In that case Ä should be an active character that expands to "A. The " should be defined as a letter (used in hyphenation).

The citation habits are different in Swedish and English. The same character is used before and after the citation, " or the guillemet (looking something like «) for outer citations and ' for inner citations. The guillemet is absent from the standard fonts and " gives too much space before a word.

We found the Computer Modern Roman fonts slightly too bold on the LGP10 so we made some small changes in CMBASE.

Typographical measures, font size and baseline distance

Part of the tradition of typography is manifest in the measures used. These were established during the Age of Enlightenment, the 18th century.

As unit of measure for font sizes the diameter of an ordinary full stop point was chosen. One point was also found to be a suitable step between adjacent small font sizes.

The size of the point was established at about the same time in France and in England. The English (pica point) and the Continental (didot) point turned out to be very close to each other but slightly different—and still are. The latter is about 7% bigger. The closeness indicates that the order of magnitude of the unit of measurement is appropriate.

$$1 \text{ didot point} = 1/2660 \text{ meter} = 0.3759 \text{ millimeter}$$
$$1 \text{ pica point} = 0.013837 \text{ inch} \approx 1/72.27 \text{ inch} = 0.3513 \text{ millimeter}$$

There are bigger units equalling 12 points:

$$1 \text{ cicero} = 12 \text{ didot point} = 4.511 \text{ millimeter}$$
$$1 \text{ pica} = 12 \text{ pica point} = 4.216 \text{ millimeter}$$

The "size" of the font was defined as the height of the metal body on which the typeface was cast. In that technology this constitutes the smallest possible baseline distance in a text typeset with the font.

In phototypesetting there is no "type body" that indisputably defines the type size, which has lead to anarchy in the denotation of font sizes. Still, a useful definition of font size is the *smallest acceptable baseline distance*.

In good typography there should be no risk of overlapping between letters on consecutive lines. Therefore the baseline distance should at least be the sum of the depth of the lowest descender below the baseline and the highest ascender above. For English, disregarding rare accents on capital letters, this is the "Hp-height". For Swedish, where capital Å is a regular part of the language, the corresponding measure is the Åp-height, which in a typical, good Swedish font is 115–120% of the Hp-height, (Romberger-Sundblad 1984). Another often used measure is the "cap-height" or "H-height" which typically is 75-80% of the Hp-height and 65-70% of the Åp-height. Thus the same font can have different "size" in English than in Swedish and other languages with diacritical marks on capital letters.

A description of how a text is typeset must contain both the font with "size" and the baseline distance. A common way to express this is "10 points on 11". With the definition of font size advocated above the densest allowable setting is obtained with baseline distance equal to font size.

Interesting ideas for denotation of font size and baseline distance are used in phototypesetting systems from Dr. Böger Photosatz (Scangraphic 1983). Font size is expressed as *CH* (Capital Height, i.e. H-height) in millimeters or in traditional measure (Hp-height in didot or pica points). Accents on capital letters are not taken into account, which must be corrected with extra spacing in German and, even more so, in Swedish. Baseline distance, denoted *LF* (Line Feed), is given in millimeters. Each font has a normal *LF/CH-factor*, which is typically 1.6 with recommended variations in steps of about 5% (0.08).

We have made an experimental version of SweTeX which use similar ideas. Its "font size macros" give by default a "normal" baseline distance about 10% higher than the minimal (Åp-height). The macros also define the following "sub-macros" for baseline distances, expressed in *mbd*, minimal baseline distance.

Macro:	Baseline distance	For amr10
/dense	*mbd*	3.8 mm
/halfdense	*mbd* + about 5%	4.0 mm
/normdense	*mbd* + about 10%	4.2 mm
/sparse	*mbd* + about 20%	4.5 mm
/verysparse	*mbd* + about 30%	4.8 mm

All distances are rounded to tenths of millimeters. An example is /tenpoint /sparse, which gives amr10 with a baseline distance of 4.5 millimeters. The body text here is typeset in amr10 with a baseline distance of 15 pica points, about 5.3 millimeters.

Hyphenation

The hyphenation algorithm in TeX is due to (Liang 1983). It uses a database of hyphenation patterns, an exception list supplied by the user and discretionary hyphens. It has been demonstrated that the algorithm works very well for English.

It is highly desirable to have a hyphenation algorithm in a typesetting program. It is more important to avoid bad hyphenations than to find all feasible ones. It is also desirable to be able to switch between several hyphenation strategies in multilingual documents. In English, accented words tend not to follow the ordinary rules. In Swedish ÅÄÖ must be taken into account to make a useful algorithm.

The hyphenation algorithm is applied only to sequences that consist solely of characters that are letters in TeX's meaning. Such sequences are not hyphenated before the second or after the third to last letter. Only characters with codes below 128 whose /lccode is different from 0 are letters in this meaning. The explicit kerning which is part of the accenting mechanism breaks the sequence.

Two solutions have been proposed: to represent national letters by ligatures or to extend TeX's set of letters with the national letters.

Hyphenation of Swedish is difficult mainly due to the great number of compound words which should be hyphenated between the parts. Syllabic pre- and postfixes may be hyphenated. In the remaining cases hyphenation can be made between adjacent vowels or before the last consonant before a vowel. These rules are contradicting and competing.

The word **finskor** can have either of the meanings "fine shoes" and "Finnish women". In the first case it is a compound word which should be hyphenated **fin-skor**. In the second case it can be hyphenated **fins-kor** according to the "consonant rule" or **finsk-or** according to the "suffix rule". The words **storskrak** (goosander) and **torskrom** (roe of cod) are hyphenated **stor-skrak** and **torsk-rom**. An extra l is added when **tillägg** (addition) is hyphenated **till-lägg**.

Conclusions

Plain TeX is intended for English text and typography. It is necessary to make nontrivial adaptations to TeX to meet the typographic requirements of other languages. These adaptations can partly be made as definitions supplementing plain TeX. For languages that contain special, intrinsic, national characters special designs with META-FONT may be necessary to achieve really good typography. Some of these adaptations are valid only for a specific language such as national standards for characters and keyboards. They are the responsibility of the TeX community using that language. Other adaptations are more general such as the arrangement of characters in fonts, requirements on hyphenation and the use of special characters in macro packages. They should be based on international standards which should be carefully considered by the TEX community. This is in particular important for production of multilingual documents.

Bibliography

Adobe Systems Inc: *Postscript Language Manual and Font manual.* Palo Alto, California, 1984.

Becker, Joseph D.: *Multilingual Word Processing.* Scientific American, Vol 251, July 1984, pp 82-93.

Désarménien, Jacques: *How to Run TEX in a French Environment—Hyphenation, Fonts, Typography.* TUGboat, volume 5 (1984), No. 2, Providence 1984.

ISO, International Organization for Standardization: *Information processing—Coded character sets for text communication.* Standard No. ISO 6937, 1983.

———: *Information processing—ISO 7-bit and 8-bit coded character sets—Code extension techniques.* Standard No. ISO 2022, 2nd ed., 1982.

———: *Information processing—ISO 7-bit coded character set for information interchange.* Standard No. ISO 646, 2nd ed., 1983.

———: *Programming languages—Pascal.* Standard No. ISO 7185, 1983.

Knuth, Donald E.: *The TEXbook.* Addison-Wesley, Reading, 1984.

Lagerström, H.: *Bokstavsformer i typtrycket.* (in Swedish, Eng.: Letterforms in type.) Nordisk boktryckarekonsts fackbibliotek, Vol. xi, Lagerströms förlag, Stockholm, 1927.

Liang, Frank M.: *Word Hy-phen-a-tion by Com-put-er.* Ph.D. Thesis, Department of Computer Science, Stanford University, Report No. STAN-CS-83-977, 1983.

Nordqvist, N.: *Antikvan och vetenskaperna.* (in Swedish, Eng.: The roman typefaces and the sciences.) Bokvännerna, Stockholm, 1965.

Romberger, Staffan and Sundblad, Yngve: *Size Measures and National Characters in Computer Generated Text with Typography.* Proc. PROTEXT I, Boole Press, Dublin, 1984, pp 227-233.

Scangraphic: *Scantext 1000.* Dr. Böger Photosatz GmbH, Hamburg, 1983.

Schulze, Bernd: *German Hyphenation and Umlauts in TEX.* TUGboat, volume 5 (1984), No. 2, Providence, 1984.

Xerox Corporation: *Character Code Standard in Xerox System Integration Standard.* Stamford, Connecticut, 1984.

THE USE OF TeX IN FRENCH: HYPHENATION AND TYPOGRAPHY

by

Jacques DÉSARMÉNIEN*

ABSTRACT:
We explain how, together with our collegues of the Laboratoire de typographie informatique, we made TeX work properly in a French environment. The main issues discussed here are: the input, the hyphenation and related problems (notably the need to produce specific fonts) and the typographic conventions. Finally, we show why the problem of hyphenation can be solved for TeX in Italian in a much easier way.

1. Introduction:

Text-processing softwares allow anybody to produce beautiful, typeset-like documents by merely typing the manuscript on a terminal, using a keyboard very similar to that of an ordinary typewriter.

Unfortunately, most of these softwares come from English-speaking countries and use typical American conventions for input codes, typography and hyphenation. To make it satisfactory to use such a program in French (or in Italian, or in any other language), one must modify it to satisfy the corresponding conventions of his own language.

The only reasonable solution to the first problem seems to build a preprocessor: it retains the universality of ANSI codes and leaves the possibility of communication. Such a software is STRATEC, developed in Strasbourg by D. Foata, J.-J. Pansiot and Y. Roy [9].

---

* *Laboratoire de typographie informatique, Université de Strasbourg, 7, rue René-Descartes, F-67084 Strasbourg Cedex, France.*

TeX for Scientific Documentation   D. Lucarella, Editor
Copyright ©1985 Addison-Wesley Publishing Company, Inc.

Contrary to most of its concurrents, TEX is flexible enough to handle the last two problems. Even if its algorithm for hyphenation was specifically designed for English, it is possible to generate by hand the *patterns* for French hyphenation. Among the problems that arose was the necessity of having extended fonts and the need for a coherent set of rules for French hyphenation. The result—in our opinion—is much better than any other automatic hyphenation program for French. For Italian, extended fonts are no more needed, and the rules for hyphenation are very simple: This makes Italian extremely easy to adapt on TEX.

It is even possible to simutaneously hyphenate in two languages without extending TEX. The trick we use is crude but it proved to be effective.

2. The input problems:

Let us just mention here, and briefly discuss, the question of inputting TEX in French. In our opinion, TEX can reach success only if it is used by secretaries—and not only by wizards. This implies that a replica of the usual French keyboard must appear on the terminal. In France, some extra characters—é, è, ç, à, ù—have to be included where they usually appear. Some other keys have to be displaced: for example, a and q have to be permuted and the digits retain their positions but must be typed by using the SHIFT key. Finally, the ^ and the ¨ constitute a special 'dead key'.

It is possible to find 'French' terminal keyboards. Unfortunately, none of them fully satisfy the typewriter keyboard specifications. Moreover, a number of ASCII codes are used for accented characters: @ for à, \ for ç, { for é, } for è and | for ù. As most of those codes have special meaning for TEX, it is almost impossible to use such keyboards. As M. Mlouka pointed out [14], part of those problems are caused by the inadequacy of the French ASCII/AFNOR standards.

Thus, D. Foata, J.-J. Pansiot and Y. Roy chose to develop a preprocessor for TEX on the VICTOR/SIRIUS: This micro computer is commonly found in laboratories all over France, and presents the advantages of a fully programmable keyboard and extended display capabilities. It was then possible to build out a specific text editor derived from P-MATE, called STRATEDI, allowing the user to type all the symbols as they appear on a typewriter. By using a third level (ALT), and the extra keys, one can input regular ANSI characters, accented capitals, Greek letters, mathematical symbols, and some special characters. All those characters will actually appear on the screen.

The STRATEC program itself then translates those extended codes to standard ASCII. For example, the é will be transformed into \'e. It was even possible to reproduce the effect of the dead key: typing ^i produces î on the screen, which becomes \^\i after processing by STRATEC. The special characters correspond to those having particular meaning for TEX, such as subscript and superscript marks, and to low-level macros such as changes of fonts. Details about STRATEC can be found in [9].

3. The hyphenation problems:

The main concern in processing French text is hyphenation. It is a strange irony: The first patented (in 1954!) computer-assisted typesetting program is a French invention, called 'Procédé B.B.R.' [2]. (Needless to say, this invention never reached the commercial stage, like most of the French technical innovations, at least in the 50's!) It included an algorithm for hyphenation, outlined in [1, 4]. This algorithm, which worked very well, was later adapted to English, with poor results. Conversely, any program for English hyphenation will behave badly in French. The procedures are fundamentally different, not only because etymology has much more importance in English, but also because the syllabifications do not obey the same rules in both languages. The same word might not be hyphenated the same way in French and in English: ma-gni-fi-cence *vs.* mag-nif-i-cence.

To 'feed' TEX's hyphenation algorithm, one needs a set of *patterns*, automatically generated by a special program, called PATGEN from a dictionary indicating legal breakpoints. This approach is not feasible for French: No French dictionary ever indicates legal breakpoints. We will emphasize this point when discussing pattern generation for French.

Thus, before attempting to make TEX hyphenate French properly, we had to set up rules for French hyphenation. Strangely enough, this was not an easy task. To summarize, everybody agree that division usually takes place between syllables [11, 16]. Unfortunately, no proper definition is given of how to find syllables, and our last example showed that it is by no means obvious. Moreover, in French, spoken syllabification do not necessarily coincide with written syllabification. (There is even a third kind of syllabification: that of poetry; for example passion is syllabified pa-ssion when spoken, pas-sion when written and pa-ssi-on when declaimed.)

To our knowledge, only Frey [10] in the 19th century and Thimonnier [17] more recently, give precise rules for finding written syllables. But their rules are incompatible. Very close to Latin (and Italian), Frey's rules are not usable in contemporary French, not because they are wrong, but because typographic traditions evolved in the last century. For this reason, we basically used the rules we derived from Thimonnier. We study this matter with more details in [6, 8].

The set of rules we established is divided into two groups: purely phonetic rules and etymological rules. Only the rules from the first group have precise formulations:

> The following groups must be considered as *single* consonants: bl cl fl gl br cr dr fr gr pr tr ch kh ph rh th gn chl phl chr phr thr. With this convention, it is possible to divide before a consonant immediately followed by a vowel, except:
> - if it is preceded only by consonants or by a single vowel,
> - before a consonant only followed by e or es (*i.e.* a mute final),
> - between the l's in the sequence ill, when they represent the semi-vowel sound yod,
> - finally, the division takes place between the g and the n instead of before the g in wagnérien, stagnant, and the words derived from them.

Let us give some examples: abs-ti-nence, ex-pli-ca-tion, ins-pec-tion, ma-gni-fi-cence, phta-léine, grillage, vil-lage, stag-na-tion. The last three examples illustrate the various exceptions to the general rule.

At that point, it must be noted that the decision on how to hyphenate a word containing ill is not purely graphical.

The second set of rules deals with etymological hyphenations. It is mostly a matter of personal taste:

> Must be divided according to their etymology, if it is obvious, those words that retain their etymological sense.

For example, we divide bron-cho-pneu-mo-nie, pa-ra-psy-cho-lo-gie, sub-lu-naire, ana-strophe. On the other hand, apostrophe has evolved too far from its etymology, so we divide apos-trophe. In case there is a conflict between pronunciation and etymology, we always adopt the phonetic rules: mi-cro-scope (etymology) *vs.* té-les-cope (phonetic). The division téle-scope would provoke the transformation of the sound represented by the e from è to 'neutral' e.

4. The French fonts:

The need for special fonts comes primarily from the way TEX hyphenates [12]. Let us just say that TEX attempts no hyphenation after the third letter preceding a non-letter or 'explicit kern', where TEX considers a letter to be a character with category code 11 or 12, having a non-zero lower-case code (\lccode).

PLAIN TEX produces the accented characters by superposing an accent over a letter. This is achieved by means of explicit kerns. It follows that no hyphenation is possible in a word containing accents, after the third letter preceding the first accent.

Unfortunately many French words contain accented characters, the most frequent being the é: out of the 49,962 entries of our on-line French vocabulary [5], 15,970 contain at least one accented letter and among them 13,477 contain at least one é.

Another problem arises when typesetting accented characters with TEX. Many times, the placement of the accent is deficient. Even if the rounding and conversion of the DVI units to the raster units is improved—which is the case in recent versions of TEX—some accents still have to be adjusted. Over some lower-case letters, they have to be slightly shifted, and they are too high and too steep over the capitals. Of course, some of these defects can be corrected by inserting extra kern, or even by rewriting the macros for the accents. Nevertheless, the best solution is to include all the accented characters as entities in the font: It gives the best positioning of the accents and enables TEX to hyphenate.

French uses thirteen accented characters: â, ê, î, ô, û, é, à, è, ù, ë, ï, ü and ç, plus the ligature œ. Even if the corresponding upper-case characters are missing from 'French' fonts as distributed by some type foundries, at least the accented upper-case E's and the C cedilla cannot be dispensed with. In fact, good typography requires all fourteen upper-case special characters [10].

TEX can handle 'extended' fonts of up to 256 characters, but only the first 128 are defined in the fonts currently used, leaving a lot of room available for extra characters. The solution seems obvious: Place the extra characters in the second half, with character codes from 128 to 257. Unfortunately, this is unfeasible at the moment. The main reason is that only characters with codes from 0 to 127 are allowed to have a nonzero \lccode. One further restriction comes from the fact that the 'old' METAFONT cannot generate fonts of more than 128 characters. This last difficulty will be eliminated when the 'new' METAFONT is fully operational.

Consequently, we tried to devise a temporary solution, allowing us, at least, to build and trest our hyphenation patterns. This made it necessary to include a minimal number of accented characters.

By comparing the Computer Modern font tables and the standard ASCII character codes, it appears that only the codes from 0 to 32 and 127 are fully available. (Some others could be used, except in the 'typewriter' fonts.) As it was impossible to move all these characters to positions over 127, we had to get rid of a certain number of them. The best—if not the only—candidates were the unslanted Greek capitals, occupying positions 0–10. Not even the accents can be removed: The acute is needed on any vowel if a quotation from Spanish is to be typeset, and the same is true with the grave accent in Italian, the umlaut accent in German, and the circumflex in Esperanto.

Therefore, we had to abandon some of the accented characters. The ü is never used in modern French, except in a few proper names. The ù is used in one word—où (where)—and à in a few words, all of which are too short to be hyphenated. Each of the others may occur in the middle of words (though very seldom will ë and ï). We decided to include them. They are the ten accented letters: â, ê, î, ô, û, é, è, ë, ï and ç. The ligatures œ and Œ already appear in the 'Computer Modern' fonts.

As it is safer for a lower-case letter to be equal to its \lccode—this last parameter is an essential element of the \lowercase primitive—the code 0 cannot be used for a lower-case letter. It could be possible to assign this code to the É, which appears quite often at the beginning of a word. But the lower-case é could not be converted to the upper-case É via \uppercase: a character with 0 as its \uccode remains unchanged. So we did not retain this possibility, hoping that, very soon, new fonts and/or a change to the restrictions about the \lccode will allow more flexible capabilities of adding extra letters.

We also removed the Spanish open question and exclamation marks and replaced them by the opening and closing guillemets, for which we wrote some lines of (old) METAFONT code. Fortunately, these guillemets now have the same character codes as the ASCII characters '<' and '>'. Moreover, the guillemets usually are not available in typewriter style, and so do not conflict with the characters '<' and '>' in the typewriter fonts.

The accented characters have been produced by adding the METAFONT codes for the accent to the code for the letter, and slightly adjusting the horizontal positioning of the former.

Finally, we modified and increased the number of kerning instructions in the METAFONT code so that the spacing is consistent: the same implicit kern is inserted between x and é as between x and e, for example. We added the same kern before and after œ as before o and after e, and did the same for Œ. (In our opinion, this could be included in the ordinary fonts.) We noticed that the spacing was wrong between f and î in roman style, and inserted the italic correction. For the same reason some kern had to be specified between the apostrophe and the accented î. The result is acceptable. Unfortunately, no satisfying result could be devised in the case of the sans-serif fonts, especially in such a word as fît (it exists!), where the rhythm of the strokes is important. This confirms the point that the design of the accented characters has to be part of the work of the designer at a relatively early stage.

A sample of one of our 'French' fonts can be found in appendix II.

5. The patterns for French:

Let us just give a short account of the way we constructed a set of patterns to be used when typesetting French. This work is more extensively described in [6, 8]. We suppose that the reader has some knowledge of the hyphenation algorithm used by TeX. It is explained in [12] and, in a French context, in [6].

The set of patterns currently used by TeX for hyphenating English was produced by F. Liang (see [13]) by applying his PATGEN program to a slightly edited version of the *Webster's Pocket Dictionary*. The same approach was impossible in French: no French dictionary indicates the feasible break positions. The task of building out a hyphenated dictionary needs probably more work than directly producing the suitable patterns. Moreover such a dictionary would be extremely large: The on-line vocabulary we used [5] countains about 50,000 entries. Its 'extended' version (containing every possible ending for every possible word) is five times as large.

The first set of rules were translated into 412 'phonetic patterns'. Most of them could be devised directly without checking the vocabulary. They take care of the 'general' rule. For example, the pattern 1ré produces the break pa-rée. The patterns 1t2r and 1ph2r displace the hyphenation point respectively before te t and the ph, as in en-trée and né-phrétique. Such patterns exist for every consonant and every vowel, and for every compound consonant. Then, some mistakes have to be corrected: The preceding patterns would wrongly hyphenate ara-ch-néen or ya-cht. This is prevented by 2chn and 2cht, which give the right divisions arach-néen and yacht. Such cases have to be looked for individually through the vocabulary.

We now arrive to the exceptions to the general phonetic rule. To avoid ph-taléine, or similar breaks, it must be added patterns such as ·ph4. (Remind that the '·' means the end of a word.) Such case are uncommon. Then comes a series of patterns to prevent hyphenation before a mute final syllable. Some examples are 4res·, 4ches·, 4che· and 4gue·.

Concerning the group ill, we had to check the pronunciation of every word containing it. We finally decided to prevent il-l with the pattern i12l, and look for exceptions, and possibly for exceptions to exceptions. For example, we have vi13l to allow vil-lage and avil4l, which will not allow the break in gravillon. Finally, the reasons for ·sta2g3n and wa2g3n are obvious.

The generation of 'etymological' patterns was a longer task to perform. As we mentioned, etymological division is, to a great extend a matter of personal choice. With the rule we stated, we had to look for good candidates to such a division, and build corresponding patterns.

Such a division is needed in about 3.5% of the words (compound words, neologisms and scientific terms). Most of them are obtained by adding a prefix to an already existing term. We could then divide our search in search for prefixes and search for radicals. The set of 392 patterns ensures the right etymological hyphenations where they are needed, and in most nonexistent but possible cases (scientific terms, neologisms). As their formation really requires a good knowledge of French to be understood, we do not explain how we produced them, referring to [6], and to appendix III.

Finally, we added patterns substituting the apostrophe to the left delimiter '·' when followed by a vowel, to produce the same result whether the word to hyphenate is preceded by the apostrophe or by a space.

The resulting set of 804 patterns was finally tested by checking once more the French vocabulary, which led to some minor corrections.

The conclusion is that 100% of the French words are correctly hyphenated—in our opinion, since no precise rule establishes when the etymological hyphenation has to be preferred to the phonetic one. No permissible hyphenations are missed, and no impermissible ones are introduced. Some words of foreign origin are specified in the \hyphenation list.

One of the advantages of the method used to produce the patterns is that the meaning of each of them is clear: They can be removed, modified, and some more can be added. If enough care is taken, the effect of such manipulations will be perfectly predictible. Hence it is easy to adapt the set of patterns to anyone's needs, and to correct the possible errors.

In order to load the patterns, and to ensure a proper hyphenation of the words containing extra characters, we must assign these characters lower-case codes. These are obviously equal to the character codes. To allow \uppercase to work in an acceptable way, we assign to the accented characters the upper-case codes of the corresponding unaccented capitals. This does not apply to the ligatures œ and Œ: they just exchange their lower-case and upper-case codes like ordinary letters. Finally, the apostrophe is given a \lccode equal to its character code, 39.

The only admissible characters in the patterns are letters and digits, the latter, in our case, serving as coefficients (see [12]). In particular, no control sequences are allowed in the list of patterns. Consequently, the extra characters must be specified through the 'double hat' notation, used for specifying the ordinarily 'inaccessible' ASCII characters. For example, the é is denoted by ^^F, corresponding to the code 6. (This kind of obscure encoding is used only when loading the patterns.) In our case, all of the special characters, except ë and ï, but including œ and the apostrophe actually appear in the patterns (^^A to ^^G, ^^I, ^^[and ').

Some of the codes used for accented characters have been assigned special category codes in the PLAIN file: ^^A, the ASCII code 1 (on SAIL the 'downarrow'), can be used for subscripts (category 8), and the ASCII tab, ^^I, is synonymous with the space (category 10). Just before loading the patterns, these category codes have to be changed to 12 ('other character'). The initial values are restored just after loading. Obviously, no 'tab' (temporarily equivalent to è!) may appear in between. For the same reasons, in case some other ASCII characters are given a special meaning (due to a peculiarity of the local system for example), care must be taken to avoid any confusion with special characters.

6. French typography:

Except for the very special case of quote-in-quotes, adapting French typography to TEX is comparatively easy. The main differences are as follows.

The semi-colons, exclamation points, and question marks are usually preceded by a thin space, which must not shrink nor stretch. The colons should be preceded by the inter-word space of the current line, which may vary from one line to another. The ordinary inter-word space follows any punctuation. Obviously, no line break is allowed before a punctuation mark. Moreover, these four punctuation marks usually are preceded and followed by a space when typed on a keyboard by French typists. The solution we have adopted is to make these characters active (category code 13). When they occur, they first test the current mode. If in horizontal mode, they remove the last glob of glue, if any (*i.e.*, the space before the punctuation is significant) and in this case replace it with an explicit kern (for the first three marks) or with unbreakable inter-word glue (for the colon). The explicit kern is such that its value is .4 times the inter-word space except in typewriter style, in which case it is exactly the inter-word space.

To the last typesetting convention we were unable to devise the correct macros: When a quotation is made *inside* another quotation, it begins with the same mark (*i.e.* opening guillemets). But, until the end of the inner quotation, the opening guillemets are repeated at the beginning of each line and are aligned with the left margin. In a sense, the lengths of the lines are shorter by the width of the opening guillemets during the inner quotation. The difficulty comes from the fact that it is impossible to modify the lengths of the lines inside a paragraph, unless the number of lines to be modified is known in advance.

The French quotes-in-quotes convention are shown in the following paragraphs. They could appear in a review of our article [6].

Les problèmes posés par la division étymologique sont ainsi résumés par J. Désarménien :

« Tout le monde s'accorde à trouver légitime la division : **extra-ordinaire**. Le cas des mots composés est le seul à rencontrer cette unanimité. Dans les autres, les opinions sont très partagées. Frey est le plus catégorique : il n'admet de division selon la formation que pour des mots de composition complètement française, et la rejette sinon ... Le *Code typographique*, tout en adoptant ce même point de vue « ... [recon-« naît] néanmoins que certains auteurs de travaux scientifiques préfèrent la division « étymologique qui fait ressortir la racine grecque ou latine ». Quant à Gouriou, il écrit : « On préférera cependant garder la coupure étymologique chaque fois que les « composants sont *aisément* reconnaissables. » (L'italique est de Gouriou.) Telle est aussi l'opinion de Girodet. »

The solution we give essentially builds a first list of lines, until reaching the inner quotation; then it removes the last line from the list and appends what remains to the page. Then, this last line is used as the beginning of a second vertical box with different indentation parameters. Once more, the last line is removed and the rest is appended to the page with opening guillemets at the beginning of each line. Finally, this new last line is appended to the page as a horizontal list, and it is followed by the end of the current paragraph. A number of 'dirty tricks' were used to avoid the use of arguments inside the macros, to allow the right spacings and penalties between lines, and to avoid having two opening guillemets at the beginning of the first line of the second section when the last line of the first section is almost \hsize long.

The TeX source of these macros is given in [7, 8].

7. Italian hyphenation using TeX:

The ideas we developed for French hyphenation can be applied to Italian. In this last language, the situation is even more favorable. First, there is no font problem, as the accented vowels may occur only in the last position inside a word and, consequently, do not interfere with hyphenation. Second, the rules for hyphenating Italian are well known, established and agreed upon by most authors. As a reference, we used A. Camilli's book [3], from which we derived the following rules.

> Compound consonants are: **p**, **b**, **t**, **d**, **c**, **g**, **f** and **v** followed by **l** or **r**; **ch**, **gh** and **gn**; **s** followed by any consonant (single or compound) except **s**.
>
> It is possible to divide before a consonant (single or compound) when followed by a vowel.
>
> We never attempt a division according to etymology.

A few examples: au-ra, ac-qua, pa-sta, tran-sa-tlan-ti-co.

As in French, the apostrophe must be made a letter. With the help of G. Letta, we checked the hyphenations around apostrophes. Our conclusion was to allow it before l', gl' and st', but not before any other consonant followed by the apostrophe: del-l'altra but not nessu-n'altra. Finally, the possibility of dividing at the apostrophe, which is encouraged to by A. Camilli is unfeasible: it was impossible, in that case, to prevent the insertion of a hyphen.

Making the patterns was almost a straightforward operation. It was possible to concentrate the rule concerning the s in only two patterns, by noting that hyphenation is always possible before an s and never after it, except when it is doubled.

The resulting 88 patterns are given in appendix IV.

8. Conclusions:

We tried to illustrate the three different kinds of problems one is faced when adapting an Anglo-American text-processing software to a new language. The solution to the input problem is essential. Unfortunately, it does not seem possible, for the moment, to solve it independently of the material. Our laboratory is now working on a text editor specific to TEX, making it more interactive, and we do not know, yet, how portable it could be. We also are associated with the Électricité de France research laboratory for adapting STRATEC to the French MICROSTAR micro-computer. This last work is under good way.

The hyphenation problem is strongly dependant on the language. There are two kinds of European languages: Those, like English or German, which have rules that are difficult to state independantly of the semantic context. The solution is then to use PATGEN. That is the way B. Schulze produced a set of patterns for German [15]. For the other languages, like French or Italian, where phonetic rules predominate, it is not difficult to produce directly good sets of patterns. For those languages, the objection usually formulated by people is: TEX does not use the best algorithm, finite state automata do as well and corresponding programs are only a few lines long. This is true. Nevertheless, TEX offers the advantage of universality: The same basic algorithm is used for any language, only the set of patterns differs. Moreover, for such a language as French, where some rules are not purely typographic, the capability of making exceptions part of the rules results in a very effective hyphenation algorithm.

The main problem we were faced came from the way TEX handles diacritics. Combined with the limitations of ASCII standards, it resulted in a solution not as good as we would like, mostly because we had to make new fonts. B. Schulze was faced with the same problems with German 'umlauts'. We just hope that the new METAFONT will help us provide new fonts (it cannot be dispensed with) at a lower cost. Those French fonts would also be more complete, including accented capitals. As META-FONT will allow producing fonts containing 256 characters, it could even be possible to build fonts common to more than one language. Finally, as no more PXL nor TFM (binary) files will be sent, but only METAFONT source codes, it will be possible to easily communicate those special fonts.

Finally, concerning the various local typographic conventions, the flexibility of TeX allows to include them as part of a local format file, as that described in [7].

References.

[1] Bafour (G.), A New Method for Text Composition, *Printing Technology*, 5(1961), 65–75.

[2] *Le Procédé B.B.R. de composition automatique des textes*, (2 vol.), Imprimerie nationale, Paris, nov. 1958.

[3] Camilli (A.), *Pronuncia e grafia dell'italiano* [terza ed.], Sansoni, Firenze, 1965.

[4] Chéreau (L.), Le système B.B.R. et les applications des machines à calculer électroniques en imprimerie et en documentation, *Bull. Bibliothèques de France*, 9e année, **2**(1964), 43–61.

[5] Courtois (B.), DLAS, vocabulaire français informatisé, Laboratoire d'automatique documentaire et linguistique, Université Paris VII.

[6] Désarménien (J.), La division par ordinateur des mots français avec le logiciel TeX, submitted to *T.S.I.*

[7] Désarménien (J.), How to run TeX in a French environment: hyphenation, fonts, typography, *TUGboat*, 5(1984), 91–102.

[8] Désarménien (J.), *How to run TeX in French*, Stanford University report No. STAN-CS-1013, 1984.

[9] Foata (D.), Pansiot (J.-J.) and Roy (Y.), STRATEC, *un logiciel de traitement de textes mathématiques en amont de TeX*, Publ. I.R.M.A. Strasbourg 225/D-06, 1984.

[10] Frey (A.), *Nouveau Manuel complet de typographie*, Paris, 1857, reed. by Léonce Laget, Paris, 1979.

[11] Grevisse (M.), *Le Bon Usage* [onzième éd.], Duculot, Paris-Gembloux, 1980.

[12] Knuth (D.), *The TeXbook*, Addison-Wesley, Reading, Mass., 1984.

[13] Liang (F. M.), *Word Hy-phen-a-tion by Com-put-er*, Stanford University report No. STAN-CS-977, 1983.

[14] Mlouka (M.), private communication.

[15] Schulze (B.), German Hyphenation and Umlauts in TeX, *TUGboat*, **5(1984)**, 103–104.

[16] Sève (A.) and Perrot (J.), *L'Ortho vert*, Éditions Sociales, Paris, 1976.

[17] Thimonnier (R.), *Code orthographique et grammatical*, Marabout, Verviers, 1978.

Appendix I

The STRATEC keyboard

Appendix II

Text font 'French roman'

	0	1	2	3	4	5	6	7
'000		â	ê	î	ô	û	é	ç
'010	ë	è	ï	ff	fi	fl	ffi	ffl
'020	ı	ȷ	`	´	ˇ	˘	¯	˚
'030	¸	ß	æ	œ	ø	Æ	Œ	Ø
'040	´	!	"	#	$	%	&	'
'050	(	)	*	+	,	-	.	/
'060	0	1	2	3	4	5	6	7
'070	8	9	:	;	«	=	»	?
'100	@	A	B	C	D	E	F	G
'110	H	I	J	K	L	M	N	O
'120	P	Q	R	S	T	U	V	W
'130	X	Y	Z	[	"	]	^	.
'140	'	a	b	c	d	e	f	g
'150	h	i	j	k	l	m	n	o
'160	p	q	r	s	t	u	v	w
'170	x	y	z	–	—	"	~	¨

Appendix III

Patterns for French

Phonetic patterns.

1ba	1bâ	1be	1bé	1bè	1bê	1bi	1bî
1bo	1bô	1bu	1bû	1by	4bes.	1b2l	4ble.
4bles.	1b2r	4bre.	4bres.	1ca	1câ	1ce	1cé
1cè	1cê	1ci	1cî	1co	1cô	1cu	1cû
1cy	1cœ	4ces.	1c2h	4che.	4ches.	2chb	2chg
2chm	2chn	2chp	2chs	2cht	2chw	.ch4	ch2l
4chle.	4chles.	ch2r	4chre.	4chres.	1c2l	4cle.	4cles.
1c2r	4cre.	4cres.	1ç	1da	1dâ	1de	1dé
1dè	1dê	1di	1dî	1do	1dô	1du	1dû
1dy	4des.	did2h	1d2r	4dre.	4dres.	1fa	1fâ
1fe	1fé	1fè	1fê	1fi	1fî	1fo	1fô
1fu	1fû	1fy	4fes.	1f2l	4fle.	4fles.	1f2r
4fre.	4fres.	1ga	1gâ	1ge	1gé	1gè	1gê
1gi	1gî	1go	1gô	1gu	1gû	1gy	4ges.
4gne.	4gnes.	1g2ha	1g2he	1g2hi	1g2ho	1g2hy	1g2l
4gle.	4gles.	1g2n	.sta2g3n	wa2g3n	4gne.	4gnes.	1g2r
4gre.	4gres.	1ha	1hâ	1he	1hé	1hè	1hê
1hi	1hî	1ho	1hô	1hu	1hû	1hy	4hes.
1j	2jk	4jes.	1ka	1kâ	1ke	1ké	1kè
1kê	1ki	1kî	1ko	1kô	1ku	1kû	1ky
4kes.	1k2h	c2k3h	.kh4	1k2r	1la	1lâ	1le
1lé	1lè	1ly	4les.	1l2l	1li	1lî	1lo	1lô	1lu
vaci14l	gil3l	hil3l	1il3l	mil3l	émil14l	rmil14l	armil5l
mil4let	semil14l	vanil3lin	vanil3lis	capil3l	papil3la	papil3le	papil3li
papil3lom	pupil3l	cyril3l	ibril3l	piril3l	thril3l	pusil3l	boutil3l
distil3l	fritil3l	instil3l	.stil3l	vil3l	avil14l	uvil14l	uevil14l
chevil14l	xil3l	1ma	1mâ	1me	1mé	1mè	1mê
1mi	1mî	1mo	1mô	1mu	1mû	1my	1mœ
4mes.	1na	1nâ	1ne	1né	1nè	1nê	1ni
1nî	1no	1nô	1nu	1nû	1ny	1nœ	4nes.
1pa	1pâ	1pe	1pé	1pè	1pê	1pi	1pî
1po	1pô	1pu	1pû	1py	4pes.	1p2h	4phe.
4phes.	ph2l	4phle.	4phles.	2phn	ph2r	4phre.	4phres.
2phs	2pht	.ph4	1p2l	4ple.	4ples.	1p2r	4pre.
4pres.	1q	4que.	4ques.	1ra	1râ	1re	1ré
1rè	1rê	1ri	1rî	1ro	1rô	1ru	1rû
1ry	4res.	1r2h	4rhe.	4rhes.	1sa	1sâ	1se
1sé	1sè	1sê	1si	1sî	1so	1sô	1su
1sû	1sy	1sœ	4ses.	1s2ch	4sch.	2schs	4sche.
4sches.	.sch4	.sh4	1s2h	2shm	2shr	2shs	4she.
4shes.	1ta	1tâ	1te	1té	1tè	1tê	1ti
1tî	1to	1tô	1tu	1tû	1ty	4tes.	1t2h
.th4	4the.	4thes.	2thl	2thm	2thn	th2r	2ths
1t2r	4tre.	4tres.	1va	1vâ	1ve	1vé	1vè
1vê	1vi	1vî	1vo	1vô	1vu	1vû	1vy
4ves.	1v2r	4vre.	4vres.	1wa	1we	1wi	1wo
1wu	4wes.	1w2r	1za	1xe	1xé	1xè	1zi
1xo	1xu	1xy	4xes.	'a4	'â4	'e4	'é4
'è4	'ê4	'i4	'î4	'o4	'ô4	'u4	'û4
'y4	2'2	1d'	d1s2	f1s2	g1s2	l1s2t	m1s2
e2s3ch	12s3ché	12s3chia	12s3chio				

Etymological patterns.

```
1alcool          i1algi           1a2nesth€si      i1arthr          a€2dre           i1€2dre
1€2drique        1€2lectr         1€2l€ment        1€2nerg          2t3heur          2r3heur
2t3houd          2s3hom           2r3hydr          1informat        o1ioni           1m2n€si
1m2n€mo          mon2t3r€al       1octet           i1oxy            3ph2tal€         3ph2tis
1p2neu           1p2n€            1p2psych         1p2t€r           1p2t€r           1s2caph
1s2cl€r          1s2cop           e2s3cop          €pi2s3cop        €pi3s4cope       di2s3cop
1s2lav           1s2lov           1s2patia         1s2perm          1s2por           1s2ph€r
1s2ph€r          1s2piel          1s2piros         1s2tandard       1s2tas           o1s2tat
pro2s3tat        i1s2tat          1s2tein          o1s2t€ro         1s2tigm          o1s2tim
1s2tock          1s2tomos         o1s2tom          o1s2trad         o1s2tratu        o1s2triction
1s2troph         a2s3tro          apo2s3tr         u2s3tr           1s2tructu        1s2tyle
.anti1a2         .anti1e2         .anti2enne       .anti€2          .anti1s2         'anti1a2
'anti1e2         'anti2enne       'anti1€2         .bi1a2c          .bi1au
.bio1a2          .bi1u2           .bi2s1a2         .ci2s1alp        co1acc           co1acq
co1a2d           co1ap            co1ar            co1assoc         co1assur         co1au
co1ax            co1en            co1ex            co1€2            .con4            .cons4
co2nurb          .co1o2           .co2o3lie        .d€1a2           .d€1io           .d€1o2
.d€2s            .d€3sacr         .d€3sastr        .d€3satell       .d€3s€gr         .d€3sensib
.d€3sert         .d€3sexu         .d€3sid          .d€3sign         .d€3sili         .d€3sinen
.d€3sinvo        .d€3sir          .d€3sist         .d€3sod€         .d€3sol          .d€3sopil
.d€3sorm         .d€3sorp         .d€3soufr        .d€3sy           .d€3s2c          .d€3s2p
.d€3s2t          .d€3su           .d€4sun          .di1a2c€         .di1a2cid        .di1ald
.di1a2mi         .di1a2tomi       .di1e2n          .di2s3h          .dy2s1a2         .dy2s1i2
.dy2s1o2         .dy2s1u2         .dy2s3           .en1a2           'en1a2           e2n1i2vr
.en1o2           'en1o2           .eu2r1a2         .eu2r1a2         extra1           h€mi1€2
h€mo1p2t         hypera2          hyper€2          hypere2          hyperi2          hypero2
hypers2          hyperu2          hype4r1          hypo1a2          hypo1€2          hypo1e2
hypo1i2          hypo1o2          hypo1u2          hypo1s2          .in1a2           .in2a3nit
.in2augur        .in1€2           .in2€3lucta      .in2€3narra      .in1e2           .in2effab
.in2ept          .in2er           .in2exora        .in1i2           .in2i3miti       .in2i3q
.in2i3t          .in1o2           .in2o3cul        .in2ond          .in1s2tab        .in1u2
.in2uit          .in2u3l          'in1a2           'in2a3nit        'in2augur        'in1€2
'in2€3lucta      'in2n€3narra     'in1e2           'in2effab        'in2ept          'in2ert
'in2exora        'in1i2           'in2i3miti       'in2i3q          'in2i3t          'in1o2
'in2o3cul        'in2ond          'in1s2tab        'in1u2           'in2uit          'in2u3l
.intera2         .inter€2         .intere2         .interi2         .intero2         .interu2
.inters2         .inte4r3         'intera2         'inter€2         'intere2         'interi2
'intero2         'interu2         .inters2         'inte4r3         .ma2l1a2dres     .ma2l1a2dro
.ma2l1ais€       .ma2l1ap         .ma2l1a2v        .ma2l1en         .ma2l1int        .ma2l1oc
.ma2l1o2d        .m€2goh          .m€2sa           .m€3san          .m€2ses          .m€2si
.m€2sus          .m€ta1s2ta       .mono1a2         .mono1€2         .mono1e2         .mono1i2
.mono1o2         .mono1u2         .mono1s2         .no2o1nlobs      omni1s2          oxy1a2
pal€o1€2         .pa2n1a2f        .pa2n1a2m€       .pa2n1a2ra       .pa2n1is         .pa2n1o2ph
.pa2n1opt        .para1s2         .pa2r1a2che      .pa2r1a2ch€      .pa2r3h€         .per1a2
.per1€2          .per1e2          .per1i2          .per1o2          .per1u2          per3h
.pe4r            p€2nul           .p€r1ios         .p€r1i2s3s       .p€ri2s3s        .p€r1i1u2
photo1s2         poly1a2          poly1€2          poly1€2          poly1e2          poly1i2
poly1o2          poly1u2          poly1s2          .pos2t3h         .pos2t1o2        .pos2t3r
.post1s2         .pr€1a2          .pr€2a3la        .pr€au           .pr€1€2          .pr€1e2
.pr€1i2          .pr€1o2          .pr€1u2          .pr€1s2          .pro1€2          .pro1s2c€
radio1a2         .re1s2           .re2s3cap        .re2s3cisi       .re2s3ciso       .re2s3cou
.re2s3cri        .re2s3pect       .re2s3pir        .re2s3plend      .re2s3pons       .re2s3quil
.re2s3s          .re2s3t          .re3s4tab        .re3s4tag        .re3s4tand       .re3s4tat
.re3s4t€n        .re3s4t€r        .re3s4tim        .re3s4tip        .re3s4toc        .re3s4top
.re3s4tr         .re4s5trein      .re4s5trict      .re4s5trin       .re3s4tu         .re3s4ty
.r€1a2           .r€2a3le         .r€2a3lis        .r€2a3lit        .r€2aux          .r€1€2
.r€1e2           .r€2el           .r€1i2           .r€2i3fi         .r€1o2           .r€1u2
.r€2uss          .r€tro1a2        sesqui1a2        st€r€o1s2        .su2b1a2         .su3b2alt
.su2b1€2         .su3b2€3r        .su2b3l1imin     .su2b3l1in       .su2b3lu         subis2
.su2b1ur         supero2          supers2          supe4r1          .su2r1a2         .su3r2a3t
.su2r1e2         .su3r2eau        .su3r2ell        .su3r2et         .su2r1€2         .su2r3h
.su2r1i2m        .su3r1inf        .su2r1int        .su2r1of         .su2r1ox         t€l€1e2
t€l€1i2          t€l€1o2b         t€l€1o2p         t€l€1o2          thermo1s2        tran2s1a2
tran3s2act       tran3s2ats       tran2s3h         tran2s1o2        tran2s3p         tran2s1u2
.tri1a2c         .tri1a2n         .tri1a2t         archi1€2pis      moye2n1€2g       po1astre
v€lo1s2ki        vol2t1amp
```

Appendix IV

Patterns for Italian

1ba	1be	1bi	1bo	1bu	1b2l	1b2r	1ca
1ce	1ci	1co	1cu	1ch	1c2l	1c2r	1da
1de	1di	1do	1du	1d2r	1fa	1fe	1fi
1fo	1fu	1f2l	1f2r	1ga	1ge	1gi	1go
1gu	1gh	1g2l	1g2n	1g2r	1la	1le	1li
1lo	1lu	1l'	1ma	1me	1mi	1mo	1mu
1na	1ne	1ni	1no	1nu	1pa	1pe	1pi
1po	1pu	1p2l	1p2n	1p2r	1p2s	1q	1ra
1re	1ri	1ro	1ru	1s2	2s3s	1ta	1te
1ti	1to	1tu	1t2l	1t2r	1va	1ve	1vi
1vo	1vu	1v2r	1za	1ze	1zi	1zo	1zu

Appendix V

How to simultaneously hyphenate two languages

The solution to this problem comes from the way TeX hyphenates. More precisely, after a word has been delimited, TeX first converts its letters into the characters specified by their \lccode, and actually hyphenates the resulting sequence of characters before reverting to the original word.

It is then possible to interchange upper- and lower-case codes for one of the languages to hyphenate. For example, in French mode, the codes are as usual. On the contrary, in English mode, we set, among others, \lccode'a='A, \lccode'A='A, \uccode'a='a and \uccode'A='a. TeX then acts as if lower-case letters actually were upper-case, and *vice-versa*. Thus, when trying to hyphenate while in English mode, TeX will look for patterns made of upper-case letters, ignoring those consisting of lower-case ones.

When loading the patterns, those for English, converted to upper-case, are added to those for French left unchanged. To ensure the proper loading, locally to this operation, all characters are specified as lower-case, by saying, among others, \lccode'a='a and \lccode'A='A.

Then it is even possible to redefine the \lowercase and \uppercase primitives. The only serious restriction is the impossibility, at last in English mode, to prevent hyphenation of words beginning with an upper-case letter via \uchyph=0.

The Hyphenation of Non–English Words with TeX

Wolfgang Appelt

*Gesellschaft für Mathematik
und Datenverarbeitung mbH, Bonn*

Abstract: Using TeX for the processing of Non–English text leads to some problems with hyphenation if the language contains letters with accents or other characters that are usually constructed or addressed by control sequences. We describe a solution to make TeX hyphenate German words which we are implementing at GMD.

```
Overfull \hbox (106.00117pt too wide) in paragraph at lines 513--529
[]\tenrm Dies    ...   Gew^^?ahrleistungsanspruchsverj^^?ahrungsfrist|
```
— TeX (1984)

1. The Problem

When processing German text with TeX one is faced with the following problem: Many German words contain "umlaute" (ä, ö, ü, Ä, Ö, Ü) and/or the sharp S (ß). These letters are normally produced by control sequences (\"a ... \"U or \ss). When TeX, however, finds a control sequence within a word, it will never find a hyphen *after* that position in the word, i.e. the number of possible breakpoints for TeX's line breaking algorithm is reduced. Since furthermore the average word length in German is considerably larger than in English, TeX very often cannot find a solution for the line breaking algorithm even if the \tolerance is increased to a rather high value. This means that the user has to insert many discretionary breaks (\-) into the text.

To make TeX hyphenate words with umlaute these must be coded as normal letters somehow. The most obvious solution is a modification of the font tables that are used when processing German text, i.e. the umlaute are included into the fonts somewhere. There is, by the way, not much choice for a reasonable "somewhere": The umlaute *cannot* be placed above ASCII '177 and be addressed by, say:

TeX for Scientific Documentation   D. Lucarella, Editor
Copyright ©1985 Addison-Wesley Publishing Company, Inc.

```
\def\"#1{\if#1a{\char'200}\fi
         \if#1o{\char'201}\fi
...
         \if#1U{\char'205}\fi}
```

Why this idea will not work will be clear when reading Appendix H of the *TEXbook*: TEX abandones it's hyphenation algorithm if it finds a token whose category code is not "letter" or whose `\lccode` is zero. But a character above ASCII '177 can neither be catcoded as "letter" nor have a nonzero `\lccode`.

A reasonable place for the German umlaute might be the positions '32 ... '37 in the Computer Modern text fonts where normally the Scandinavian ligatures are placed. This approach, however, would require a modification of the TFM files and of the corresponding pixel files. Since at GMD we are currently running TEX on five different computer systems using seven output devices with six different pixel resolutions we would have to update several hundred files.

The modification of the TFM files would be a minor problem since writing a program that performs the required changes on a PL file (property list file; output from the `TFtoPL` program) is easy. A good text editor might be sufficient for such changes. The modification of the pixel files, however, would be a rather tedious task for several reasons that shall not be discussed here.

We therefore tried to find a solution for the handling of umlaute that did not require an update of the pixel files.

2. Fooling TEX

To make TEX process umlaute like normal letters we proceed as follows: We redefine the \"–macro of plain TEX and make the double quotes be accepted by TEX's hyphenation algorithm:

```
\def\"#1{"#1}
\catcode'\"=11  \lccode'"='"
```

The usual coding of the German umlaute thus simply expands to a letter pair ("a ... "U).

We furthermore make modifications to the TFM files: Each of these six letter pairs shall be replaced by a ligature. These ligatures are placed above the position '177 in the font tables, say at position '200 ... '205. The ligature programs might be written by the following piece of code in a PL file:

TEX for scientific documentation

```
(LABEL C ")
(LIG C a O 200)
(LIG C o O 201)
(LIG C u O 202)
(LIG C A O 203)
(LIG C O O 204)
(LIG C U O 205)
(STOP)
```

and the ligature characters might be defined as:

```
(CHARACTER O 200
   (CHARWD R 0.5)
   (CHARHT R 0.4305553)
   (VARCHAR
      (TOP O 177)
      (MID C a)
      )
   )
```

The widths and the heights we assign to those letters are the widths and the heights of the corresponding letters without the umlaut dots.* (Example: The character '200 ("ä") has the width and height values of the letter "a".) We furthermore assign VARCHAR-attributes to those letters: The MID- and TOP-value are just the characters that TEX would use when creating the umlaute by the normal plain TEX macro.

Though the final result of this two step procedure to place umlaute above '177 into the font tables is the same as with the \"-macro in the first chapter — the dvifiles would be identical — we have fooled TEX a little bit with this trick: TEX will now hyphenate such nice words like "Gewährleistungsanspruchsverjährungsfrist"** since any ligature substitution will take place *after* a possible hyphenation. As hyphenation patterns we have to use the "expanded" form of the umlaute, of course (e.g. ""u14l"o" instead of "ül4lö").

On the other hand TEX will use the correct values for the widths and heights of the umlaute since when TEX computes the position of the characters on the page the

---

* We have done this just for convenience. While the width values are o.k., the height of an umlaut is of course larger than the height of the corresponding unaccented letter. But letting TEX do it's computations with wrong height values for the umlaute can lead to undesired results only in very extreme situations. It is of course no problem to compute the correct values and put them into the TFM files.

** The result is `Ge-w"ahr-lei-stungs-an-spruchs-ver-j"ah-rungs-frist`, when using our German hyphenation patterns, which is absolutely correct. We found this word when we compiled a book an a juridical topic with TEX.

ligature substitution has already taken place. (TEX will not be confused by the TOP and MID attributes of the umlaute since these values are only used in math mode.)

3. Processing the Dvifile

Instead of updating the pixel files which seems to be necessary now, we modified our drivers a little bit: Whenever we find a command to set a character above '177 we assume that this character is an umlaut.* By taking the TOP and MID values of the character we know what umlaut we have to create.

The creation of the umlaut is done exactly the same way as TEX would do it. We just looked at the code of the *make_accent* procedure in TEX's source code and transfered the algorithm into the driver: We set the character that is addressed by the MID value, compute the position of the accent (addressed by the TOP value) and finally set the accent. In other words, the printed output looks the same as if we had created the umlaute by the normal plain TEX macro (not taking into account, of course, that TEX might have found more hyphenation points).

If a driver is written as a changefile to the DviType program (as a decent driver implementation will be) the required modifications within the changefile are rather small. The creation of the umlaute as described above is just a few lines of code. The only major change that affects several modules is due to the fact that we have to read more information from the tfmfiles as DviType does: Besides the widths of the characters the driver needs to know the height of each character plus the x-height and slant parameter of the font (to compute the accent position) and, of course, the TOP and MID attributes of the umlaut ligatures.

It should be noticed that the procedure for handling umlaute as described above keeps TEX source files portable to other installations. If an installation neither has the modified tfmfiles nor a driver that can create umlaute it is sufficient to redefine the \"-macro to its original meaning and the TEX file can be processed. There might of course arise some problems because the number of hyphenation points that TEX will find is reduced and discretionary breaks will have to be inserted into the text.

4. Extensions/Modifications

The method we have described can be used for other languages with accented letters, too. The extension is obvious for all characters that are build by the \accent primitive (ò, ó, ŏ, ö, ō, ô, ȯ, ő, õ). It is only necessary to make appropriate modifications of the

---

* Up to now we have no fonts that have more than 128 characters.

tfmfiles, redefine the macros that create the accented characters and the driver will generate all those characters as it does for the umlaute.

The situation becomes a little bit more complicated for characters where the accents go underneath (ǫ, o̦, o̱) because the \accent primitive is not sufficient in this case and some macros have to be used (see Appendix B of the *TEXbook*). Since these macros, however, only concern the positioning of two characters atop of each other and have no side effects it is possible to write appropriate code within a driver that does the computations of the macros. In other words, these macros can be handled like the \accent primitive and instead of letting TEX do the computation of the character positions, this task could be done by a driver as well. The characters with accents underneath should have a MID and a BOT attribute: Depending on the fact which of the values are present (TOP and MID or MID and BOT) the driver can decide which algorithm for computing the character positions has to be applied.

In Non–English speaking countries people often use keyboards with their terminals that contain letters of their native language. (In Germany, e.g., the umlaute and the "ß" are usually on the keyboards.) In that case it is not necessary — and the users will surely not like it — to code the accented letters via the usual TEX macros, but the corresponding keys can be used. To make TEX understand such a text a simple preprocessor can be written that translates each of the characters in question into the corresponding TEX control sequence. Another possibility (usually used at GMD) is extending TEX's character set by the additional characters on the keyboard and declare them as active characters that expand to the desired result (an "ä", e.g., in a TEX input file is an active characters that expands to ""a").

Acknowledgements

I am especially obliged to Jaques Désarménien who had done a profound investigation into the problem of running TEX in a French environment and gave me a lot of useful hints concerning the hyphenation problem for Non–English languages.

TeX and ISO/STPL standard

Le van Huu

Università degli Studi di Milano, Istituto di Cibernetica

In this paper we want to examine the most important STPL aspects and make a comparasion with those of TeX, with an attempt at answering the question whether TeX could be integrated with STPL such a way as to become a standard.

Introduction

D. Knuth in his book "TeX and METAFONT New Directions in Typesetting" published about 1979 writes "... Perhaps some day a typesetting language will become standardized to the point where papers can be submitted to the American Mathematical Society from computer to computer via telephone lines ... Of course I am hoping that if any language becomes standard it will be my TeX language ...". Many years have elapsed: we can now say his wish has been partly fulfilled, even if TeX has not been officially accepted as standard formatting system. Our affermation is as well proved from the fact that many important publishing houses and universities prefer TeX to many existing systems for their document production.

In the last few years, while TeX imposed itself as the standard system for these environments, a committee of ISO, the International Organization for Standardization, has worked at a project, called CLPT (Computer Language Processing Text), oriented to define standards relating to languages and functionality for text processing activity, as defining the logical and physical text structure, editing, formatting, storing and retrieving, interchanging... of documents.

The objective of the project, to which Knuth collaborates as expert, is to increase and simplify the intercommunication among them. The various standards are grouped under the name STPL (Standard Text Processing Languages), renamed then with "Information Processing Systems - Text Preparation and Interchange ...").

It is natural that we wonder what is the role of TeX in this proposal; in other words could TeX be integrated with STPL such a way as to become a standard? In this paper we want to examine the most important STPL aspects and make a comparasion

TeX for Scientific Documentation   D. Lucarella, Editor
Copyright ©1985 Addison-Wesley Publishing Company, Inc.

with those of TeX, with an attempt at answering the question whether TeX could be integrated with STPL such a way as to become a standard.

STPL

The standard STPL was drawn over a period of six years. Its main components specify:

- a text processing programming language (called TPPL) for an application that deals with text. A TPPL foundamental characteristic is that it can be included into the text upon which it may be operate. Although oriented to string and text treatment, it keeps the functionality needed for general purpose application.
- functions commonly used in text entry and editing applications
- functions commonly used in text processing and composition applications
- a generalized markup language (SGML) to describe the structure of a document. It provided a coherent and unambigous syntax for describing whatever an user chooses to identify within a document.
- functions needed by applications that process documents prepared with the markup language. It constitutes a link between the programming language and the markup language, in fact the features of the the parts may be combined into a single application.
- the binding to the Graphical Kernel System, that provides the capability of containing within one data set the entire abstract version of a document including pictures. There is no working draft of this part.
- the application to WYSIWYG processing. There is no working draft of this part.

The standard STPL is drawn to be compatible with Open System Interconnection Model. It functions as a member of the Application Layer of that Model.

Briefly we explain the important aspects of some of those parts that should be put in connection with TeX system. The first is the standard SGML (Standard Generalized Markup Language).

SGML

This standard is proposed for the definition process of documents to be submitted to others activities. Generally a document can be defined by means of additional information inserted into the text. These pieces of information, "markup elements", form a real description language with their own syntactic and semantic rules.

A markup language, according to information that its elements are able to represent, can be inserted into one of the following classes:

a) Procedural markup, where the markup specifies operations that must ordinately apply to text logical elements. This type of language is constituted by a set of low level commands which allow the user to drive and to control the formatting process (underline a phrase, change the font ...) exactly at the point of the text where the markup is inserted.

b) Declarative markup, which concentrates on the logical structure of the document objects bringing out their attribute values (figure with the figure caption, first paragraph ...) and the relations between an element and the others (a figure inside a paragraph, footnote of the preface ...). In this way, the processing which affects the various parts of the text is left to the formatting system, which must give them a proper layout, according to their attribute values.

SGML belongs to the second cathegory, so it is viewed as a declarative markup language, capable of describing the document logical structure and its attributes.

In SGML a document is a logical construct called "document element", which is the top of a tree of elements that make up the document's content. A book, for example, could contain a "chapter" element that in turn contains "paragraph" and "picture" elements, then the "paragraph" element could contain in turn "text", "example", "note" elements. Each of these elements could finally contain characters sequences that represent its "content".

Every element of such logical structure is identified by a symbolic name, called "generic identifier" (we will refer to it as GI) and by a set of attribute values. Moreover, every element has its own "value model" made of a set of attribute values and by eventual subelements. So, a physical portion of the text will be associated to a particular GI if its characteristics correspond to the value model of that GI: for example, it must be placed in an exact point of the document or it must have all alphabetic and not numeric characters ... Again, two text portions can be considered different even if identified with the same GI when they have two different attribute values.

The markup elements of SGML are divided into 3 classes:

- Markup declaration: to define characteristics of every document element. There are two types of markup declaration: structure declaration, to specify the logical structure of an element defining its "value model", and attribute declaration to specify its attribute model, i.e. attribute names and attribute values.

For example with this structure declaration phrase:

<!STRUC cover (title, author) >

we define the structure of the cover, which is consituted by the "title" element, followed by the "author" element, and with this attribute declaration:

<!ATT author type (principal : co-author) >

we define an attribute of "author" element, named "type", which possible values are "principal" and "co-author". (*)

However in this paper we prefer use the old SGML version to facilitate the illustration of its concept.

- Markup descriptive: to mark every segment of text which content corresponds to an element of the document structure using relating GI name.

  For example in the following document

  1 <!STRUC cover (title, author) >
  2 <!ATT author type (principal : co-author) >
  3 <cover>
  4 <title>
  5   The SGML standard proposed by ISO.
  6 <author type = "principal">
  7   Le van Huu
  8 </cover>

  lines 4, 6 are markup descriptive sentences that mark the text representing the title, the author name and the value of its attribute (type = "principal"). The location of these element is conformed to the structure established by the logical structure declaration (lines 1 and 2).

- Processing instruction: to indicate, in particular cases, some procedures to be activated.

To describe a document using SGML we should:

(*)We note that the above SGML syntax has been changed by the last versions of the language, according to them the structure declaration markup and the attribute declaration markup are included in a single delaration sentence, called "ELEMENT" declaration. In this way the following syntax
    <!STRUC gi (value-model) >
    <!ATT gi attribute-name (attribute values) >
becomes:
    <!ELEMENT gi (value-model)

1) Define the logical structure of our document type using "markup declaration" SGML phrases. At this stage we don't specify any "markup descriptive" because we are creating only the skeleton of a document type.

2) Describe our particular document according to the logical structure created by the above stage. The GI names of that structure will be used to form the "markup descriptive" phrases. We construct in this way the physical structure of our particular document.

But to obtain the final layout of the document we must add to these stages other activities, such as:

- Parsing the source document mapping every text portion of a logical element to a composition procedure. These procedure formats the document by creating a device independent file
- Print out the final pages.

SGML and TEX

From the above considerations we notice that a formatter must have not only the capability to describe the document structure, but even low level functions able to resolve typesetting problems. Then it is easy to realise that SGML and TEX can be inserted in this context, where the power of TEX to treat typesetting elements is enhanced by the elegance and the semplicity with which SGML describes the document logical and physical structures.

Let's examine a TEX input document:

\hsize 2 in
\vskip 1 in
\ctrline{ STPL and TEX }
\vskip 36pt
\ctrline{ by Le van Huu }
\vskip 2.54 cm

Almost text processing activities .... I will examine its properties in the next paragraph.

\par
\vfill
\end

and the same document decribed with SGML notations:

```
<!STRUC article (title, author, paragraph* ) >
<article>
    TeX and METAFONT - New Directions in Typesetting
<author>
    Donald E. Knuth
<paragraph>
```

Almost text processing activities ... I will examine its properties in the next paragraph.

```
</paragraph>
</article>
```

In the last document we notice that every reference to typesetting functions has disappeared, however in return we can know what every component of the document represents, for example the line "TeX and METAFONT - New Directions in Typesetting" is the document "title" and "Donald E. Knuth" is the "author" name.

Naturally from that source document SGML cannot produce a page out put like that produced by TeX. There must exist somewhere a mapping from the logical elements onto the correspondent low level commands. Then integrate TeX with SGML it is necessary to create a mapping table where every logical element of SGML is associated to a set of TeX control sequences. For example from the above documents we can see that the input line <title> corresponds to TeX sequences

```
\hsize 2 in
\vskip 1 in
\ctrline
```

or </paragraph> that indicates the end of a paragraph is equivaled to TeX phrases

```
\par
\vfill
```

It is obvious to think that this association could be provided simply using TeX macros definitions facility, but sometimes it may be difficult to find a correspondence between a SGML element and TeX control sequences. The reason is that since SGML is a descriptive language with its variables and parameters, the mapping must depend on the current global state of these SGML objects. A solution may be to use the SGML parser to transform document described with SGML notations into TeX source document, thus mapping every GI to TeX control sequences, and to submitted the transformed document to TeX system which will yield the final layout.

In this context we can again benefit from TeX macros definition facility. Precisely we can first define a set of TeX macros with parameters, then realize a mapping between them and SGML elements. The actual values of parameters of TEX macros are flexible, i.e. they depend by status of SGML variables, so they are resolved by the SGML parser.

But the main problem for the SGML and TEX integration is derived from the scientific formula specification in a SGML document. For this we can follow two different approaches:

a) To specify the formula by TEX syntax

b) To describe the logical structure of the formula and to refer to its components by mean of SGML markup sentences.

The first approach is based on adeguate SGML markup that allow a text portion to be considered not as the content of the document but as the control sequences for other systems e.g. NROFF, TEX ... In this way, within that portion we can specify the formula following the TEX syntax. The example of a document described with these markup is shown below:

01 <!DATA tex "Formula notation from TEX formatting language" >

02 <!DATA lowres "Low resolution scanner input produced by SCAN.MODULE" >

03 <!DATA eqn "eqn notation" >

04 <!STRUC formula CDATA >

05 <!ATT   formula data NOTATION (tex : eqn) >

06 <article>

07 This is the notation of the following formula:

08 <formula data = tex >

09   $$ \sqrt { 1 - x \over { n + 1 }} $$

10 </formula>

where the particular attribute "data" of the element "formula", indicated in line 08, specifies that the text portion (line 09) represents the control sequences for TEX.

The second approach is based on the assumption that every formula, even if complicated, is in any case a structured object, and as such, it can be decribed by SGML markup. Therefore a formula may be decomposed step by step elementary subcomponents, each of them is identified by a GI.

Since every element represents a formula component, we can associate to its attributes some adeguate values to indicate the symbol of the math font table that TEX must select to produce the formula component.

In this way to produce the formula

$$m + n^2$$

we can use the following markup descriptive sentences:

```
01   ..........
     ..........
12   <formula mode = display >
13   <sqr font = font-sqr >
14   <component >
15     m
16   <operator font = font-plus >
17   <power >
18   <base >
19   <component>
20     n
21   <esponent >
22   <component>
23     2
24   </formula >
```

To simplify, in the above example we omitted the structure declaration of the formula, but from the markup descriptives reported we can do many considerations. In the first place with the values "display" and "text" of the attribute "mode" associated to the element "formula" (line 12) we can choose to place the formula at the line center or in a horizontal list (these attribute value correspond to the TEX metacharacter $ and $$).

Other lines refer to the formula structure that are constituted by "sqr" element that in turn contains "power", "operator" and "component" elements, and so on ...

Every element has an attribute type called "font", the value of which specifies the symbol of the particular font that must be selected to produce the element itself, for example line 16 indicates that the symbol corresponding to the font that produces the sign "+" is "plus". The idea to decompose a formula into elements is similar to that proposed by EDIMATH, a math interactive editor. In it a formula is considered as a sequence of constructs. Every construct contains expressions which in turn contain another construct. Every construct belongs to a proper type which determines characteristics of the construct itself, as the position, the form ... The user can select these construct to build his formula and obtain immediately the graphical representation of the constructs on the screen. So we can say that our proposal tries to provide a formula description language, whereas EDIMATH provides a user interface to obtain that description.

Of course both two approaches shown above can be choosen at the same time in a document: for a complex formula we can use TEX notation, whereas if the formula is simple or if its structure is already described in some system library then the second approach could be adopted.

Formatting and composition functions.

We now consider another component of the STPL standard: the formatting and composition functions. That component consists of a completed set of primitives relating to operations which may be performed upon text, i.e primitives to which a formatter implementation could refer. More precisely, with these primitives we are able to build an interactive formatter in which the user has the total control about the layout during the source document introduction.

In this environment the most general object for the formatter is PAGE. PAGE is a component of the document physical structure. As the logical structure of the document is composed by elements "chapters", "paragraph", "note" ..., so the physical structure is built by concrete objects known as "text image area".

Text image area are rectangular in shape and can be of various types, as BLOCK, COLUMN, FIGURE, FLOAT, FOOTNOTE ... They may be nested freely, with the exception of PAGE type, and an action performed in an outer area of a nested set is propogated downward through the nest.

Numerous primitivies and system parameters, for every text image area, allow:

- the definition of the relation between it and others
- the description of its characteristics as its dimensions, its positions ...
- the definition of its appearance, as the color, the characters style ...
- the control on the operation to carry out.

In particular to define the characteristics of a text image area the user can set several system parameters with proper values, e.g the parameter "position" to specify the block position relating to the containing block, "minimum-size" and "maximum-size" for the minimum and maximum width and height of the block, or "entry-environment" to indicate if upon entry into the block the settings for all character appearance, alignment ... instructions will be taken from the parent block or they will be set to the default state for the formatter...

Others parameters allow user to describe the appareance of the text image area. He has the possibility to specify the style, the size, the type ... of every character. At last we underline an important feature of the standard consisting in the fact that it provides a simple system to describe color of characters. The system is derived from CNS (Color Naming System) and uses natural language constructs providing a wide range of color specifications. It is based on a small set of keywords relating to 3 colors attributes: chromatic hues (31 keywords), lightness (5 keywords) and saturations (4 keywords). Combinations of these keywords may be constructed to form a total of 627 separate color names. In this way an example of color specification could be:

CHARACTER-BACKGROUND-COLOR = DARK MODERATE GREEN

i.e the background color of the character is "GREEN" with a lightness of "DARK" and a saturation of "MODERATE".

TeX and STPL formatting functions

The concept of STPL text image area is similar to the boxes of TeX except some differences. One results from the fact that with STPL the user must specify every information about the text image area, while generally TeX processes boxes automatically with its paragraph builder, page builder... (even if it offers to the user the possibility to construct his own boxes, e.g. hbox, vbox ...). Another difference is that for TeX every box is independent from the others, while the state of a STPL inner block is affected from the outer, except when the user requires the contrary.

Furthermore TeX considers a box of a single character or rule as the elementary box, where its layout is establihed from its font, instead the STPL block, that contains many characters, is an elementary text image area.

Together with the instruction to define text image area, STPL provides others ones for its text placement. The user is able to make current a particular text image area to receive the input text, as well as he can suspend, resume or terminate it.

The result of the input text processing is placed into the text image area and consists of either entirely formatted text or some mix of formatted text, unresolved forward references, instructions and input text strings. In the case of mixed text, it is placed in an internal "process buffer" and processing of the input stream continues. During such subsequent processing when a reference is met, the input processing is suspended and all pages in the process buffer are examined for forward references.

Both TeX and STPL make up the page pasting boxes (text image area) together in combination, in horizontally or vertically. While the base line of every TeX box is that of the list of horizontal or vertial boxes, the lack of this reference point in a text image area causes the boundaries of the outer blocks to be considered as reference positions.

From the above considerations, it emerges that the TeX features correspond to almost all functions requested by the standard STPL. In some cases TeX provides many functions that in STPL are omitted or left to the ability of the implementer, as the use of macros commands or the hyphenation meccanism, or the formula construction. Therefore an adjustement of TeX in conform with STPL is a good way to render the first a standard formatting system. Perhaps the adjustement can principally regard two points: to supply the system with an interactive end user interface and to include the color treatment for boxes. The latter objective could be obtained, with regard to specification syntax, integrating the CNS notation in TeX control sequences. The other objective is much more difficult to reach, it could consist to increase TeX commands with text image area instrcution so that we can image to use them to design on the video our page composed by several text image areas, then to select each time one of them, to fill it with text and TeX control sequences and at last to see the result in the same block. The basic idea is to create a processor where we can define "template area" to receive input text and manipulate these area to compose the desired layout. We can think that this concept is similar to ETUDE or JANUS principles, even if in the first one the user is expected to deal mainly with the final form of the document, while in the latter manipulations are performed on the logical structure of the document.

Conclusion

To verify the possibility of the integration between TeX and the standard STPL we have compared the former with only two STPL components, the results are enough to suggest us to go on in that direction. The way is very long and we only are at the beginning, but the characteristics of two systems, as the flexibility of STPL, with which interchange or moving between implementations is possible, or the powerfull and the completeness of TeX functions, will help us in a correct start off.

Bibliography

[1] Le van Huu: *SGML: A standard language for text description*, Submitted paper - Software & Applications Conference, October 1985 - Chicago, Illinois

[2] Le van Huu: *Problemi di standardizzazione: SGML e TEX*, Proceedings from the TEX Conference - Bologna (Italy) November 1984

[3] Le van Huu: *STPL (Standard Text Processing Languages) proposed by ISO*, Convegno AICA "Elaborazione Testi e Documenti", Milano (Italy) November 1983

[4] Le van Huu: *Il linguaggio SGML proposto da ISO,* Note di Software, number 27/28 1985

[5] D.E.Knuth: *TEX and METAFONT: New Directions in Typesetting*, Digital Press (1979)

[6] G.Canzii, D.Lucarella, A. Pilenga: *"I Sistemi TEX e Metafont"*, CLUED Pub. Co., (1985)

[7] C. Lightfoot: *Draft GenCode : Generic textual element identification - A primer,* Graphic Communications Computer Association Arlington, 1979

[8] B.K. Reid: *SCRIBE: A Document Specification Language and its Compiler,* Departement of Computer Science, Carnegie-Mellon University (1980)

[9] B.W.Kernighan, L.Cherry: *A system for Typesetting Mathematics,* Comm. ACM 18 (1975)

[10] I.H.Witten: *Elements of Typography (for Computer Scientists),* Research Report N. 84/165/23 - October 1984, Departement of Computer Science, University of Calgary - Canada

[11] *ACM Computing Survey,* Volume 14 N. 3, September 1982

[12] D.C.Chamberlin, Alii: *JANUS: An interactive system for document composition,* Proc. ACM SIGLAN SIGOA Symp. Text Manipulation, SIGLAN Notices (ACM) 16, 6 June 1981

[13] M.Hammer, Alii: *The implementation of ETUDE, an interpreted and interactive document production system,* Proc. ACM SIGLAN SIGOA Symp. Text Manipulation, SIGLAN Notices (ACM) 16, 6 June 1981

[14] V.Quint: *Interactive editing of mathematics* PROTEXT I - Proceeding of the First International Conference, October 1984 - Dublin (Ireland)

Towards an interactive Math Mode in TeX

Jacques André and Yann Grundt
IRISA/INRIA-Rennes
Campus de Beaulieu
F-35042 Rennes Cedex, France

Vincent Quint
IMAG-Génie Informatique
Université de Grenoble, BP 68
F-38402 Saint Martin d'Hères, France

Abstract

One of the major difficulties when using TeX is to use the "math mode" when you are neither a mathematician, nor a programmer. This paper presents an attempt to interactively input formulae, with the Edimath system.

Edimath is an experimental system for mathematical text processing. Its first principle is interactivity: any action by the operator has an immediate effect upon the formula being manipulated and the screen displays the formula in as close a form as possible to its normal graphic representation. The second principle is that a formula has a tree structure. This allows the user to be guided by the system (e.g. the cursor indicates the position where to enter the next item). At any time it is possible to walk in the formula like in a tree, and then to correct embedded boxes.

The second pass of this product has been changed so that instead of sending its output to some printer device, Edimath produces a TeX text corresponding to the formula. This text may be processed by a TeX system.

This is implemented on a VAX/VMS with a regular VT100 terminal to display the draft formula. This system is now tested to look at the problems that arise because of the nature of TeX, and because Edimath is not yet complete, and to check conviviality of this truly interactive system.

Keywords

TeX, Edimath, Mint, interactivity, mathematical formulae

TeX for Scientific Documentation   D. Lucarella, Editor
Copyright ©1985 Addison-Wesley Publishing Company, Inc.

1. INTRODUCTION

Electronic publishing is growing very fast thanks to the availability of high resolution devices (such as bit map screens and laser printers), workstations (such as McIntosh or Sun) and software (such as TEX, Mint, Mac Write or Interleaf). However electronic publishing still presents two kinds of problems, not completely solved yet: How to insert images into a text, and how to "friendly" handle mathematical formulae. This paper is concerned with the second point.

Since TROFF/EQN [Kerninghan 75], many formatters allow for mathematical formulae manipulation. TEX [Knuth 79] (and now TEX82 [Knuth 83]) and MINT [Hibbard 84] are among the favorite systems. However, they are not interactive. Interactive document preparation systems do exist [Meyrowitz 82], such as Bravo [Lampson 79], Andra [Gutknecht 84] or Interleaf, which cannot process formulae. Despite the fact that *WYSIWYG* systems are sometimes critically judged, e.g. [Lamport 84], they are on the way and batch oriented systems get older and older.

TEX is like an assembly language, what means both quality (you get what you want) and difficulties: TEX is awfully difficult to safely use if you are not a wizzard. That's why pre- and post-processors are defined, such as macro systems (AMSTeX, LaTeX etc.), systems to help input of "exotic" languages like french (e.g. Stratec [Foata 84], [Désarménien 85]), systems to output proofs on bit map screen (like TEX82/SUN), or systems to simulate interactivity (e.g. [Aiello 82], [Agostini 85]). None of this systems is a genuine interactive one, id-est a system where you can modify a formula on the screen and obtain the corresponding modification in the TEX text.

All these improvements show that TEX needs to become an interactive product. We propose here a way to interactively enter formulae in math mode by using the Edimath system.

2. THE EDIMATH SYSTEM

Edimath is an experimental system designed at IMAG, Grenoble-France for mathematical formulae processing [Quint 82, 83, 84].

The study which led to Edimath was begun by 1981 with the aim of developing a tool for processing scientific texts: at that time existing systems, such as word processors or software packages available on various computer systems did not permit easy processing of scientific material. Edimath is an interactive editor which allows the structure of the document to be manipulated, as well as its constituent elements, such as text, formulae, and illustration.

Edimath has been designed as an interactive system in which commands are invoked by pressing function keys or by making selections from a menu, the user is provided with constant guidance, and the results of any action are immediately displayed. Edimath does not need special bit map screen: an approximation of the formula may be displayed on a regular screen like a VT100. Note that what you see is not what you get: you get better if you have got an output device with a better resolution than the screen one.

2.1 Using Edimath

The user interface is particularly important in this type of system. No matter what the intrinsic qualities of the system, if it is difficult for a non-specialist to operate and learn, it will not be used. Particular attention has therefore been paid to the user interface in order to make the system as user-friendly as possible.

2.1.1 Entering a formula

At the data capture stage, the formula is described *naturally*, similar to the way in which it would be dictated or drawned. Again, constant guidance is given to the user, in this case by the position of the cursor, which indicates the element to be entered into the formula being generated. Here are some cursor positions (indicated with an arrow $\searrow$) when entering an integral:

$$\searrow \quad \int_{\searrow} \quad \int_{a\searrow} \quad \int_{a+\searrow} \quad \int_{a+b}^{\searrow} \quad \int_{a+b}^{c\searrow} \quad \int_{a+b}^{c}\searrow$$

This method of guiding the user simplifies the process of learning to use the system, without being a nuisance for an expert user.

The formula is described by using function keys to enter the various constructs which make it up, from left to right. Characters are entered directly using a standard alphanumeric keyboard. A function key is dedicated to fonts. Pressing it and, say the key 2 (for greek font), then you get greek letters on the screen, if your terminal allows it.

Whenever a function key is pressed, the graphic symbol for the corresponding construct (if there is one: fraction, root, integral, summation, bracket) is displayed on the screen at the current position and the cursor moves to the appropriate position for input of the next expression. Characters keep the same size if the terminal screen does not give any facilities to change them, however symbol sizes are updated according to the formula state. Example:

$$\frac{1}{\searrow} \quad \frac{1}{\sqrt{\searrow}} \quad \frac{1}{\sqrt{a+\searrow}} \quad \frac{1}{\sqrt{a+\frac{b}{c}+\searrow}}$$

An **End** key terminates the current construct (e.g. after entering the numerator of a fraction) and causes the cursor to move to the next position after the construct. Note that this **End** key is equivalent to a TEX } ending a grouping started with a symbol and its implicit {. For example, pressing the **integral** key in Edimath is equivalent to type $\backslash int\{$ in TEX.

2.1.2 Internal representation of formulae

Like many systems which manipulate mathematical formulae (compilers, symbolic manipulation systems, TEX, ...), Edimath uses a tree structure for organising these constructs. Each formula is represented by a tree whose nodes are either basic or specific constructs, and whose leaves are character strings. Actualy, each construct behaves like a TEX box.

The tree structure is only used for processing within the system. For storing or transmitting a formula, an equivalent linear parenthesized form is used. However this linear representation *is not* visible to the user. Its grammar and examples are given in [Quint 83].

2.1.3 Updating a formula

At any time, either during the formula capture, or when it is completed and stored, a formula may be modified on the screen, and the immediate effect is visible on the screen and correspondingly changes the internal representation of the formula.

A formula is edited in two stages. The user first indicates on the screen which part of the formula is to be changed, and then indicates the operation which he wishes to carry out. In order to select without ambiguity a construct (constructs indeed are embedded like TEX boxes), the user is provided with an **includes** key. The user can therefore select any construct by moving the cursor and pressing the **includes** key. The selected construct will, depending on the screen, appear either in reverse video or within a box.

Five operations can be performed on the portion selected:

- **delete**: the formula is reconstructed and redisplayed with the selected part erased.
- **replace**: behaves like **delete** then enter input mode.
- **insert**: Two insert commands are necessary, **before** and **after**. The two following examples show why this is so: If the only command available were **insert before**, it would be impossible to distinguish between

$$\sqrt{a+b+c}+1 \quad and \quad \sqrt{a+b+c+1}$$

with "insert before + 1" in $\sqrt{a+b}+1$. Reciprocally, if the only command available were **insert after**, it would be impossible to distinguish

$$x^{yn} \quad or \quad xy^n$$

from "insert after x" in x^n.

- **save** a part of a formula in a buffer.

2.2 Implementation

Edimath is written in Pascal and consists of two independent programs. The first of these is an interactive program which produces and manipulates the external (linear) representation and allows it to be stored on a disk. The other program reads the disk files, interprets their contents, and produces output to a printer device. It is not interactive. See [Quint 83b] for more details.

Edimath is implemented on various computers (LSI 11, VAX, Perq, Honeywell DPS8, SM90 etc.) and works with different kinds of screens (VT100, bit map, etc.) and with different dot or laser printers (Sanders, Digital LN01 etc.).

Edimath, however, is not yet complete. It has allowed its creator to validate the approach adopted for formula handling. It is now used as one of the basic principle of a rather general editor to manipulate whole documents [Bogo 83, Quint-Vatton 85]. Futhermore, some developments are in progress to construct commercial text editors based on Edimath.

3. FROM EDIMATH TO TEX

The question is obvious: *Instead of printing Edimath output on some device like a laser printer, why not to give input to some formatter like TEX ?*. Such an attempt is in progress at IRISA/INRIA, Rennes. Although this work began few weeks ago only, some points already deserve to be quoted. Note that the same attempt is made to output formula to be processed by MINT [Hibbard 84], another formatter whose formula handling is a bit different of TEX one.

3.1 Implementation

As was said before(2.2), Edimath consists of 2 programs, one to handle the formula, one to print it. This second pass, a non-interactive one, reads the external representation (the linear form equivalent to the tree one) of the formula. It is obvious to change the parser and to output TEX text instead of driving an output device. For example, if you enter, through Edimath, on the screen

$$x = \frac{1}{a_i + b^2}$$

the pass one creates the string

$$M(C1(x=)F(N(C1(1))D(C1(a)S(C1(i))C1(+b)P(C1(2)))))$$

where $C1$ means *font number 1*, F means *fraction*, N means *numerator*, D means *denominator*, S *subscript* and P *power*. It is easy to translate this string to TEX:

$$\$x = \{1\backslash over\{a\_i + b\char`\^\ 2\}\}\$$$

with some additional {'s and }'s.

Note that a stack mechanism is generaly not usefull to parse the tree. This is not true when translating an Edimath string to a MINT text: indeed the preceding formula would be to written, in the today prefixed notation, as follows:

$$x = @Fract(1, @sub(a, i) + @sup(b, 2))$$

Let us call EdiTEX this Edimath pass 2 that outputs TEX formulae.

3.2 Ergonomy

This system has been checked by entering formulae either from *The TEXbook* or from some real papers. The first feeling, although not yet statiscally evaluated, is

- Edimath is easy to learn and to use. It produces good TEX input.
- Edimath seems to be easier to use than TEX when there are many embedded levels (braces, dollar signs etc.).
- Edimath is very quick to enter complicated formulae.

However, some problems have been immediately seen. Let us quote some of them:

3.3 Inserting text and math mode

Today, Edimath allows only for formulae manipulation, not for text handling. We have not yet been concerned with the problem of mixing formulae produced by Edimath into a TEX text. Our experiments are today concerned only by giving math mode formulae (produced by Edimath) to TEX. However, it is obvious that we need an editor where both the Edimath representation and the TEX equivalent formula are kept together so that it would be possible to either modify the TEX formula or to interactively re-edit the formula on a screen through Edimath.

3.4 Fonts

Characters and fonts handling is probably the most tricky problem in text manipulation. Indeed they are so many standards that no one uses them. TEX defines its own font tables, the printer devices use other ones such as ISO standards.

To allow some portability, Plain TeX gives a name to each character that is not a regular one. For example, \alpha means α.

In opposite, Edimath assumes the users to designate a character by a font number and the Ascii code in it. For example, to get α you have to press the **font** key, then 2 (assuming it's the greek font number), then the **a** key, assuming that **a** and α have the same Ascii code. This allows portability from a device to an other one.

The problem is that Edimath and TeX don't use the same standards, nor the same sequencing in this font tables. Obviously, translation tables may be used. However this simple problem is rather annoying.

3.5 Variables

TeX writes variable names in italic, and function names in roman. To do so, users are requested to type \sin(x) to get $\sin(x)$ instead of $sin(x)$.

To allow compatibility with TeX, two solutions are possible:
- EdiTeX is modified in a way to analyze strings and to recognize sin and change it to \sin. That is the way Mint works.
- The user is asked to type on the screen \sin instead of sin. It will be shown later on (4.4) that this kind of solution may produce unreadable screens.

3.6 Completion

Edimath is an experimental prototype and in that it is not yet as complete as TeX is. Among possibilities that are not implemented, let us quote matrix handling. However, vectors are implemented. To allow matrix handling, EdiTeX recognizes the special character @ as a separator and translates it to the TeX ampersand. In that way, if you type on the screen the 3 lines vector (remember that Edimath does not analyse character strings)

$$A = \begin{pmatrix} x - \lambda & @ & 1 & @ & 0 \\ 0 & @ & x - \lambda & @ & 1 \\ 0 & @ & 0 & @ & x - \lambda \end{pmatrix}$$

you get the TeX matrix equation

$$A = \begin{pmatrix} x - \lambda & 1 & 0 \\ 0 & x - \lambda & 1 \\ 0 & 0 & x - \lambda \end{pmatrix}$$

This works quite well, and even it seems to be easier to write this first matrix than the equivalent TeX text.

4. SEPARATION OF CONCERNS

The success of TEX partly is due to the fact that TEX offers possibilities to satisfy any kind of typographic requirement.

This section presents some problems encountered with EdiTEX to reach the same level of typographic resources as TEX. It is shown why it is difficult to do so, then a way to interactively set typographic attributes in a formula is proposed.

4.1 Alignments

The notion of alignment as used in TEX to handle "a whole bunch of formulae or different pieces of a huge formula" does not exist in Edimath which only allows for centering, puting left or right vector elements. Edimath does not offer any immediate way to put down lines with alignment, for example around the ='s like in the following situation:

$$\begin{cases} f(x)=\alpha \\ f(x+y)=\beta \\ f(y)=\alpha+\beta \end{cases}$$

The preceeding result could be obtained through Edimath by entering on the screen

$$\begin{cases} \backslash\text{eqalign} \\ f(x)@=\alpha \\ f(x+y)@=\beta \\ f(y)@=\alpha+\beta \end{cases}$$

id est by adding a new vector element: \eqalign and the @'s in the lines of the vector, so that EdiTEX gives the following TEX input to get the wanted output

```
{\left\{\eqalign{
{f(x)}&{=}\alpha
\cr
{f(x+y)&{=}\beta
\cr
{f(y)}&{=}\alpha
{+}\beta
\cr}{}\right.}
```

4.2 Display style

A second problem is related to the so called display style. This is a problem for Edimath. Indeed, let us enter on the screen

$$a_1 + \cfrac{1}{a_2 + \cfrac{1}{a_3 + \cfrac{1}{b}}}$$

Obviously, EdiTEX outputs

$$a\_1 + \{1\backslash over\ a\_2 + 1\{\backslash over\ a\_3 + \{1\backslash over\ b\}\}\}$$

what gives the following unexpected TEX result:

$$a_1 + \frac{1}{a_2 + \frac{1}{a_3 + \frac{1}{b}}}$$

Indeed, to get the first formula, EdiTEX should output the following piece of TEX:

$$a\_1+\{1\backslash over\backslash displaystyle\ a\_2+\{\backslash strut\ 1\backslash over\backslash displaystyle\ a\_3+\{\backslash strut\ 1\backslash over\ b\}\}\}$$

Note that this problem exists as well with MINT, however it is easier solved, for to have the displayed formula you just have to add **@n** in front of the formula to override the automatic font size change.

4.3 Fine tuning

An other class of typographic suggar in TEX consists of small tricks that you have to add for elegance, or "fine tuning". For example, it is better in TEX to type $\$\backslash sqrt2\backslash,x\$$ to get $\sqrt{2}\,x$ instead of $\$\backslash sqrt2x\$$ which gives $\sqrt{2x}$.

4.4 Division of labor

The preceding examples exhibit situations where, in TEX, two different kinds of information are mixed together:
- the description of a formula
- its particular typesetting.

Indeed, macros like \eqalign, \displaystyle and so many other ones (examples are given in [Grundt 85]) are not parts of the formula as an abstraction. They only refer to the layout. Even, it is some kind of "noise" that makes a formula difficult to enter and even more difficult to analyse [Lucarella 85b].

All these information could be typed on Edimath screen, as we proposed in section 4.1. Clearly, this would be equivalent to enter TEX text, and this is not the expected way to get friendly input.

We propose to return to the traditional division of labor, as recommended in software engineering [André 78] and in text manipulation systems [Furuta 82], by separating the processes of writing a formula and the processes of formatting it.

4.5 Entering typographic attributes

New programming languages, such as Ada or Modula-2, offer the principle of separating the abstract properties of a program from those which relate to a particular environment. Different methods are used for the separation between logical descriptions and their physical representation (modules, packages, etc.). We are implementing such a separation in Edimath. Work is still in progress, and this section is only to be considered as a draft specification.

4.5.1 The two aspects of boxes

Both TEX and Edimath use the concept of *box*. A box is a structure made of two entities:

- The *content* of the box: a character or a set of embedded boxes of characters, representing a (part of a) formula.
- Its *implementation*: the place where it appears (coordinates of the reference point, height, width and depth) and, in a certain manner, other information such as alignment, justification etc.

TEX gives the user the possibility to keep in touch with that two parts of the structure, through different commands that are mixed together in the input text. On the other hand, Edimath gives access to the first part (box contents) only. We propose here a way to access in Edimath to some of the information of the second class, to separate formula writing and typographic work, so that EdiTEX can produce any kind of TEX text.

4.5.2 Separate input for attributes

During Edimath Pass One (entering and editing formulae), a new key (or menu entry) is made available. When pressing it, Edimath enters the new mode "composition". In that mode, when pressing again the key, Edimath exit this mode. In composition mode, it is possible to select a logical part of a formula, like in updating mode (see above 2.1.3). Different keys (or sub-menu entries) allow the user to:

- Enter typographic attributes concerning the selected box.
- Display the typographic attributes of the selected box.

- Modify (delete, replace etc.) some of the typographic attributes of the selected box.

During this mode, the formula is displayed on the screen, and the attributes are listed nearby (or in a second window). *Typographic attributes* are written with keywords, and correspond to the typographical requirements such as "no automatic font size change", "aligment around the ='s" etc. The list is not yet fixed.

During pass two (what we called EdiTEX in section 3.1), the attributes are read, and inserted in terms of TEX orders (such as \displaystyle or \eqalign) into the formula description to get regular TEX text.

In this way, a mathematician may concentrate on maths while a typograph may add the required suggar.

5. CONCLUSION

The mixture of the abstract description of a formula together with the concrete typographical specifications makes TEX difficult to use, specially when editing and changing a formula. Clearly, a truely interactive system like Edimath may help to handle formulae. However, some improvements are still needed in Edimath in such a way to offer as many typographical possibilities as TEX does. This improvements are in progress and are designed to keep Edimath as interactive as it is, and to operate separately on the abstract and on the concrete parts of a formula, and so to become a real friendly TEX workstation.

REFERENCES

[AGOSTINI 85]

M. Agostini, V. Matano, M. Schaerf and V. Vascatto, *An Interactive User-Friendly TEX in VM-CMS Environment.*
in [Lucarella 85a].

[AIELLO 82]

L. Aiello and S. Pavan, *Towards a friendly workstation for TEX* .
Internationaler Kongress für Datenverarbeitung um Informations Technologie, Berlin 1982.

[ANCONA 83]

M. Ancona, B. Falcidieno and C. Pienovi, *Un algorithme à sémantique extensible pour la manipulation de formules.*
in [André 83], 152-163.

[ANDRE 78]

J. André, J. Bézivin, J.L. Nebut, R. Rannou and S. Schuman, *Some Remarks on Software Morphology.*
in *Constructing Quality Software* (P.G. Hibbard and S.A. Schuman eds.), IFIP, North-Holland Publishing Company, pp.285-307, 1978.

[ANDRE 83]

Jacques André (ed.), *Actes des "Journées sur la Manipulation de Documents"* , *Rennes, 4-6 Mai 1983.*
INRIA pub., 1983.

[BOGO 83]

Gilles Bogo, Hélène Richy and Irène Vatton, *Un modèle de représentation de documents généralisés.*
in [André 83], 221-235.

[DESARMENIEN 85]

Jacques Désarménien, *The Use of TEX in French: Hyphenation and Typography.*
in [Lucarella 85a].

[FOATA 84]

Dominique Foata, Jean-Jacques Pansiot and Yves Roy, *STRATEC, un logiciel de traitement de textes mathématiques en amont de TEX.*
Publ. I.R.M.A. Strasbourg 255 D-06, 1984.

[FURUTA 82]

Richard Furuta, Jeffrey Scofield and Alan Shaw, *Document Formatting Systems: Survey, Concepts, and Issues.*

in *Document Preparation Systems* (J. Nievergelt, G. Coray, J.D. Nicoud and A.C. Shaw eds.) pp.133–220, North-Holland, 1982.

[GRUNDT 85]

Yann Grundt, *Entrée interactive de formules mathématiques pour TEX*.
Rapport de DEA, Université de Rennes, 1985 (to appear).

[GUTKNECHT 84]

Jürg Gutknecht and Werner Winiger, *Andra: The Document Preparation System of the Personnal Workstation Lilith*.
Software-Practice and Experience, vol.14, p. 73-100, 1984.

[HIBBARD 84]

Peter Hibbard, *Mint User Manual*.
Computer Science Department Report, Carnegie Mellon University, Pittsburg 1984.

[KERNIGHAN 75]

B. W. Kernighan and L. L. Cherry, *A System for Typesetting Mathematics*.
CACM, 51 (1975), 151-156.

[KNUTH 79]

Donald E. Knuth, *TEX and Metafont: New Directions in typesetting*.
Digital Press, Bedford Mass., 1979.

[KNUTH 84]

Donald E. Knuth, *The TEXbook*.
Addison-Wesley pub. comp., 1984.

[LAMPORT 84]

Leslie Lamport, *The LaTEX Document Preparation System*.
Menlo Park 1984.

[LAMPSON 79]

B. W. Lampson, *BRAVO Manual*.
Alto user's handbook, Xerox PARC, 1979.

[LUCARELLA 85a]

Dario Lucarella (ed.), *TEX for Scientific Documentation*.
The First European Conference, Como, May 16-17,1985 (These proceedings), Addison Wesley, 1985.

[LUCARELLA 85b]

Dario Lucarella, *TEX Formulae Dictionnary*.
in [Lucarella 85a].

[MEYROWITZ 82]
> Norman Meyrowitz and Andres Van Dam, *Interactive Editing Systems*.
> Computing Surveys, vol.14,3, 1982.

[QUINT 82]
> Vincent Quint, *An Interactive System for Editing Mathematical Documents*.
> European Conf. on Integrated Interactive Computing Systems, Stresa, Italy, North-Holland 1982.

[QUINT 83a]
> Vincent Quint, *Une approche de l'édition interactive en deux dimensions*.
> in [André 83].

[QUINT 83b]
> Vincent Quint, *An Interactive System for Mathematical Text Processing*.
> Technology and Science of Informatics, vol.2, num.3, 169-179, 1983.

[QUINT 84]
> Vincent Quint, *Interactive Editing of Mathematics*.
> Proceedings of the First Internat. Conf. on Text Processing Systems (JJ. Miller ed.), Dublin 1984, pp.55-68.

[QUINT 85]
> Vincent Quint and Irène Vatton, *GRIF: Un éditeur interactif de documents structurés*.
> Rapport de Recherche TIGRE num. 27, Bull-IMAG, Grenoble 1985.

TEX FORMULAE DICTIONARY

D. Lucarella

Università degli Studi di Milano

Istituto di Cibernetica

This paper outlines design issues and implementation aspects of a formulae Dictionary. First standardization problems for the formulae description language are discussed and then the problem of building a Formulae Dictionary is faced with regard to the data structure and the capability to index mathematical texts.

Introduction

The attempt to build a formulae Dictionary may have several implications in different areas ranging from mathematical research to mathematical education. Moreover, it may be considered as the first step in order to set up a basic structure on which incrementally to imbed new mathematical knowledge.

In the past much work was done in this direction by G.Peano, a famous Italian Mathematician. These studies led to the production of the *Formulario Mathematico* that passed through different versions untill the last edition that was published at the beginning of this century [PEA60].

It was the result of a deep work aimed at ordering concepts and defining a basic vocabulary to specify the formulae. Particular attention was also devoted to the graphical presentation of every symbol so that the text composition could be easy and aesthetically appreciable. With reference to typographical technologies at that time, a great effort was directed to compound and correctly align symbols in the body of the formulae.

Recently, Prof.D.E.Knuth has approached the problem of devising a language capable of defining every kind of complicated formulae in a linearized way and has embodied it into the TEX composition system.

The ability to specify the graphical two dimensional structure of mathematical formulae by means of a linearized language gives the chance of building a Dictionary where the formulae can be loaded, manipulated and accessed as ordinary text strings.

Items logically related may be retrieved and eventually printed after being processed by the TeX system so that the pictorial representation of the formulae is reproduced. The proposed structure may be also interfaced in order to index and access a document collection of scientific texts assuming TeX as standard composition system. Such a Dictionary, just as the other access structures, may be referred to during queries based on formulae in a document retrieval environment.

This research activity is related to SDDS *Scientific Document Delivery System*, a joint Italian project partially supported by the Commission of European Communities [CAN84]. In the following, the TeX system is briefly reviewed with regard to the formulae description language and then the Dictionary architecture is presented.

A language for typesetting mathematics

The solution to the problem of maths typesetting is to devise a method for specifying unambiguously mathematical notations taking into account all typographical aspects. [KER75], [KNU79].

Two dimensional formulae must be represented as a one dimensional sequence of instructions that can be entered easily from every Ascii terminal without requiring special keyboards. Such a formula description is then processed reproducing the pictorial layout.

Prof. Knuth at the Stanford University has designed a language for typesetting mathematics taking into account notions of typographical aesthetics and has embodied it inside the TeX system. TeX, a trade mark of the American Mathematical Society, is suitable for the composition of scientific and technical documents.

Many typographical fonts are available under TeX and they can be extended, without any limit, by using METAFONT, a system developed at Stanford to generate fonts of every shape [KNU79].

TeX has been designed as an integrated system in which formulae and texts are handled in a unified framework. A model has been introduced based on *box* and *glue* primitives to define textual and mathematical objects. Boxes define the size of the object they contain and provide a reference point which is used to align them either horizontally or vertically. Aligning the boxes produces an enclosing box. Glue provides space between boxes. Glue has a natural size and may be stretched or shrinked according to given constraints on page space.

Within this framework every formula may be regarded as a set of boxes pieced together in various ways. "The basic idea is that a complicated formula is composed of less complicated formulas put together in a simple way; the less complicated formulas are, in turn, made up of simple combination of formulas that are even less complicated;

and so on." [KNU84]. For the description of TEX language refer to [KNU84]. The special sequence $$ forces the system to enter mathematical mode. The spaces within formulae and the font body are handled by the system according to a predefined mathematical style. So, in order to produce the following well known formula:

$$\frac{1}{2\pi}\int_{-\infty}^{\sqrt{y}}\left(\sum_{k=1}^{n}\sin^2 x_k(t)\right)(f(t)+g(t))\,dt$$

the input sequence that must be supplied is:

$$ {1\over 2\pi}\int↓ {-\infty} ↑ {\sqrt y}\bigglp\sum

↓ {k=1} ↑n \sin↑2x↓k(t)\biggrp\biglp f(t)+g(t)\bigrp\,dt$$

Just for example, in the following, a brief excerpt from the Dictionary dealing with integral transforms is reported [BAT54]:

$$g(y) = \int_0^\infty J_0(ax)\sin(xy)dx \qquad a>0$$

$$g(y) = \int_0^\infty J_{2n+1}(ax)\sin(xy)dx \qquad a>0$$

$$g(y) = \int_0^\infty J_\nu(ax)\sin(xy)dx \qquad \mathrm{Re}\,\nu > -2,\quad a>0$$

$$g(y) = \int_0^\infty x^{-1}J_0(ax)\sin(xy)dx \qquad a>0$$

$$g(y) = \int_0^\infty x^{-1}J_\nu(ax)\sin(xy)dx \qquad \mathrm{Re}\,\nu > -1,\quad a>0$$

$$g(y) = \int_0^\infty x^{-2}J_\nu(ax)\sin(xy)dx \qquad \mathrm{Re}\,\nu > 0,\quad a>0$$

$$g(y) = \int_0^\infty x^{-1/2}J_{2n+3/2}(ax)\sin(xy)dx \qquad a>0$$

$$g(y) = \int_0^\infty x^\nu J_\nu(ax)\sin(xy)dx \qquad -1 < \mathrm{Re}\,\nu < 1/2,\quad a>0$$

$$g(y) = \int_0^\infty x^{-\nu}J_{\nu+1}(ax)\sin(xy)dx \qquad \mathrm{Re}\,\nu > -1/2,\quad a>0$$

$$g(y) = \int_0^\infty x^{-\nu}J_{2n+\nu+1}(ax)\sin(xy)dx \qquad \mathrm{Re}\,\nu > -1/2,\quad a>0$$

$$g(y) = \int_0^\infty x^{2\mu-1}J_{2\nu}(ax)\sin(xy)dx \qquad -\mathrm{Re}\,\nu - 1/2 < \mathrm{Re}\,\mu < 3/4$$
$$a>0$$

$$g(y) = \int_0^\infty (x^2+\beta^2)^{-1}J_0(ax)\sin(xy)dx \qquad a>0,\quad \mathrm{Re}\,\beta > 0$$

$$g(y) = \int_0^\infty x(x^2+\beta^2)^{-1}J_0(ax)\sin(xy)dx \qquad a>0,\quad \mathrm{Re}\,\beta > 0$$

$$g(y) = \int_0^\infty x^{1/2}(x^2+\beta^2)^{-1} J_{2n+1/2}(ax) \sin(xy)dx \qquad a>0, \quad \operatorname{Re}\beta>0$$
$$n = 0, 1, 2, \ldots$$

$$g(y) = \int_0^\infty x^\nu (x^2+\beta^2)^{-1} J_\nu(ax) \sin(xy)dx \qquad -1 < \operatorname{Re}\nu < 5/2$$
$$a>0, \quad \operatorname{Re}\beta>0$$

$$g(y) = \int_0^\infty x^{1-\nu}(x^2+\beta^2)^{-1} J_\nu(ax) \sin(xy)dx \qquad \operatorname{Re}\nu > -3/2$$
$$a>0, \quad \operatorname{Re}\beta>0$$

$$g(y) = \int_0^\infty x^{-1} e^{-ax} J_0(\beta x) \sin(xy)dx \qquad \operatorname{Re} a > |\operatorname{Im}\beta|$$

$$g(y) = \int_0^\infty x^{\nu-1} e^{-ax} J_\nu(\beta x) \sin(xy)dx \qquad \operatorname{Re}\nu > -1/2, \quad \operatorname{Re} a > |\operatorname{Im}\beta|$$

$$g(y) = \int_0^\infty x^\nu \cos(x) J_\nu(x) \sin(xy)dx \qquad -1 < \operatorname{Re}\nu < 1/2$$

$$g(y) = \int_0^\infty x^{-\nu} \cos(x) J_{\nu+1}(x) \sin(xy)dx \qquad \operatorname{Re}\nu > -1/2$$

With reference to our goals, TEX has been selected as the standard composition system in order to supply formulae and texts that must be loaded on the archive.

The Dictionary structure

Once the problem has been solved of representing formulae as character strings and reproducing their pictorial layout when retrieved, we can regard these textual items as the basic objects of our archive.

The main concern is to begin from a limited area in order to experiment the system. We have chosen specific fields of the functional analysis. The first step is to arrange the formulae according to a certain classification criteria and then the information structure must be built in order to gain access from different views.

In order to guarantee a responsive access, various structures have to be provided: classification, mathematical symbols, free terms and then several indexes have to be built up. In order to avoid redundancy, index entries contain only pointers to the corresponding data items stored in a source direct access file. In fact the organization and classification of formulae material is a very difficult task considering that the same formula may be related to different semantic contexts and, with this facility, multiple views are achieved without repetitions.

Facilities must be provided to both users with specific requests and users who have only a general idea of what they are looking for. In the latter case, a browsing facility enables the user to navigate on the indexes and to inspect the source formulae attached to the index terms. In many cases, such a browsing facility could locate directly the requested formulae without supplying a query. [FRE82]. So, the system has to support formal retrieval by means of queries as well as browsing through index entries and linked items.

The classification index provides a grouping of the terms used in a given topic area. Examining it carefully, we see that a network is the appropriate structure where nodes are terms in the subject field and links are the various types of relationships between them. So, an underlying hierarchical structure has been enriched to form a network with cross connecting paths for passing to a semantically related region and data connecting paths which link a node of the tree with items of the data collection [FRE82].

Term associations are displayed to the user in order to help him in identifying the class of formulae of his interest. An easy to use interface enables him, starting from the current node, to move to broader, narrower, related nodes or to inspect attached items.

Fig. 1 shows the proposed structure outlining three levels of indexing: classification, free terms, mathematical symbols. At the moment, the free term index has not yet been implemented. So the access may be achieved by means of the classification network in order to locate a class of formulae or by supplying a set of mathematical symbols to select formulae where such symbols occur. Symbols can obviously be chained via boolean operators and such a request may be also directed to a narrower subset previously selected.

Now, we want to provide the facility of a formulae query language. With this purpose, we are experimenting the opportunity to supply a query of precoordinated TEX control sequences not completely refined in order to emphasize only some structural aspects of the searched formulae.

Such an approach has already been successfully carried out with another kind of formulae description language in Chemistry on line applications [WEL83].

For example, always referring to the Dictionary section concerning the integral transforms, the following statement leads us to identify a certain class of formulae:

g(y)=\int↓0↑\infty *\sin(xy)dx

In order to select the excerpt previously presented, the query statement must be further refined:

g(y)=\int↓0↑\infty * J * \sin(xy)dx

Clearly some problems arise with association rules for the operators. Just for example, with reference to the \int operator, you can write equally \int↓0↑infty as well as \int↓infty↑0. The same happens for control sequences that affect the formula from a typographical point of view (e.g. \quad, \qquad, ecc.) but have no mathematical meaning.

The design of a query language for formulae retrieval is not an easy task. Further research is required in order to fully specify the language and to devise a sort of similarity function that evaluates matching expressions.

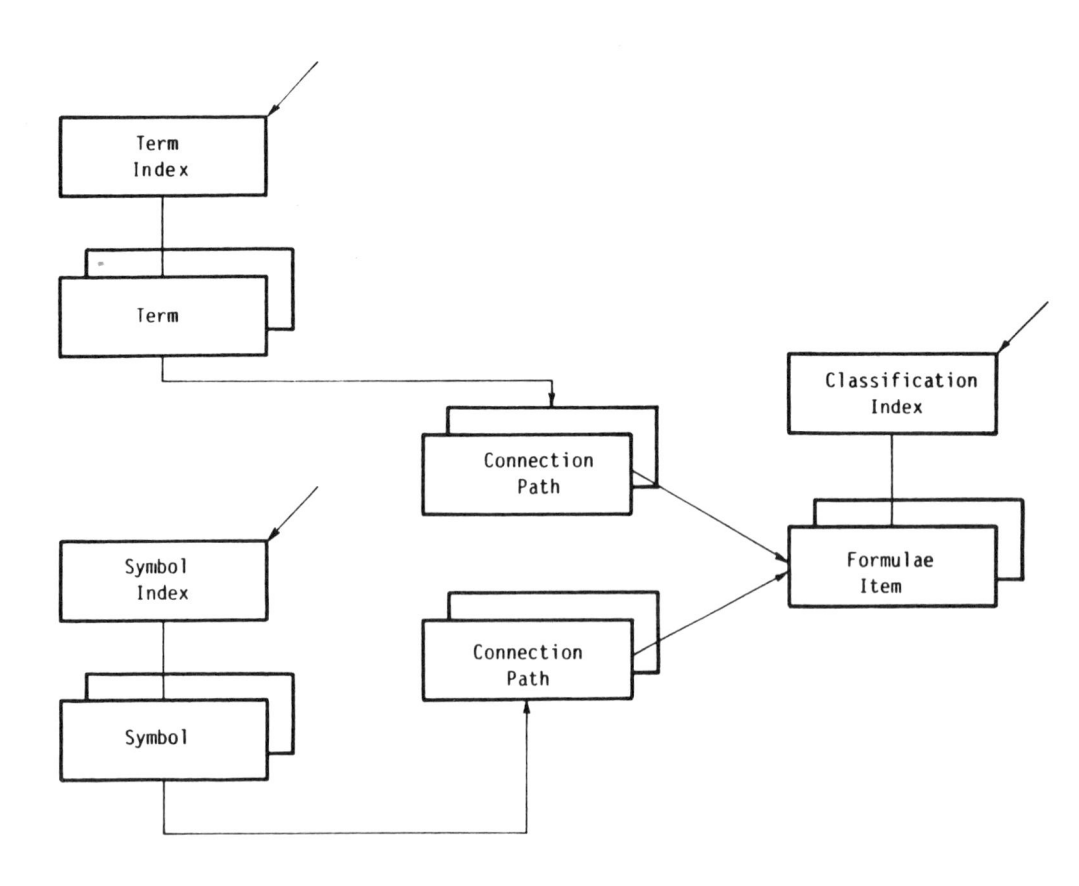

Figura 1. Dictionary Access Structure

Text Retrieval

The widely spread utilization of text composition systems [FUR82] increases the amount of textual information stored in machine readable form and allows the creation of full text archives suitable for document on line search and on demand printing.

If we assume the presence of a standard composition system, it becomes possible to scan the source text, during the filing process, looking for mathematical formulae and to consider formulae fragments and mathematical symbols just like indexing terms [LUC84].

So the described structure, as a whole, can also be considered a mathematical Dictionary referable to during queries based on formulae in a document retrieval environment. Incoming documents are scanned; imbedded formulae are identified and loaded on the Dictionary after being checked by the user. At the moment the procedure is semi-automatic in order to select only final results or relevant formulae and to verify that semantic linkages with the index entries are correctly generated. In this phase, the classification index can be interactively displaied.

This research aspect is oriented towards building an auxiliary access structure for mathematical texts loaded on SDDS data base. SDDS is aimed at providing distributed services for Electronic Publishing, Filing and Delivery of Technical Documentation and grey literature and to propose a standard language for scientific communication purposes [CAN84]. In such an environment, the user, from his workstation, can originate the manuscript and its mark-up, control its final appearance and transfer it via computer network. Collected documents are centrally stored and the user can both find a fully qualified document or locate documents relevant to his requests.

After the document has been located, it may be scanned and viewed on the terminal. This previewing capability reduces the necessity of paper copies and allows the checking of the correspondence of a large document to the needs before committing the copy. Different workstations, at distributed network nodes, are allowed to interact with, view and print the same text without recomposing it. Such device independence allows the user to choose among the available output station on the basis of the typographical quality required for document reproduction.

The implementation of the prototype, here discussed, accommodates two types of retrieval strategies:

Access based on formatted attributes

The retrieval of the document takes place when one or more attributes satisfy the selection conditions chained via boolean operators. Assuming there is for every document a formatted header according to a predefined structure.

Access based on the content

The retrieval procedure locates all documents relevant to the user query and arranges them according to a rank order. This allows the user to present an enquiry on a *subject* retrieving as answer all *objects* dealing with that subject. A document characterization with reference to the index term language is achieved during the load phase [RIJ79].

The organization is based on the file structure reported in Fig. 2 with the outlined logical links [CRO82]:

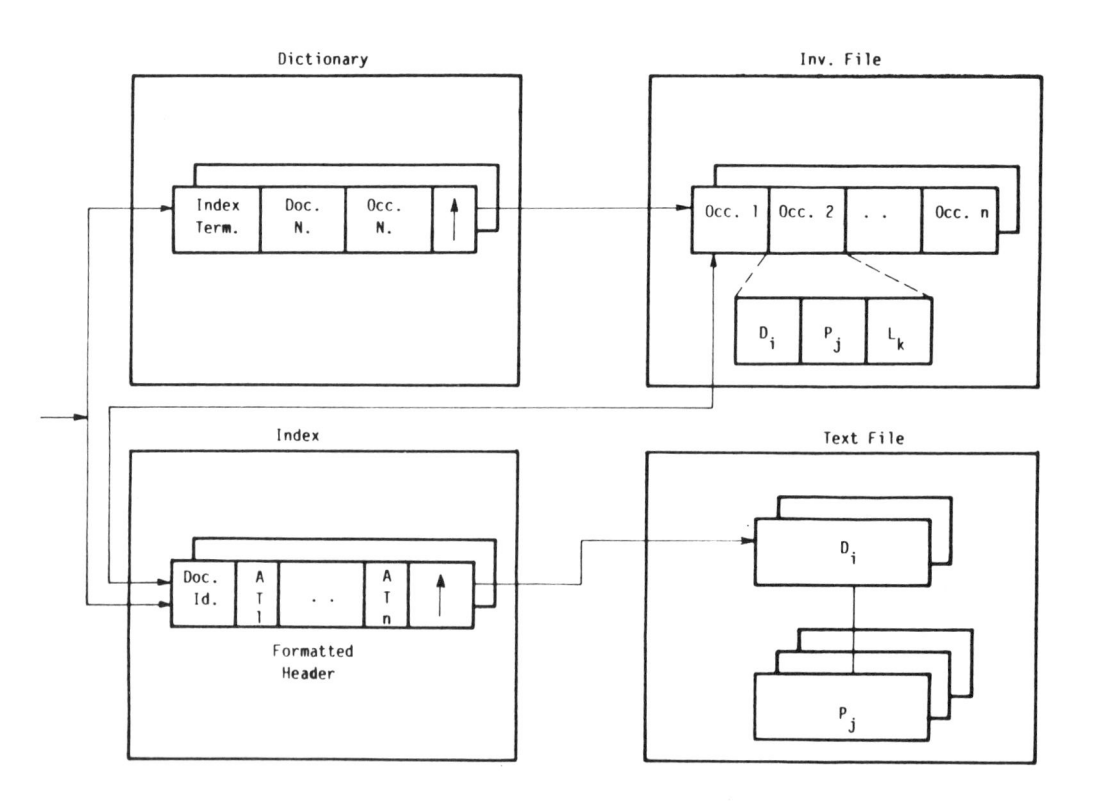

Figura 2. File Organization

Text file

This file allocates full texts stored in a number of fixed length random access pages. When the document is loaded the corresponding index file entry is created and the text is processed in order to identify significant terms. Such terms and their location are respectively used to update the Dictionary and the inverted file.

Text Index

The index file entry contains a pointer to the document in the text file, a unique document identifier and a formatted header with structured attributes. This information can also be retrieved directly using the document identifier.
The user can provide attributes content during text preparation using a set of TEX macros designed with reference to a standard model of document structure [LAM85].

Dictionary

The Dictionary allocates index terms with pointers to the inverted file. With regard to the Mathematical Dictionary, each entry provides, passing through the inverted file, the reference to all locations in which the formula occurs.

Inverted File

The inverted file entries contain pointers to the formatted bibliographic headers stored in the Text index allowing, in this way, the document retrieval.
Each entry in the occurrence list provides the reference in the form of a triple (D_i, P_j, L_k) identifying document, page and line where the item occurs.

The presented organization enables the end user to look up formulae in the mathematical Dictionary. The document location proceeds via inverted file and the page, in which the required formula is imbedded, may be presented to the user workstation.
In order to experiment with the suggested techniques we have developed a prototype in Pascal/vs on IBM 3081K under MVS Operating System. The VSAM organization is extensively used as file interface [WAG73].

Conclusion

In the previous pages we have presented the implementation of a formulae Dictionary with emphasis on access structures. With our requirement of TEX as composition language, it is not easy to envisage the integration of these capabilities within the existing mathematical literature. Of greater benefit, but in the longer term, would be the full implementation of such facilities for the online access to mathematical information.

In the shorter term, it seems reasonable to carry out experiments and to consider TEX as basic language for Dictionary compilation, typesetting and searching. However, in this field, further research is needed to fully define a query language for formulae retrieval and to devise a similarity function in order to evaluate the relevance of various information items to a given request.

Aknowledgments

Thanks are due to Prof. G.DegliAntoni for discussions about the system architecture and implementation issues.

References

[BAT54] A.Erdelyi(Ed.): *"The Bateman Project"* California Inst. of Technology, McGraw-Hill, 1954

[CAN84] G.Canzii, G.DegliAntoni, D.Lucarella, A.Pilenga: *"A Scientific Document Delivery System"*, Electronic Publishing Review, Jun84, Learned Inf. Oxford and New Jersey

[CRO82] W.B.Croft: *"The Implementation of a Document Retrieval System"*, Research and Development in Information Retrieval, Proceedings, Berlin, May 1982, Springer-Verlag Ed. G. Salton

[FRE82] M.Bartschi, H.P.Frei: *"Adapting Data Organization to the Structure of Stored Information"* Research and Development in Information Retrieval, Proceedings, Berlin, May 1982, Springer-Verlag Ed. G. Salton

[FUR82] R.Furuta, J.Scofield, A.Shaw: *"Document Formatting Systems: Survey, Concepts and Issues"*, ACM Comp. Surveys, Vol.14,n.3, Sept.82

[KER75] B.W.Kernighan, L.Cerry: *"A System for Typesetting Mathematics"*, ACM Comm. Vol. 18, N. 3, March 75

[KNU79] D.E.Knuth: *"TEX and METAFONT: New directions in Typesetting"*, Digital Press, 1979

[KNU84] D.E.Knuth: *"The TEX book"* Addison-Wesley Comp, 1984

[LAM85] L.Lamport: *"The LaTEX Document Preparation System"*, Addison-Wesley. Publication in progress (1985).

[LUC84] D.Lucarella: *"TEX Document Retrieval"* Proceedings of First Text Processing Conference, Trinity College, Dublin Oct. 1984, Ed. Boole Press, 1984

[PEA60] G.Peano: *"Formulario Mathematico"*, Edizioni Cremonese, Roma, 1960

[RIJ79] C.J.van Rijsbergen: *"Information Retrieval"*, Second Edition Butterworths, London (1979)

[WAG73] R.Wagner: *"Indexing design considerations"*, IBM Syst.J. n.4 (1973)

[WEL83] S.M.Welford, alii: *"Towards simplified access to chemical information in patent literature"*, J.Inf.Science 6 (1983), North-Holland.

STRATEC AND A RATIONALIZED KEYBOARD FOR INPUTTING TEX

by

Dominique FOATA, Jean-Jacques PANSIOT and Yves ROY [*]

ABSTRACT:
This paper describes the main features of the preprocessor STRATEC, invented in order to take into account the typing habits of and the keyboards used by English and non-English writers and to facilitate inputting the TEX files. The system STRATEC that was implemented on the micro-computer VICTOR has been in use at a number of places including Strasbourg for more than a year and has worked to everyone's greatest satisfaction.

1. Introduction

TEX has now been implemented on various computers making possible the realization of splendid typographic layouts for those who can master the appropriate commands. TEX was primarily conceived for English typists. The real problem for the other users was that special software systems had to be created, which would produce correct TEX files from a non-English keyboard.

The English language is fortunate enough not to have accented letters in common use. To type the letters "é", "è" or "à", the TEXbook recommends the control sequences:

\'e, \'e and \'a.

---

[*] *Laboratoire de Typographie Informatique, Université Louis-Pasteur, 7, rue René-Descartes, 67084 Strasbourg, France.*

'TEX' is a trademark of the American Mathematical Society.

'VICTOR' is a registered trademark of Victor Technologies, Inc.

TEX for Scientific Documentation   D. Lucarella, Editor
Copyright ©1985 Addison-Wesley Publishing Company, Inc.

But there is no hope of convincing any French typist that for the beauty of TEX one should have to type three keys instead of one — the traditional French keyboard, the so-called AZERTY (not the QWERTY *), does have "é", "è" and "à"-keys.

As many microcomputers possess an extended keyboard, it is reasonable to use the extra keys to implement the most frequently used mathematical symbols. As an example, the keyboard of the *VICTOR*, rebuilt to include the facilities of *STRATEC*, includes the key:

$$\boxed{\begin{array}{c}\Sigma \\ + \\ \oplus\end{array}}$$

allowing the user to type the $\sum$ instead of the sequence

\sum.

Finally, the most common errors encountered in TEX typing come from erroneous bracketing of formulas. Some text editors check the balance of the bracket commands, but it is perhaps more reasonable to do the checking *before* running TEX... *STRATEC* does this.

STRATEC is a preprocessor that includes:

(1) an easy way to type the TEX files. In particular, the use of the full-screen editor *PMATE*** greatly facilitates instant correction. Moreover, what is actually typed in is much more compact and readable than TEX.

(2) mathematical symbols directly accessible from the keyboard appear as such on the screen.

(3) automatic transformation of each *STRATEC* file into a true TEX file. In particular, whenever a mathematical symbol from the keyboard is typed, it will be automatically transformed into its TEX control sequence.

(4) verification of the syntax of the file (changes of modes, bracketing levels).

Minor changes adapt *STRATEC* to other languages, for example English.

STRATEC is entirely *compatible with* TEX, in the sense that a file containing both *STRATEC* and TEX commands will always be transformed into an executable TEX file.

---

* Look at the line of keys above the natural resting place on the keyboard of the right hand.

**'*PMATE*' is a registered trademark of Phoenix Software Associates Ltd.

The paper is organized as follows. In section 2 a full description of the keyboard is given. Then, section 3 contains a flow chart of the various files created by *STRATEC*. Finally, examples of files are reproduced in section 4.

2. The Stratec keyboard

Consider the *STRATEC* keyboard (reproduced at the end of the paper). It is divided into seven parts numbered 1 to 7, as shown in Fig. 1. Each of these parts is called a subkeyboard.

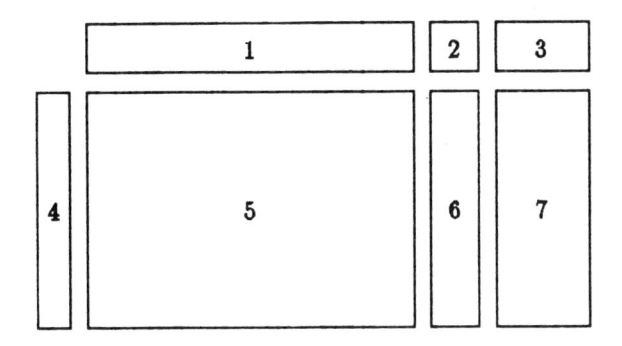

Each key has three modes: lower case or normal, upper case or shift and "alt". In drawing up the *STRATEC* keyboard each key was represented by a rectangle containing three symbols. The middle symbol is the normal mode. The upper symbol is obtained by pressing the key and the shift simultaneously as on a normal typewriter. The bottom symbol is obtained by pressing the key and the alt simultaneously.

The main subkeyboard is part number 5. The AZERTY is shown here, rather than the QWERTY dear to anglophone users. It is worth noting that *all* printable ASCII symbols are accessed from that subkeyboard, so an ordinary computer keyboard with only the keys of subkeyboard 5 allows every TEX file to be typed using the *STRATEC* system.

2.1. Subkeyboards 1, 2, 3 and 4. — A few useful keys for special commands; for instance, the editor exit key (labelled sortie éditeur) that allows immediate return to the operating system, and the "Init imprim" key which is used to load the typefonts on the low-cost printer connected to the microcomputer.

2.2. The main subkeyboard. — Aside from all the traditional letters we have included all the common accented letters of the French language: "é", "è", "à", "ù" together with their capitals: "É", "È", "À", "Ù". The c cedilla "ç" is also there, as is usual on French keyboards. Other languages have their own special needs which could be accomodate as necessary.

The Greek alphabet is so important in mathematics that we felt we had to make special provision for the eleven uppercase Greek letters that do not appear in the roman alphabet and for the entire Greek alphabet in lower case. What a relief not to have to type \alpha, but only α !

As usual, the dead key

to the left of the P-key was preserved. Following the French typing tradition "ê" is obtained first by pressing the dead key and then the e-key. What is important is the fact that the real "ê" appears on the screen of the microcomputer, and not a sequence of commands, such as "^e".

2.3. The subkeyboard 6. — It was found convenient to have a special symbol to switch the mathematical mode on and a second one to switch the mathematical mode off.

For instance, the sentence:

The sum $\sum_{i=1}^{i=n} x_i^2$ is equal to z.

is STRATEC typed as:

```
The sum [∑↓{i=1}↑{i=n}x↓i↑2] is equal to [z].
```

Notice the symbol "[" to turn on the mathematical mode and "]" to turn it off.

There is also a symbol to switch to the Display mathematical mode ("[[") and another one ("]]") to switch off that mode, as in the following example:

The sum
$$S = \sum_{i=1}^{i=n} x_i^2$$
is a polynomial of the second degree.

which is STRATEC typed as:

```
The sum
   [[S=∑↓{i=1}↑{i=n} x↓i↑2]]
is a polynomial of the second degree.
```

Special symbols for the *italic* ("➚" and "➘"), the **boldface** ("▶" and "◀") and the roman ("▶" and "◀") are convenient.

For instance

The sentence:
boldface against roman and *italic*.
can be typed:

▶boldface ▶ against roman and ◀ ◀ ➚ italic ➘.

2.4. The subkeyboard 7. — There we find all the usual mathematical functions which the reader will have no trouble recognizing. However, certain symbols have been introduced, that, as such, do no exist in TEX :

$$ \cdot/\cdot, \ \{, \ \}, \ \downarrow, \ \uparrow. $$

The symbol "$\cdot/\cdot$" replaces the control sequence "\ over" used in TEX for building up the fractions.

Example. — For typesetting the following fraction in display math

$$ F = \frac{a+b}{c+d} + e $$

one has to type:

[[F={a+b·/·c+d}+e]]

Boldfaced braces "**{**" and "**}**" stand for \{ and \} , as required in TEX.

The downarrow "↓" and uparrow "↑" are the commands for constructing subscripts and superscripts in mathematical mode. In common with several other TEX implementations those symbols replace the TEX commands "_" and "^".

3. Using Stratec

The *STRATEC* preprocessor has been implemented on the micro-computer *VICTOR* under the *MS-DOS* system,* taking advantage of the full-screen editor *PMATE* and has been adapted to handle files that are to be processed by TEX.

The flow chart of Fig. 2 shows how a particular *STRATEC* file — call it myfile — gives rise to four different files :

myfile.screen   myfile.print   myfile.log   myfile.tex

---
* 'MS-DOS' is a registered trademark of Microsoft Corporation.

The last two files are saved on the the micro-computer disk. The first two are of a different nature.

3.1. The myfile.screen. — When returning to the operating system after the typing is finished, a file called `myfile.screen` unfolds ("scrolls") on the screen. It is a transcription of `myfile`. The special codes such as [,], ◥, ◢, ▶, ◀, disappear leaving the mathematical formulas (that were typed between two [and] signs) displayed in reverse (see example 4.1). Italicized words are then underlined and sections between the signs ▶ and ◀ appear in boldface.

More important, the scrolling stops as soon as a syntactic error has been detected, such as an inadmissible change of modes, or an erroneous change of fonts, or a missing bracket. To continue the scrolling one must then press carriage return. This is a first indication of an incorrect entry in `myfile`.

3.2. The myfile.log. — While `myfile` is being analyzed, `myfile.log` is being constructed. Each error detected, together with its nature and its line number is stored in `myfile.log`. At the end of the analysis the user can read `myfile.log` and make the corrections immediately in the original `myfile`.

3.3. The myfile.print. — A version of the manuscript can be printed which is as close to the final document as the technology of the low-cost printer will allow. This file is created only upon request and only in the case where the microcomputer is connected to a low-cost printer. Particularly for the novice, this is a great convenience.

3.4. The myfile.tex. — This is really the *STRATEC* product. A veritable TeX file is stored on the disk once the analysis of `myfile` is made and `myfile.log` is empty showing that there are no more error entries. As a matter of fact, `myfile.tex` never appears on the screen, unless the user asks for it. If the microcomputer is connected to a computer on which TeX is implemented, only `myfile.tex` is transferred.

4. Examples

The following text is an example of a *STRATEC* file. French is used in order to illustrate accented letters. Notice that `myfile` is more compact than `myfile.tex`.

TEX *for scientific documentation* 111

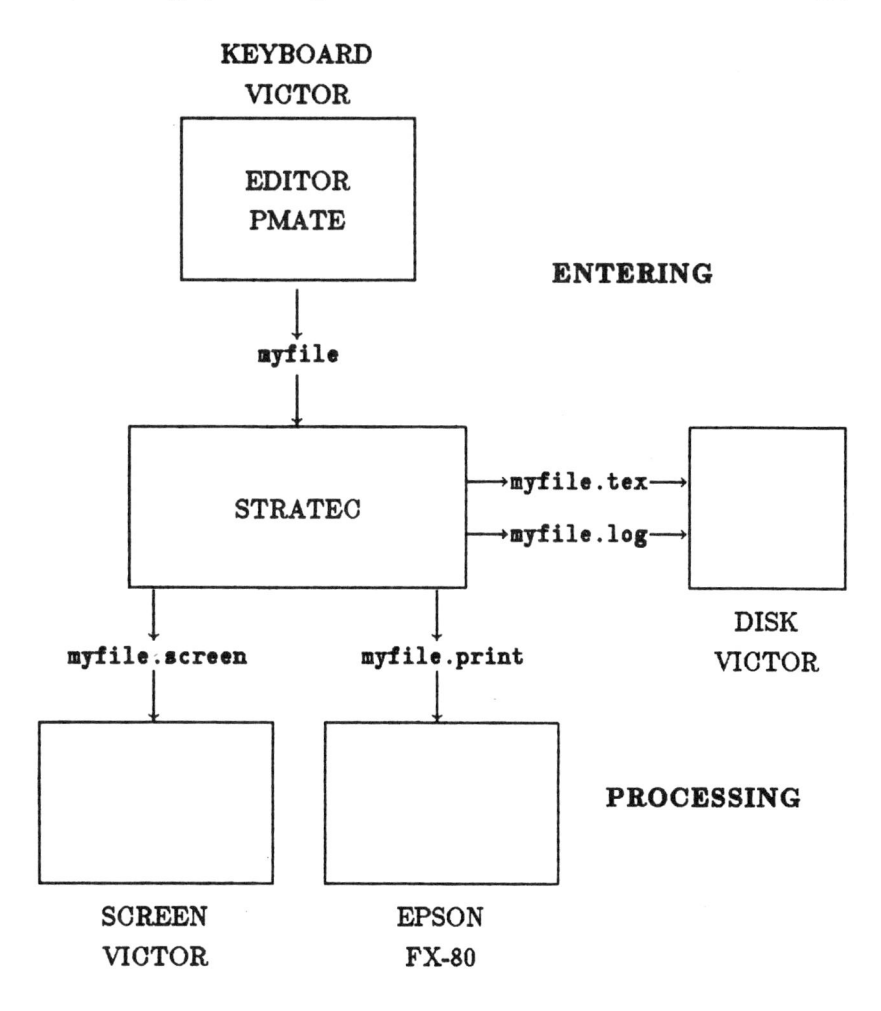

Fig. 2

4.1. Myfile.

```
Dans l'algèbre [K{X}] on peut former les produits
[xxy] et [x⊗y]. Les quantités
  [[Π↓{i=1}↑{i=n} x↓i\qquad ⊔⊔↓{i=1}↑{i=n}y↓i]]
ont aussi un sens. Si [g:↦x+√{x↑2+1}]
et [f:x↦√{x+2}] sont deux applications, leur
produit de composition [h=f∘g] prend en [x]
la valeur
  [[h(x)=√{x+√{x↑2+1}+2}.]]
Enfin, l'intégrale
  [[∫↓0↑{+∞} {dx/x↑2+1}]]
est convergente.
```

4.2. Myfile.screen. — Notice that mathematics appears in reverse mode.

```
Dans l'algèbre K{X} on peut former les produits
xxy et x:y. Les quantités
   ↓{i=1}↑{i=n} x↓i\qquad _↓{i=1}↑{i=n}y↓i
ont aussi un sens. Si g:↦x+√{x↑2+1}
et f:x↦√{x+2} sont deux applications, leur
produit de composition h=f∘g prend en x
la valeur
   h(x)=√{x+√{x↑2+1}+2}.
Enfin, l'intégrale
   ∫↓0↑{+∞} {dx/x↑2+1}
est convergente.
```

4.3. Myfile.print. — Notice that the mathematical text is in elite, while the rest of the text is in pica.

```
Dans l'algèbre K(X) on peut former les produits
xxy et x⊗y. Les quantités
   Π↓{i=1}↑{i=n} x↓i\qquad ⊔↓{i=1}↑{i=n}y↓i
ont aussi un sens. Si g:↦x+√{x↑2+1}
et f:x↦√{x+2} sont deux applications, leur
produit de composition h=f∘g prend en x
la valeur
   h(x)=√{x+√{x↑2+1}+2}.
Enfin, l'intégrale
   ∫↓0↑{+∞} {dx/x↑2+1}
est convergente.
```

4.4. Myfile.tex. — This is a traditional TEX file. Notice that a space is systematically inserted after each control sequence. For example, \sqrt{ is not produced by STRATEC, rather \sqrt { appears.

```
Dans l'alg\`ebre $K\langle X\rangle $ on peut former les produits
$x\times y$ et $x\otimes  y$. Les quantit\'es
   $$\prod _{i=1}^{i=n} x_i\qquad \coprod  _{i=1}^{i=n}y_i$$
ont aussi un sens. Si $g:\mapsto  x+\sqrt {x^2+1}$
et $f:x\mapsto  \sqrt {x+2}$ sont deux applications, leur
produit de composition $h=f\circ g$ prend en $x$
la valeur
   $$h(x)=\sqrt {x+\sqrt {x^2+1}+2}.$$
Enfin, l'int\'egrale
   $$\int _0^{+\infty } {dx\over x^2+1}$$
est convergente.
```

4.5. The final document. — No example of myfile.log is reproduced. Once myfile.tex is processed by TEX, the final document appears and looks like :

Dans l'algèbre $K\langle X\rangle$ on peut former les produits $x \times y$ et $x \otimes y$. Les quantités

$$\prod_{i=1}^{i=n} x_i \qquad \coprod_{i=1}^{i=n} y_i$$

ont aussi un sens. Si $g : \mapsto x + \sqrt{x^2+1}$ et $f : x \mapsto \sqrt{x+2}$ sont deux applications, leur produit de composition $h = f \circ g$ prend en x la valeur

$$h(x) = \sqrt{x + \sqrt{x^2+1} + 2}.$$

Enfin, l'intégrale

$$\int_0^{+\infty} \frac{dx}{x^2+1}$$

est convergente.

REFERENCES

[1] KNUTH (Donald E.). — *The TEXbook.* — Reading, Massachusetts, Addison-Wesley, 1984.

[2] ROY (Yves). — *TEX/WEB et le traitement de textes mathématiques.* — Paris, Masson, 1984.

[3] DÉSARMÉNIEN (Jacques). — How to run TEX in a French environment, *TUGboat*, t. 5, 1984, p. 91-104.

[4] FOATA (Dominique), PANSIOT (Jean-Jacques) et ROY (Yves). — Stratec, un logiciel de traitement de textes mathématiques en amont de TEX, Publ. I.R.M.A. Strasbourg, 255/D-06.

ACKNOWLEDGEMENTS. — The authors would like to thank Wilbur JÓNSSON for helping the authors edit the manuscript.

The brochure and the floppy disk with all the *STRATEC* files can be ordered by writing to anyone of the authors.

T_EX *for scientific documentation*

F1	F2	F3	F4	F5	INIT IMPRIM	SORTIE ÉDITEUR

{ \ [	1 * @	2 é É	3 " #	4 , $	5 (<	6 - >	7 è È	8 - ~	9 ç Ç	0 à À	&) |	} !]	BS ⇐
Γ TAB Δ	A a α	Z z ς	E e ε	R r ρ	T t τ	Y y η	U u υ	I i ι	O o θ	P p π	¨ ^ Υ	` ^ Ξ	
caps caps ⇕ shift	Q q χ	S s σ	D d δ	F f φ	G g ψ	H h Φ	J j Ψ	K k κ	L l λ	M m μ	% ù Ů	⇐ CR	
SHIFT ⇑	W w ω	X x ξ	C c γ	V v Λ	B b β	N n ν	? , Θ	. ; Π	/ : Σ	+ = Ω	⇑ SHIFT		

ALT					⇑ SCROLL ⇓

STRATEC Keyboard

Strasbourg, November 1984

AN INTERACTIVE USER-FRIENDLY TEX IN VM/CMS ENVIRONMENT

M.Agostini [1], V.Matano [1], M.Schaerf [1], M.Vascotto [2]

Abstract

Documents produced using TEX [3] can satisfy all sorts of aesthetic and functional requirements when printed using high quality output devices.
However the use of TEX may be quite difficult for a user lacking programming experience and typographical skills.
The work described in this paper is intended to overcome these drawbacks offering to the TEX users two facilities:

- a simple declarative language (SGML like), with high level commands for document composition with TEX;
- some degree of interactivity which allows to edit and preview on a screen the text formatted by TEX.

These facilities, which extend the capabilities of TEX82 without modifying its features, are implemented under VM/CMS. Their modularity allows the portability of those modules which are not system dependent.

The work has been carried out at the IBM Scientific Centre of Rome in close cooperation with the Computer Centre of the University of Rome "La Sapienza".

---

[1] *University of Rome "La Sapienza"*
[2] *IBM Scientific Centre of Rome*
[3] TEX is a trademark of American Mathematical Society

TEX for Scientific Documentation   D. Lucarella, Editor
Copyright ©1985 Addison-Wesley Publishing Company, Inc.

1. Introduction

With the recent increase in the number of computer users (from home computers to large systems) there has also been a considerable increase in the number of people using a document formatting system.
This growth in quantity must be counterbalanced by improving the quality of printed matter produced by formatters.

On one hand, results must be achieved which meet the favour of those who have technical and aesthetic skills of a typographical source, meant in a broad sense. On the other hand, there is a wide public of *"inexperts"* that, being immersed in a world where the visual media has a dominating role and offers sophistication levels noticeable in its every expression (cartoons, advertising, etc.), are used to receive the eminent part of communication information through its formal components.

TEX allows us to reach high aesthetic results, thanks to its formatting algorithms, particular care given to math formulas and tables and to some typographical devices (ligatures, kernel, etc.), which in addition to their rather restricted local influence, have an important impact on the presentation of a publication as a whole.

The TEX82 version, on which we have based the work described in this article, gives us the opportunity to introduce figures (raster or vectorial images) in the text: nowadays, this is an essential point for the effectiveness of any written communication, whether it be a degree thesis, an article or any other publication.

For a general TEX user it could be complex and time-consuming to define the layout of his publication and reach the desired results using the low level standard commands. Such a difficulty can lead either to a minor utilisation of the formatter, or to the adjustment to a standard defined elsewhere, as in the case of AMS articles.
On the contrary, we feel that the typical *"Opening"* of TEX (public domain, device independent file, etc.) can and should permit a deeper and more flexible usage for a wider range of users.

In considering the possibilities of TEX82 and VM/CMS operating system, which will be described later on, we thought of a offer of a most immediate usage of TEX for following categories of users:

- the *"expert"*, who can be either the one in charge of the graphical aspect of an organisation publications or a researcher who wishes to exploit the new methods of automatic document formatting;
- all common users of a computer who need to write a document.

The following are the main areas in which to operate to simplify and extend further the use of TeX:

1. the creation of interfaces that allow the common user to produces a text file and command to submit to TeX without knowing the language (for example, trough panel procedures or by placing directions in a *"free"* format);
2. the definition of document styles through a set of high level commands with a flexible syntax. The aim is to give user a progressive learning of the formatting commands, with the possibility of reaching immediately a non-particularly sophisticated result;
3. the gradual introduction of *"interactivity"*: a first facility, the control of pre-formatted pages without resorting of the printer was already available; these could be the following steps:

    - the offer of just one environment to carry out the writing, preview and print the document;
    - the incremental processing of the text in input.

Since our users, because of their *"forma-mentis"*, are supposed to know how to skilfully manage with the constraints imposed by strict language syntax, yet in use with computers, we have preferred to develop the second and the third of the quoted points.

For the second point we followed a standard suggestion for document composition languages, namely SGML, realising in TeX and Pascal languages a declarative language with additional instruments for a greater flexibility in the preparation and check of a document format (see sect.2).

To our opinion, the third point (interactivity) is an important requirement for the optimisation of productivity of authors and designers of new types of document.This becomes rather necessary when the publication contains figures, math formulas and particular graphical devices and pagination.

In the third section we will speak of what has been done to offer the interactivity advantages to TeX82 users in VM/CMS environment.

2. A declarative language for TeX

A document is a set of objects placed in a logical order that reflects the natural structure of the document itself [3].

Therefore, we can think of a document as made up of two different object configurations: **abstract** or **logical** objects and **concrete** objects.

In the preparation of a document (*editing*) we work on abstract objects describing their aspect through the system definition language. During the display or print we obtain their concrete configuration; the transformation of abstract objects into the corresponding concrete objects is carried out by the system in the formatting process, according to the chosen properties from the commands inserted in the text. The way of stating these properties depends mainly on the type of language definition used by the system.

Many systems see the formatting process as a sequence of operations applied to logical objects, described with the same formalism of language programming. In such a case, the definition language is extremely powerful and the user can describe in details any logical object and maintain the full control of the transformation from abstract to concrete objects. This kind of language is called "**procedural**".

The TeX language is highly procedural, being made up of low level commands that allow us to describe thoroughly the form of the document and all the logical objects of which it is composed.

In other systems the definition language is "**declarative**": the document is seen as a series of declarations on its logical objects and their contents. Every command is associated to a logical object of the document and determines synthetically all necessary functions for the complete formatting of the corresponding concrete object. The passage from abstract to concrete objects is checked by the declarations in a very clear way for the user. This type of approach has the disadvantage of the limited flexibility of the language: the commands allow us to obtain just one representation of concrete objects and therefore, of the document itself.

Two provisions can make declarative language more powerful:

1. attention to the flexibility of commands, required so as not to limit the choice of the user and to allow the setting up of different document styles;
2. the use of "template files" to describe, in a parametric manner, the pages layout of the document. The parameters (for example: width, length; space,

margins) represent the pagination characteristics which vary according to the document style and the needs of the user.

In the work stated here, our objective is to facilitate the use of TEX by having available its standard language as well as a high level language of a declarative type.

For the generic command we have used a particular structure where the presence of several optional attributes, through which we get different realisations of a document or of its concrete objects, is balanced by the predefinition of default values. Thus, we avoid the risk that a high number of obligatory choices produces for the user the same psychological and practical effects of a procedural language.

In the project we have followed the "standard" language suggested for document production systems accepted by ANSI/ISO: SGML, Standard Generalized Markup Language [4,5] .

In this language the logical objects of a document are identified by a uniform symbolism through high level commands, named "**tags**".

A tag is a mnemonic label made up of a string of characters preceded by an escape character (':'), differentiating it from the rest of the text:

1. it separates and identifies the logical objects of a document;
2. it synthetically specifies the set of actions that determine the whole formatting of the identified concrete object.

To comply with the aims of the project we have realised a language containing a limited but flexible set of tags.

There are about 30 tags available and represent the objects most common to the various types of documents. It was neither realistic nor of our interest to define "ad hoc" tags for a certain style; however, with the definite ones we can print several types of publications using proper values for attributes.

The objects marked-up by the tags can thus be divided into two categories, according to their position in the document structure:

1. first level tags: correspond to objects that have a rather stable position in the document structure (front matter, abstract, chapters, sections, sub-sections, bibliography, table of contents, etc.).
2. second level tags: correspond to objects that do not have a set position in the document structure, but can be considered as belonging to the paragraph

(simple, ordered or unordered list, bibliographical quotations, footnotes, figures, etc.).

The attributes of the tags set up refer to the outline variables of the concrete aspect of an object (font, position in the page, position compared with other objects, etc.). For each object there is also a concrete default representation that allows the user to obtain immediately a non-particularly sophisticated result.

The last commands available are those for the definition of templates. Information as the width and length of a page, the value of space, formatting on one or two columns etc., is not inherent to particular objects but defines the layout of "pattern pages" that could appear in the document (front-matter, appendix, etc.).

The defined language can be an useful instrument for the designer of types of documents. In fact, by the use of the tags flexibility, he can try different forms for all the document objects searching for and setting the value combination of tags attributes that define the new style. This combination is stored in an input file for TEX, in it are also joined the designer's chosen layout parameters for the different pages of the document. Therefore, the language tags have been constructed parametric in regards to these values.

Once outlined all the characteristics of the new style, the final user can refer to it by placing at the beginning of his input file the command "\input ⟨name file⟩", (the name of the file is chosen by the designer) and to obtain the proper aspect of the document he must mark his text with tags of the chosen style. In the case the user doesn't ask for a specific predefined style, but wishes to make use of the tags marking-up his text, he must load a macro library inserting at the beginning of the input file the command:"\input macrodoc".

In writing tags with TEX language we have used the following TEX82 characteristics:

- the availability of constructs of the structured programming (conditional branches, case instruction, loop with conditional phrases);
- the possibility to accept in input several text and/or commands files and manage 16 auxiliary files for reading and writing or 16 auxiliary files for reading and 16 for writing.

A tag is a control sequence to which a macro, leading the system to the formatting of the identified object, is associated selecting (through conditional branches or case instructions) the procedure corresponding to the chosen values for the attributes.

A generic tag syntax is represented in fig.1. The value of the attributes, chosen in a predetermined set, is placed at the right of the tag identifier. The macro's *"field of action"* is generally a part of the text, corresponding to the object identified by the tag, enclosed in grouping characters of TeX. In some cases the field of action may not be specified: in this case it could be either the whole text, a paragraph or the whole text up to the following tag. In order to insert the default action in the macro the TeX is forced to *"look ahead"* so as to identify the possible specifications present in the tag attributes. An example of tag defined for TeX is \rhead, it identifies the *"running heading"* of a document. Its syntax is the represented in fig.2.

```
\tag     attribute₁ = "value"
         ⋮
         attributeₙ = "value"
         { field of action }
```

Fig.1 This is the tag's syntax.

The tag argument is a wording relative to either running chapter title or document title or identification of production environment (e.g. Computer Centre of the University of Rome). As default we use the running chapter title, either on the even page or the odd one; it is placed to the right followed by the page number. The attributes specify the following characteristics of the concrete object corresponding to the tag:

```
\rhead    select = Even/Odd/All
          pos = Left/Center/Right
          page = y/n
          { text }
```

Fig.2 An example of tag: \rhead for running heading in a document.

- 'select': it selects the odd page heading ('Odd'), the even page heading ('Even'), both pages heading ('All');
- 'pos': it determines the text position on the line;
- 'page': if the value of this attribute is 'y' the page number will appear with the tag's text, according to the following rules: to right if the page is odd or it has been selected the same paging for both pages, to left if the page is even.

Some tags are more complex by the necessity of storing information about the processed objects on auxiliary files. Among these are the tags for the table of contents, the index and the bibliography that require from TeX, as from any other compiling or interactive system, several processing steps of the input file.

For the composition of the bibliography and index in any document, without performing all the necessary functions for their reproduction, we use two Pascal programs: BIBLIO, for the bibliography, and INDICE, for the index. Both programs process the information written from TeX in the first passage to auxiliary files producing other files that contain the commands for the formatting of the relative objects. Therefore, these files, are read by TeX in the following passages for the definitive version of the document.

On the other hand, the table of contents, also if it requests more than one passage, has been realised as a normal macro TeX. In the realisation of BIBLIO two modules were also joined (a "preprocessor" for predetermined types of documents and an editor for the composition and management of a data base of bibliographical items) deriving from a previous work on TeX [7].

The task of calculating and carrying out the number of further processing steps needed to obtain the definite version of the document is done by the PERFECT system procedure. Not only can it be called directly by the user, but it is also integrated as a second level module in the interactive scheme described in the following section.

3. Toward an interactive TeX

The system here described aims to simplify and facilitate as much as possible the processing phases of a document.

In producing a text with the use of TeX it is not always easy to figure the aspect of the formatting output, especially if we use low level commands or we require some unusual facilities.

On the other hand, even the user who utilises high level commands (e.g., tags as described in the preceding section) but who still wishes to create documents containing formulas, tables and figures, needs to know the exact position of each object in the definite page.

In both cases it is important to display the formatted document and the marked-up one at the same time. Therefore, we either have a two-display workstation [an alphanumeric video and a graphic screen with suitable resolution) or just one screen divided into *"windows"*.

If we use only a graphic screen that is easily divided into windows we can depend on the alternate display of the marked-up and formatted document. The first choice seems the best: it is easier to correlate abstract and concrete objects and the display resolution is better used.

This type of workstation is not sufficient to guarantee an efficient interaction with the user. It is advisable to have just one environment where to insert the text, request the display of any page or start to print, and keep the response time within acceptable limits.

A solution of this kind characterises the interactive systems for text processing. In these systems, the incremental processing of input together with the listed characteristics, gives the user an immediate check on the reached results. In fact, in a document of n pages, the control of page j, with $1 \leq j \leq n$, requires the formatting of pages 1 to j; a change in page i, with $i \leq j$, requires the formatting of the pages i to j for a new check of page j.

Since a workstation with two screen was available, in an interactive TEX we have marked out two objectives:

1. the direct control of pages, e.g., being able to request the display or print the document without leaving the editing environment;
2. the partial reprocessing; the formatter deals with only the part modified after the last formatting.

With the first objective we avoid a strenuous repetition (after any variation we want to display) of commands to recall TEX and activate the system procedures that display or print the text. Therefore, the three phases of editing, formatting and print which in a normal use of TEX are done separately, here they seem joint to the user (see fig.3). Anything that can be done for the second objective aims to reduce the response time, which would be quite high if after every change we had to reformat the entire manuscript.

In some objects of a document reference can be made to other objects (e.g., name or number of a section or of the following chapter). Therefore, a change in one section can cause changes to be made in all sections that have reference to it. The SCRIBE system [4] manages automatically references [8]. In our case the partial reprocessing creates temporary versions of the document, while the

---

[4] SCRIBE is a trademark of Unilogic Ltd.

definite version is created by one or more complete processing recalled by the PERFECT module. Here the processing not only produces the table of contents and bibliography but they can also resolve crossed references.

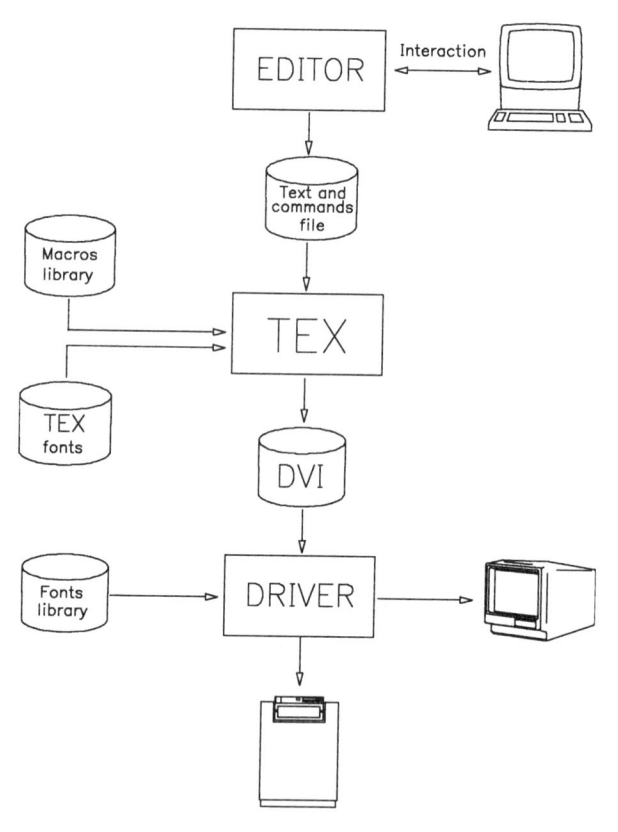

Fig.3 Unified phases.

3.1 Functions of interactive processing

An interactive system should be able to take up the processing at any point in the document and take into account all changes made. With this aim, during every processing session an *"information block"*, containing the current *"state"* of the system, is saved for every page in auxiliary storage. This block contains all the program active variables and the format specifics. An ordinal number is associated to every *"block"*, indicating the position of the corresponding page within the document.

Furthermore, at any request for the display or print of a page, given in an *"editing"* environment, the system questioning the editor, must identify the lowest line of the input file in which, in the current session, there is a change:

- if this change follows the requested page then the page will be formatted (if it hasn't already been done) and immediately outputted on the required device;
- if the change precedes the page then the system picks up the processing from the part changed up the requested page enabling its display or print.

In the interactive processing with TEX, piloted in the editing environment, we can identify the following main functions:

Starting Function; used to create a new document or to make changes in a existing document. This function controls the work of editing, formatting and print. Its tasks include:

- creating or recalling TEX files (passing from the operating system environment to the editing one);
- the definition of an auxiliary storage area where support files are placed and used in interactive processing;
- the assignment of a set of total variables to which all functions may accede.

Formatting Function; it is set up, just like all functions following, in the editing environment. It automatically supplies the whole processing of the text if it hasn't already been formatted or, in case of changes being made, it makes a partial processing. Information on the input to be processed is given by minor functions which will be examined later.

Output Function on devices; beginning with DVI, using proper drivers, outputs an formatted page on the printer or on the screen addressed by the parameters supplied to it.

At a lower level we have:

Inter-Editor Function; it supplies information on all changes made in the input file and on other parameters. For example , it determines the number of the general line of editing, required to support correctly the marked-up and formatted document.

Database Function; as we have stated, in order to reprocess only a part of the text and at same time keep the document as an only logical entity, at every complete or partial processing we must store a number of data:

- the division of the document into pages and consequently, which and how many are the lines for every formatted page;
- the internal "*state*" of the system for every "*end of page*" clearly identifiable.

Therefore, for every document is created an information database on auxiliary TEX files.

These files, of no interest for users, are placed in the area defined at the beginning of the session. The functions available are those of "Dbstore" to store information during every processing session, and of "Dbfetch" to find the stored information. Saving the whole "*state*" of the system is needed to "*simulate*" the new starting point from which TEX may continue to process the text as if there had been no interruptions and to allow all the operations of the partial reprocessing among which the recovery of information from database.

3.2 The set up system

We will now describe the set of commands provided by the project and dwell upon their relation with the functions listed previously. The user starts the session with 'INTERTEX' command, which as a parameter requires the identifier of the main input file.

The procedure associated to the command sets up the starting function; in particular, provides the retrieval of all the work carried out in the preceding sessions, if the file is already existing and if it hasn't been changed after the last session. After performing the command, the user has a wide editing environment in which, besides the normal sub-commands, he finds the macro of the editor corresponding to the following operations:

- formatting (sub-command of 'PAGEUP'); sets up the formatting function on a sub-set of the document;
- display (sub-command of 'SHOW') of any page or of the page corresponding to the text on the screen (the corresponding information is obtained by the "Inter-Editor" function). If the requested page is not yet available, it is automatically formatted. In this manner the user does not see the intermediate passages of this file, remaining disengaged from the command syntax of the operating system;
- print (sub-command of 'PRINTEX'); the action is similar to the above sub-command: the only thing differs is the addressed device;

- final formatting (sub-command of 'PERFECT'); is requested by the user when he has reached the definite aspect of the document. With PERFECT we recall the outer modules for the creation of the bibliography and the tables of contents and carry out the passages required for all the operations of the document.

The available sub-commands are shown on the fig.4.

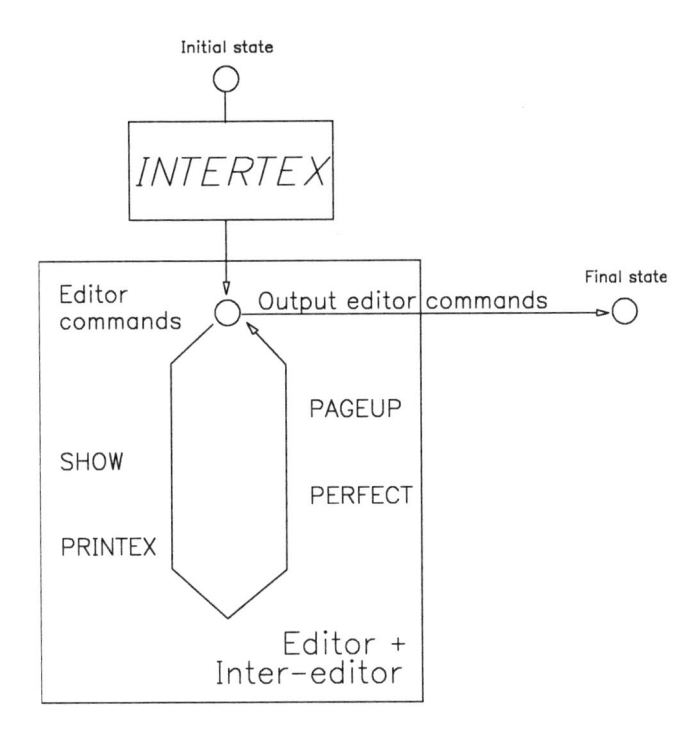

Fig.4 Available sub-commands.

There is a series of optional parameters provided for every sub-command to which if not already supplied with, we assign standard values (for example, SHOW without any parameter displays the current page).

The VM/CMS operating system has offered a friendly environment and at the same time plenty of software and hardware support for the development and set up of the project.

Among the facilities (used or available for future applications) let us just recall the programs to obtain graphics and drawings, for the image processing, the communication facilities, and the DBMS.

We have referred to the "System Product Editor" (XEDIT); its macros and system procedures have been written with the "System Product Interpreter" (REXX language).
The other procedures were set up in partly in TeX (definition of TeX macros, management of in and out files, etc.) and partly in Pascal.

In the realisation phase of the system prototype, some translation programs and drivers already available have enabled the output function on devices, which was treated as a *"black box"*.

We have tested two display solutions: a two-display workstation made up of an IBM 3277 Graphics Attachment and a TEKTRONIX 614 graphic screen and single terminal (IBM 3278 or IBM 3279) with an alternate display of marked-up and formatted document. The print sub-command offers two possibilities: an IBM APA6670 printer (with a 240 ppi resolution) and an electroerosive IBM 4250 printer (600 ppi resolution).

In the first phase of the project no changes were made on TeX source. This brought about the need of an initial processing of the whole manuscript; later it will be possible to reprocess just the changed part of the document.

Another problem solved only temporarily is the way of resuming the formatting: the processing starts from the last end of page clearly evident before the lowest line of the text changed, thus the quantity of information pertaining to the state of the system stored in the database is limited.

4. Conclusions

The results reached concerning both the declarative language and the problem of interactivity are by themselves satisfactory.

The first point needs only one refinement and a check of the available tags.

Interactivity has already shown its advantages: a single work environment reduces both the effort on the part of the user and the time required to carry out any function.

The first survey of performance times shows that the interactive use of TeX is convenient if compared to the traditional 'batch' (complete processing plus a check on the screen of formatted pages), especially where changes have been made in the last pages of a document. Therefore, it is worthwhile to continue in this direction studying improvements (automatic storing of the state of the system, etc.) that, although requiring an interaction with the TeX source for better efficiency, guarantee a high level of system portability.

REFERENCES

1. AIELLO, L., PAVAN, S., Un sistema per la produzione di documenti basato sul TeX. *Rivista di Informatica Vol.13*, n.3 (July 1983).

2. CHAMBERLIN, D., KING, J., SLUTZ, D. AND TODD, S., JANUS: an interactive system for document composition. In *Proceedings of the ACM SIGPAN SIGOA Symposium on text manipulation*, ACM SIGPLAN NOTICES, Portland, Oregon, June, 1981, pp. 82-92.

3. FURUTA, R., SCOFIELD, J., SHAW, A., Document Formatting Systems: survey, concepts and iusses. *in ACM Computing Surveys Vol.14*, n.3 (September 1982), pp.417-472.

4. GOLDFARB, C. F., A Generalized Approach to Document Markup. In *Proceedings of the ACM SIGPLAN SIGOA Symposium on text manipulation*, ACM SIGPLAN NOTICES, Portland, Oregon, June, 1981, pp. pp.68-73.

5. GOLDFARB, C.F., *International and American National Standard for Computer Languages*. Third Working Draft; December 1, 1982.

6. KNUTH, D.E., *The TeXbook*. Addison Wesley, 1984.

7. PAVAN, S., Un sistema per la produzione di documenti ad alta qualità tipografica. Degree Thesis, Università di Pisa, Pisa, October, 1981.

8. REID, B.K., A high-level approach to computer document formatting. In *Conf.Rec. 7th Annual ACM Symp. on Principles of Programming Languages*, ACM, Las Vegas, January, 1980, pp. 24-31.

TeX FOR RIAD COMPUTERS

Janusz S. Bien, Hanna Kolodziejska

Institute of Informatics

Warsaw University

RIAD family consists of IBM 360 and 370 compatible computers produced in Poland and other COMECON countries. In this paper we present the progress report of our effort to adapt TeX to a Pascal dialect available on RIAD computers. We hope that our experience can be useful for other teams undertaking similar tasks

Introduction

Although our goal is to run TeX on a RIAD computer at the Warsaw University Computing Service, we preferred to install it first on the IBM 370/148 at the IBM Support Center in Warsaw, using the VM/SP and CMS operating systems and the RIAD dialect of Pascal (PASCAL/VS is not available on this installation).

We started our interest in TeX late enough to avoid being involved in TeX78, but too early to set the distribution tape in the IBM/CMS format with the TeX executable module. In consequence, we had only the generic source tape of release 0.8, which was kindly provided for us by Jan Madey, D.Sc., at his own expense.

There are two Pascal dialects available on RIAD computers: OS/JS Pascal (IMM 1977, 1977a) and Pascal 360 (Iglewski, Madey, Matwin 1984); both of them restrict the language in some way, but Pascal 360 comes closer to the standard. In consequence, our choice was Pascal 360, which we obtained from its authors in the form of the distribution tape for the OS operating system.

Extending Pascal 360

The first step was to install Pascal 360 under VM/CMS. The Pascal 360 compiler consists of two separate parts: the proper compiler and the running system, supervising the execution of a Pascal program. The Pascal 360 compiler is itself implemented in Pascal 360, except of the running system, called MASTER, which is implemented in the assembly language. Some small changes to MASTER allowed to get rid of the

TeX for Scientific Documentation   D. Lucarella, Editor

Copyright ©1985 Addison-Wesley Publishing Company, Inc.

cumbersome OSRUN command and made possible to execute both the compiler and the Pascal programs directly under VM/CMS.

It soon became clear that two substantial extensions were needed to make TEX installation feasible. First, TEX makes an extensive use of the general form of the **case** statement, which includes a so-called default case. As this was not available in Pascal 360, the appropriate modifications of the compiler source code were necessary. The default case is introduced by the label "**else:**".

The next extension was, however, much more important and indispensable. This second drawback of Pascal 360 concerned file usage. Each file variable used in a Pascal program had to be declared three times:

a) in the program header, i.e.
   program name-of-program (file-variable,...);

b) in the declaration part, i.e.
   var file-variable: **file of**...;

c) in data definition statements required by the operating system, in the case of CMS in the FILEDEF commands, i.e.
   FILEDEF file-variable DISK external-file-name options

The connection between the file variable and the external file name from the FILEDEF command was permanent and did not allow any modification; there was no possibility to assign an external file name to a file variable inside a Pascal program. In consequence, it was impossible to open a file with the name read in at run time. Since such operations on files very often occur in TEX, it was obvious that the appropriate extension of Pascal 360 was needed. Auxiliary external procedures were written in the assembly language:

procedure setname (**var** file-var: file-type; name: name-type); pascal;
procedure closef (**var** file-var: file-type); pascal;
where
file-type = **file of**...;
name-type = **packed array** [1...20] **of** char;

The modification allows the specification of the file name by calling the routine 'setname (f, name)', where 'f' is the file variable and 'name' contains an external file identification in the format:
   'MM:NAME.TYPE ...'
(MM stands for CMS file mode).

'Setname' should be called prior to any 'reset' or 'rewrite'. The 'closef' procedure closes the file associated with the variable.

Later it also appeared that the constant in the compiler code limiting the number of external references from one Pascal procedure or block was to be increased. The constant was set to 40 by the authors of the compiler, while the 'main-control' procedure of TEX calls nearly 90 other procedures.

Last but not least, the compiler caused us a serious problem when it appeared that there was a bug in it. Locating it was difficult and time consuming but, fortunately, the bug was rather quickly corrected by the authors of the compiler.

Preparing tools

The auxiliary programs TFtoPL, PLtoTF, POOLTYPE, TANGLE and DVItype were installed rather smoothly but with WEAVE we experienced the difficulties which later appeared crucial for TEX (cf. sec. 5). We have also found it convenient to add another auxiliary program, called XTRACT; it searches for the indicated WEB modules and copies them into another file. The modules can be then conveniently edited into an appropriate change file for WEB. We adopted the policy of exchanging complete modules rather than single lines.

It is worth mentioning that we worked with the version 1.0 of WEB. This version causes some problems which do not occur any longer in the last versions. In the version 1.0 the method of merging data from the web file and the change is as follows: If the change file is not empty then the web file should have at least one line that exactly matches the first line of the change file. At the first such match, TANGLE and WEAVE will start to read lines from the change file, until encountering the next '@z' that appears at the beginning of a line. This method replaced the corresponding material in the web file up to the next '@z' or the beginning of the next module. If the change file is not exhausted at this moment the process continues in the same way. This method causes some problems with modification of the first line of a module. In the new version of WEB, where each change in the change file has the form:

@x <old lines> @y <new lines> @z

the problem does not exist.

System dependent changes

The most important system dependent changes were induced by the specific way of handling of input/output in Pascal 360. As it was primarily designed for the OS operating system, mastering the TEX, Pascal 360 and VM/CMS interaction was not a trivial task; some subtle aspects of it had to be discovered experimentally.

In the examples below, by 'term-in' we understand the file variable when the terminal is considered an input file, and by 'term-out' the file variable when it is considered an output file. One of the problems encountered was:

- calling 'reset(term-in)' causes the program to wait for input data;
- calling 'reset(term-in)' and pressing the 'ENTER' key rises the EOF condition instead of the EOLN one.

It was for these reasons that the TEX procedure which inputs a line from the terminal had to be modified.

The system dependent operations called 'update-terminal' and 'clear-terminal' were introduced to synchronize the terminal input/output. To make sure that all characters had left the computer's internal buffers and appeared on the terminal, 'update-terminal' was defined as follows:

define update-terminal = write-ln (term-out,' ')

The definition of 'clear-terminal', called to cancel the input that the user may have typed ahead, was a little more complicated. The definition:

define clear-terminal = read-ln (term-in)

was better, but we found out that the execution of 'read-ln' caused the program to wait for input data and pressing the 'ENTER' key was necessary to finish the input operation. In this way we came to the present definition:

define clear-terminal =
    if not eof(term-in) **then**
        while not eoln(term-in) **do** read(term-in, ch)

where 'ch' is an auxiliary character variable.

Overcoming compiler limitations

The Pascal 360 compiler has an intrinsic limitation for the length of a procedure code (8192 bytes), caused by the addressing method of Pascal 360. Several procedures in WEAVE and TEX run out of this limit, so it was necessary to split them into smaller ones. The general method was very simple. Let's suppose that we want to split the procedure called 'too-long' which exceeds the limit, and that this procedure containg the module M:

```
procedure  too-long (...);
   .....
begin
   .....
   @<Module M @>;
   .....
end; (* too-long *)
```

We can make a parameterless sub-procedure from the module M, without much effort, in the following ways:

```
procedure  too-long (...);
   .....
   procedure  M;
   begin
      @<Module M @>;
   end; (* M *)
   .....
begin
   .....
   M;
   .....
end; (* too-long *)
```

Of course, sometimes it may be necessary to make more than one sub-procedure in the way shown above. We should only pay attention to the labels which must be declared in the created subprogram if they occur there.

However, when a **case** statement was to be split, careful editing by hand was the only solution.

The next disadvantage of the Pascal 360 compiler is connected with files, because arrays of files are not available and, moreover, the total number of files used in a program is strongly limited.

There are three arrays of files used in TEX: read-file, write-file and input-file. There was no other choice than to define each file separately and to use an appropriate **case** statement in every place where a file array was referenced. Sometimes, however, the **case** statement was not sufficient and we had to add some auxiliary procedures. For example, the 'a-open-in' function is used in TEX to open a text file for input. Its header is:

function a-open-in (**var** f: alpha-file): Boolean;

We added two functions to distinguish the calls of that function for an input file from the calls for a read file. We received:

function a-open-read (n: small-number): Boolean;
begin
  case n **of**
    0: a-open-read := a-open-in (read-file-0);
    1: a-open-read := a-open-in (read-file-1);
    . . . . .
  end
end ;

and the similar function for the input files:

function a-open-input (n: small-number): Boolean;
begin
  case n **of**
    1: a-open-input := a-open-in (input-file-1);
    2: a-open-input := a-open-in (input-file-2);
    . . . . .
  end
end ;

At the same time we replaced the appropriate calls of the 'a-open-in' function respectively by the calls of 'a-open-input' or 'a-open-read'.

It was not our only problem with files. TEX gives the possibility of using 16 read files, 16 write files and some input files (their number is defined by the 'max-in-open' constant, which value is set in TEX to 6). As there are also some other files, like e.g. pool-file, log-file, tfm-file, fmt-file, we have over 40 different files used in TEX. Pascal 360 addresses the files directly and keeps their description in one block of 4096 bytes. For example, the description of a single text file needs exactly 128 bytes. Additionally, the information about some other objects is also kept in the same block. In consequence, we had to substantially reduce the number of files. It was easy in the case of the input files when it was sufficient to decrease the 'max-in-open' constant (it was set to 2). It was more difficult with the read and write files; they may have numbers from 0 to 15 and these limits are not defined by any constant. File numbers are checked in the 'scan-four-bit-int' procedure; since the procedure is also used for other purposes, the limits cannot be changed simply by modyfing the procedure body. The new 'scan-two-bit-int' procedure (with the limits: 0 . . 3) was written, replacing 'scan-four-bit-int' when appropriate.

Testing

At the time of this writing TeX is installed and operational, i.e. it generates correct DVI files. It was tested in accordance with the procedure described in the report "A test file for TeX" by prof. D.E. Knuth. The TRIP file from the distribution tape was processed exactly as required. We did not set any other differences between our output data and the supplied ones than it was allowed, with only one exception of discrepancies caused by the limit 0 . . 3 of the read and write file number (cf. sec. 5). The whole process of testing was successfully finished in april, 1985.

For the time being, we use the IBM 3287 colour dot-matrix printer as an output device. It was chosen because it is directly connected to IBM 370/148 and provides the fast turn-around time for TeX jobs. The printer has the horizontal resolution 100 dots per inch and the vertical one 70 dots per inch; we use for it the 240-dot-per-inch fonts from the distribution tape. Of course, the resulting quality allows only to experiment with TeX posters (cf. Sauter 1981), but this is sufficient for the very first steps towards mastering the TeX usage.

We prepared the driver program for this printer. It is based on the DVItype program from the distribution tape. Pascal 360 provides the possibility to call external procedures written in FORTRAN, and this way was used to access the FORTRAN interface to the IBM Graphical Data Display Manager System (GDDM). When DVItype gives some information about a char to be printed, or about moving the current position on a page, etc., the appropriate GDDM's routine is called in DRIVER. Fortunately for us, all the actions described by DVItype could be replaced by the GDDM's routines. We defined the imaginary coordinates of a page in pixel points and we use them in all our drawing instructions. The most frequently used GDDM's routine is the one called 'GSIMG', which draws an image at the current position on a page. The width and depth parameters of GSIMG determine the horizontal and vertical dimensions of the image. An image specification consists of an array of bits representing pixels; 1 sets the associated display point on, 0 leaves the associated display point unchanged. A similar method is used to code raster information for characters in PXL files. Therefore, to print a specified character it was sufficient to read the appropriate fragments of the PXL file into an auxiliary array and, after having calculated the other parameters, just to call the GSIMG routine for this array.

GDDM has one disadvantage which concerns the page size. The dimensions of the biggest available picture is about 250mm × 300mm.

Conclusions

The task of adapting TeX 0.8 to Pascal 360 appeared much more difficult and resource consuming than it had been expected, but the knowledge and experience gained should make installation of TeX 1.1 a straightforward process. As Pascal 360 is widely used on RAID computers and some graphic dot-matrix printers are produced in Poland, this will make TeX available to the Polish academic community.

Acknowledgment

The work presented here would not be possible without the help of our colleague Piotr Carlson.

References

[IBM81] *Graphical Data Display Manager,* Release 2, User's Guide. SC33-0101-1.

[IGL84] Iglewski J., Madey J., Matwin S.: *Pascal. Jezyk wzorcowy. Pascal 360. Wydawnictwa Naukowo-Techniczne,* Warszawa 1984.

[IMM77] *OS/JS Pascal – opis jezyka.* Zaklad Doswiadczalny Instytutu Maszyn Matematycznych, Warszawa 1977.

[IMM77a] *OS/JS Pascal – przewodnik prosram prosramisty.* Zaklad Doswiadczalny Instytutu Maszyn Matematycznych, Warszawa 1977.

[KNU82] Knuth D.E.: *A test file for TeX. Preliminary draft,* September, 1982.

[SAU81] Sauter J.: *"Poor Man's TeX".* TUGboat Vol. 2, No. 3, pp. 34-35.

Experiments in teaching METAFONT

Richard Southall
Computer Science Department
Stanford University
Stanford, CA 94305, USA

Jacques André
IRISA/INRIA-Rennes
Campus de Beaulieu
F-35042 Rennes Cedex, France

Abstract

In January 1985 a one-week winter course was organized in Rennes, France on Typography and Computer Science. The course was mainly devoted to type design. A set of lectures and practical work was organized on METAFONT and the design of typefaces.

METAFONT differs from other systems of character digitization because a META-FONT program tells an output device how to draw the characters it describes, rather than simply what shapes they are. Designers working with it are therefore faced with problems in three areas: the normal problems of type design, the normal problems of font production and the special problems that arise from the nature of METAFONT.

The practical work on the course was intended to investigate one important problem from each of these areas. Participants were given METAFONT programs that produced elementary shapes on a printer/plotter. They were asked to alter the programs and make visual assessments of the resulting output.

The present paper explains why METAFONT was taught in this way, discusses some of the problems that were encountered, and shows some results of the practical work.

TEX for Scientific Documentation   D. Lucarella, Editor
Copyright ©1985 Addison-Wesley Publishing Company, Inc.

1 Introduction

Between Gutenberg's time and the beginning of the 1980s, there were really only three truly significant events in the history of the manufacture of printers' type. In the years following 1882 the cutting of steel punches, which was the first stage in the production of metal type, changed from a handicraft to an industrial process. Between 1965 and 1970, the advent of photocomposition changed the product of the type-composing process from a three-dimensional assembly of pieces of metal to a two-dimensional assembly of character images on photographic paper or film. And from about 1977 (though the technique had been in commercial use since 1966) these character images were synthesised in the photocomposing machine by electronic means, rather than being provided as prefabricated master images on a photographically-produced character matrix.

With the arrival of extremely fast microprocessors and high-performance reproducing devices (laser printers and bit-mapped visual displays) at lower and lower cost [Bigelow 85], printers' type has moved out of the printing works into the office systems environment. More and more people, most of them without any experience of letterform design or type manufacture, are becoming involved in the production of digital type: designing systems to produce digitized characters, and designing the characters themselves.

The central problem in industrialized type manufacture has always been the problem of communication between the designer and the producer of the type. This problem is especially important in today's situation, because the producers of type, instead of being people, are now systems of computer programs and the machines on which they run. Among these systems, METAFONT is particularly significant because it is more than a way of describing the shapes of characters: a METAFONT program contains a schematic description of how to produce a series of fonts. Using META-FONT to make technically satisfactory fonts requires of the user both craft knowledge (for deciding on the shapes of the characters in the fonts) and programming skill (for writing the programs that specify the shapes). Using METAFONT well, and teaching it, are therefore both difficult enterprises.

The present paper describes an approach to teaching METAFONT that was used during the winter course on Typography and Computer Science at Rennes in January 1985.

2 The 1985 winter course on typography at Rennes

In 1983 a symposium on Document Preparation Systems was organized in Rennes [André 83]. The participants and lecturers were either typographers and type designers (like Charles Bigelow, Ladislas Mandel and Adrian Frutiger) or computer specialists (like Peter Hibbard, Brian Reid, Patrick Baudelaire and C. Newmann). However, it was noticed that these two categories of people did not mix together very much, and the feeling was that typographers and computer scientists do not speak the same language. It was therefore decided to organize another course to bring computer scientists and typographers (or graphic designers) together a second time. This course was originally planned to take place during the summer of 1985, but it had to be held earlier, during the winter of 1984-85.

The course was organized by the Institut National de Recherche en Informatique et en Automatique (INRIA). It was held at the Institut de Recherche en Informatique et Systèmes Aléatoires (IRISA), an INRIA laboratory for computer science located on the University campus at Rennes. The course contained the following parts [André Sallio 85]:

- Lectures on type design (by Ladislas Mandel and Richard Southall), after an introductory survey by Jacques André and some discussions on legibility;
- Lectures on character description techniques and font handling (discussions of spline curves and character digitization algorithms by Gérard Hégron, the PostScript page description language by Patrick Baudelaire, and laser printer interfaces by Roger Hersch);
- Two lectures on commercially important systems for the production of digital type: IKARUS by Peter Karow and the Camex/Bitstream Letter Input Processor (LIP) by Jim Flowers;
- Lectures on copyright questions (Nicole Croix) and the problems of handling non-latin scripts on computers (Jacques Piolle);
- and finally three lectures and four sessions of practical work on type design and METAFONT by Richard Southall.

3 Why METAFONT?

On such a course, it would evidently be valuable to have practical experience of a system for character digitization and font production. But which one? At the time the course was planned there were only a dozen or so systems extant for handling high resolution digital fonts [Ruggles 83], and new ones like IMP [Carter 84] were not yet available. None of the extant systems was really useable in a course context: they were too expensive, or unsuitable for use by a group; and in general they were too thickly veiled in commercial secrecy. Thus special attention was paid to METAFONT [Knuth 79], which, like TeX, belongs more or less to the research community. Alas, the first version of METAFONT (METAFONT79) was written in SAIL, a rather exotic language that runs only on DEC-10 computers and hence was not available at Rennes. Fortunately, however, a new version of METAFONT was being developed that was supposed to be as portable as TEX82. Since the new version of METAFONT was announced in 1984, a few months before the course, we decided to go for this new product.

4 The 1984 Stanford course on METAFONT

A course on 'Topics in digital typography' was organized at Stanford University during the Spring quarter of 1984 [Knuth 84]. The subject of this course was type design in general and the use of the new METAFONT in particular. It was taught by Charles Bigelow, Donald Knuth and Richard Southall. Southall's lectures were on the general topic of 'Designing typefaces'; Bigelow discussed the history and development of letterforms from ancient times to the present day; and Knuth lectured on the new METAFONT, which he was developing while the course was in progress. The first homework assignments were exercises done with cut paper, to illustrate the important differences between 'what you see' and 'what is there'. The first META-FONT assignment was to draw parts of El Palo Alto (the tall tree) for a new version of the Stanford symbol. During the second METAFONT assignment, each student was asked to create two letters of a new typeface, using macros written by Knuth in the new language that drew pen-like strokes and arcs. The last assignment was to design a set of eight characters with METAFONT, that could be used for setting typographic borders. Some results of this work appear in [Knuth 84].

5 Installing and running METAFONT

Once we had decided to try to teach METAFONT at Rennes, it was clear that we had to have practical exercises with it on a computer. Initially, we thought of using METAFONT on Sun workstations, as at Stanford. Although METAFONT is essentially batch-oriented rather than interactive, a high-resolution screen like the Sun's allows the output of a METAFONT run to be displayed next to the program that generated it. Unfortunately, the Sun workstation was not yet available in France at that time; and an interactive version of METAFONT for the Perq was still being developed [Leitch 85]. It was therefore decided to install METAFONT on a VAX running VMS at the IRISA, with a Versatec printer/plotter as output device. However, many problems arose, particularly in the few days before the course began:

- Both the VAX with VMS and the Versatec were new equipments at the IRISA. There was no wizard easily available who had the ability to make a quick installation of the TEX system (parts of which were needed to process METAFONT output for the Versatec). Fortunately a VAX specialist was able to come from

Lausanne to help. In the event, it took more than a week to get TEX running, since we had problems with the distribution tape and very little information on installation procedures.

- We were not able to get a distribution tape of METAFONT. Eventually, thanks to Lynn Ruggles' efforts at Stanford, we obtained a pre-release version. This worked well, except that the 'gray fonts' for making proof-mode output on the Versatec were missing. However, programs for making these were on the tape, and we successfully made both 'gray' and 'black' fonts for the Versatec with METAFONT.

- The VT100 terminals we were waiting for arrived too late: so we had to use old Questar terminals that could not handle the VMS screen editor, and had to use the line editor instead. In terms of running the practical classes, this gave us our greatest difficulties.

- We planned to use at least 15 terminals (one for each pair of participants). Because the VAX had only 8 ports, we had to connect the terminals via the IRISA NetOne network. We needed a special cable for the Versatec, so that it could work at reasonable speed in the room where the course was held: this cable did not arrive until after the course had begun. The VAX had no spooler for the Versatec, so that only one file could be sent to it at a time. This was a major difficulty until Jorge Eggli made us a 'pseudo-spooler', that interrogated the Versatec repeatedly on behalf of each user who was waiting to have a file printed.

- The VAX was being used by IRISA personnel for their own research during the course, and at times it was rather slow. We even had a power failure on the NetOne network.

In absolute terms, we had fewer technical problems at Rennes than there were on the Stanford course [Knuth 84; personal experience (RS)]. However, because of the limited capability of the IRISA equipment, the intensity and short duration of the course and the relative lack of technical support, the problems seemed more acute at Rennes than they did at Stanford.

6 Teaching type design and METAFONT

METAFONT is a programming language for instructing a computer to draw shapes on a bit-mapped output device. It differs from other systems like IKARUS [Karow 83] or LIP [Flowers 84] not only because it is batch-oriented, but also because a META-FONT program tells an output device *how to draw* the characters it describes rather than simply *what shapes* they are. Because METAFONT is primarily intended for the production of new designs rather than the reproduction of existing ones, designers working with it are faced with problems in three areas:

- the normal problems of type design;
- the normal problems of font production;
- the special problems that arise from the nature of METAFONT, where shapes that designers normally make manually and assess visually have to be described in symbolic form.

Richard Southall's lectures at Stanford had been mainly concerned with trying to explain the distinctions between the different tasks involved in what is generally described as 'type design'. The experience of the Stanford course showed (not altogether surprisingly) that there tended to be great differences in habits of thought between computer scientists and graphic designers. We decided to continue at Rennes the attempt to discuss the design process in terms which would be comprehensible to non-designers.

We planned to tackle this task by two means:

1 A series of three lectures about the nature of the type design task [Southall 85b]. These lectures were adapted and condensed from lectures given in the Stanford course. They had the titles *What is a typeface?*, *Quality criteria for typefaces*, and *What does a type designer have to do?*.

2 Practical work with METAFONT, to investigate one important problem from each of the areas of type design, font production and the symbolic description of shapes.

Because of the short duration of the course, we could only devote three afternoons and part of a morning to the lectures and practical work on this subject. For logistical reasons, we had to divide the participants into two groups for part of the time: this meant that each group had a total of about 10 hours for this part of the course.

6.1 Information about METAFONT

Because of the lack of time, it was out of the question to adopt a formal approach to teaching METAFONT, as Knuth had on the Stanford course. We therefore decided to let people learn about METAFONT by osmosis. The participants were given the following texts:

- A draft version of the first five chapters of The METAFONT book [Knuth 85] as it was available in December 1984;
- A copy of Knuth's paper *The Concept of a Meta-Font* [Knuth 82] in a French translation [Knuth 83];
- A paper on 'METAFONT and the problems of type design' [Southall 85a]. The latter two items formed part of the *support de cours* [AndreSallio 85].

We should say straight away that the course participants did not read these documents soon enough. For this reason, and because of the technical difficulties described earlier, the first session of practical work was rather turbulent. We should have scheduled at least an hour for an introduction to METAFONT, and some additional time to discuss the programs that the participants were given for the practical project.

6.2 The practical work

Once again because of the lack of time, it would have been absurd to ask the course participants to design a complete typeface, and we felt that making individual characters in the absence of a well-understood unifying graphic idea lacked pedagogical value. On the other hand, it seemed relatively easy to investigate some of the basic problems of type design, font production and symbolic description by generating and manipulating elementary shapes by means of METAFONT programs and looking at the results.

The participants worked in pairs. To minimize the difficulties arising from the use of the VMS line editor and computer terminals with no graphic capability, particular attention was paid to mixing participants coming from the world of graphic design with experienced computer users.

Each pair was given a computer account, some files containing METAFONT programs to produce elementary shapes, and listings of these programs and of Knuth's **plain.mf** macro file [Knuth 85].

The brief for the practical project is given in Appendix A. In outline, the objective was to make elementary shapes – solid and hollow rectangles, circles and triangles – by running METAFONT programs; to change the values of parameters in the programs to alter the shapes that were produced; and to assess their appearance visually. Participants were asked to make sets of shapes – first solid, then hollow – that when viewed from about 5 metres away appeared to be equal in size, aligned at top and bottom, evenly spaced and (for the hollow shapes) equal in apparent boldness. Participants were asked to put their output up on the walls in order to assess it visually, and to try to find reasons for the visual effects they observed.

(The final objective described in the project brief, to produce a set of technically satisfactory glyphs, could not have been achieved because we lacked some of the necessary software. In any event, very few of the participants reached that stage.)

7 Some results

Beside the 10 lecturers, 54 people took part in the course. Of these, 22 were connected with typography or graphic design (printers, publishers, teachers in colleges of art). The others came mainly from university research centers or from software development houses.

fig.1

fig.2

The evaluation forms distributed at the end of the session showed that the participants had enjoyed the lectures. In particular, many computer scientists discovered a completely new world.

What about METAFONT? The lectures on type design were successful, and an extra one was added on the last day. The practical work, on the other hand, was not a complete success. Some of the reasons for this are as follows:

- As we said in section 5, the system (particularly the part that sent files to the Versatec for printing) was not working properly in time for the first session: some people got discouraged.
- As we said in section 6.1, many participants did not read the documentation about METAFONT before the first session, and so did not understand what was being asked of them.
- Surprisingly, computer scientists are not good at putting their own work up on the wall and discussing it. In consequence, the 'studio atmosphere' and the spirit of group involvement on which this particular project depends for its complete success never materialized.

In spite of this, many participants made correct modifications to the shapes (Figure 2). Some took the set project as far as they could, and then played with some of the example programs from [Knuth 85] and modified them (figure 3).

From our point of view, the most important thing was that participants generally seemed to understand that type design for computer-based systems is not only a matter of spline drawing and digitization algorithms.

Acknowledgements

Thanks are due to the people who helped us to get METAFONT: Lynn Ruggles, David Fuchs and John Hobby at Stanford; and to the people who made it run on the IRISA machines: MM. Cedelle, Angelini, Portier and Le Bechec. Jorge Egli from EPFL-Lausanne deserves a special mention for his exceptional efforts, without which the course could not have worked as well as it did.

Special thanks are due as well to the participants in the course.

APPENDIX A: Practical Project Brief

1. Choose from the range presented in the terminal room a **nominal drawing size** d and a **boldness** b for the shapes you will make.

    1.1 Write Metafont programs to make the following solid shapes:
    - A square of side d
    - A circle of diameter d
    - A triangle of height d and base d
    - Two half-squares of height d and width $d/2$

    1.2 Assemble the shapes in the sequence *half-square, square, circle, triangle, half-square* with what you feel to be natural amounts of space between them. Adjust the sizes and alignments of the square, circle and triangle so that they appear to be the same size as the half-squares, and aligned with them at top and bottom, when seen from about 5 meters away.

    1.3 Modify your Metafont programs to make the square, circle and triangle into hollow shapes, with stroke thicknesses d/b. Instead of the half-square, make rectangles of height d and width d/b.

    Make an assembly like the one you made in 1.2. Adjust the sizes, spacing, alignments and stroke-weights of your shapes until, when seen from about 5 m away, they appear to be:
    - Equal in size with each other and the rectangles
    - Aligned top and bottom with each other and the rectangles
    - Evenly spaced
    - Equal with each other in "colour" (apparent boldness)

    You will now have produced a set of elementary shapes that are technically satisfactory in terms of the criteria that apply to drawings of typeface characters.

2. Now choose a **nominal font size** f from the range presented in the terminal room.

    2.1 Modify your Metafont programs to produce an assembly like the one you made in 1.3, but with rectangles of height f rather than d. Repeat the adjustments you made in 1.3, and make other changes to your programs as necessary, until your small shapes have the same evenness of apparrent size, alignment, spacing and colour that your large shapes had. You will now have produced a set of technically satisfactory **glyphs** (components of a font).

    2.2 Experiment with changing the values of f and b, to produce differents fonts. Modify your Metafont programs so that they produce technically satisfactory glyphs for all the values of f and b you use.

3 Write down what you think are the reasons for the visual effects you saw at different stages in the project.

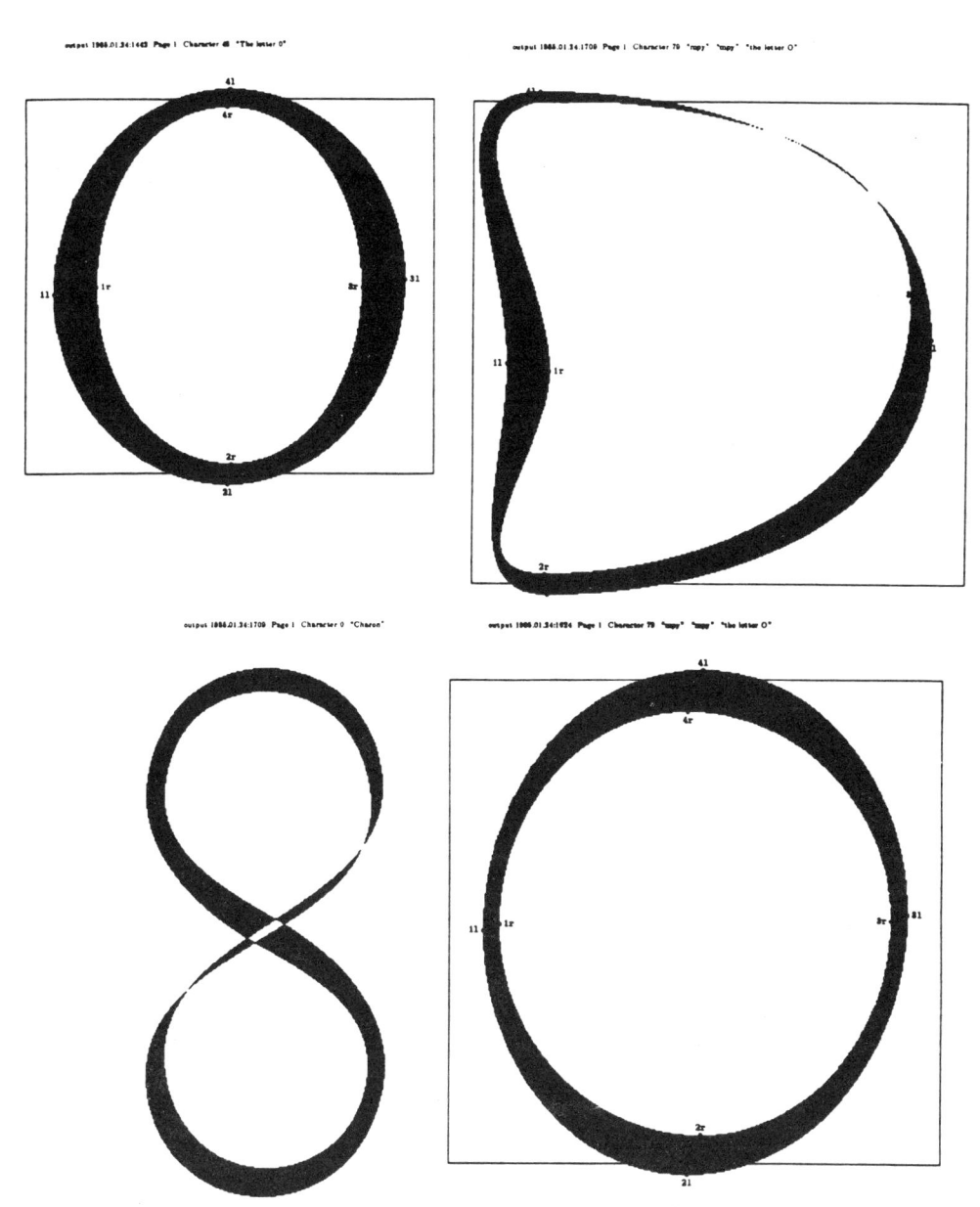

fig.3

References

[ANDRE 83]
Jacques André (ed.), *Actes des Journées sur la Manipulation de Documents (Rennes, 4-6 Mai 1983)*.
Rocquencourt: INRIA, 1983.

[ANDRE SALLIO 85]
Jacques André et Patrick Sallio (eds.), *Typographie et Informatique. Support du cours INRIA, Rennes, 21-25 Janvier 1985*.
Rocquencourt: INRIA, 1985.

[BIGELOW 85]
Charles Bigelow, *Font Design for Personal Workstations*.
Byte, vol. 10 no. 1, pp. 255–270 (1985).

[CARTER 84]
K.A. Carter, *IMP — A System for Computer-Aided Typeface Design*.
in T. Miller (ed.), *Proceedings of the First International Conference on Text Processing Systems*, Dublin, 1984, pp. 114–119.

[FLOWERS 84]
Jim Flowers, *Digital Type Manufacture: An Interactive Approach*.
IEEE Computer, May 1984, pp. 40–48.

[KAROW 83]
Peter Karow, *IKARUS for Typefaces in Digital Form*.
Hamburg: URW, 1983.

[KNUTH 79]
Donald E. Knuth, *TEX and Metafont: New Directions in Typesetting*.
Bedford, Mass.: Digital Press, 1979.

[KNUTH 82]
Donald E. Knuth, *The Concept of a Meta-font*.
Visible Language, vol. 16 no. 1, pp. 3–27 (1982).

[KNUTH 83]
Donald E. Knuth, *Le concept de Metafonte*.
Communications et langages, vol. 55, pp. 40–53 (1983).

[KNUTH 84]
Donald E. Knuth, *A Course on* METAFONT *Programming*.
TUGBoat, vol. 5 no. 2, pp. 105–118 (1984).

[KNUTH 85]
>   Donald E. Knuth, The METAFONT book.
>   Reading, Mass.: Addison Wesley (in press), 1985.

[LEITCH 85]
>   S. Leitch, *Implementation of* METAFONT *on ICL PERQ*.
>   in "TEX for Scientific Documentation" (D. Lucarella ed.), these proceedings, 1985.

[RUGGLES 83]
>   Lynn Ruggles, *Letterform Design Systems*.
>   Stanford University Technical Report STAN-CS-83-971 (1983).

[SOUTHALL 85a]
>   Richard Southall, *Metafont and the problems of type design*.
>   in [ANDRE SALLIO 85].

[SOUTHALL 85b]
>   Richard Southall, *Metafont and the design of typefaces*.
>   Supplement to [SOUTHALL 85a], 1985.

GENERALISED ALGORITHM FOR DRAWING NON–PARAMETRIC SPLINES

S.Leitch and F.J.Smith

Departement of Computer Science

The Queen's University of Belfast

A short history is given of the drawing of curves on a raster. Cubic splines are then shown to be sufficiently accurate and smooth for modelling curves in general. An algorithm for rasterising cubic splines fitting single-valued functions is described using finite differences, which are shown, under defined conditions, to be sufficiently accurate. This algorithm is then extended to multi-valued functions by dividing the graph of the letter into sections where Y is a function of X, and in the following section, X is a function of Y.

Introduction

The mathematics of curve-fitting is now fairly well-known, but drawing curves on a raster poses different problems not all of which have been solved. Most computer graphics software includes routines to draw straight lines, circles or other conic sections such as ellipses, but routines for drawing more general curves are conspicuously absent. One reason is that curve-fitting needs many floating-point operations, and modern small computers do not usually have processing power adequate for computer graphics. Another reason is that rasterisation of curves must preserve continuity of the curve to make it look smooth and this is not easy when the curve must be represented by points on the raster.

History

One of the first attempts to overcome the limitations of computing power and continuity was Bresenham's algorithm in 1965 for joining close points on a curve with straight lines [2]. Previously, in 1964, Ferguson had published his paper showing how cubic splines could be used for modelling curves [4]. However, although there have been several suggestions for plotting conics on raster screens since then, little has been written on the drawing of splines, in spite of their usefulness as close fits to any smooth curve. One paper by Barsky and Fournier [1] gives an exposition of the use of finite differences for drawing a spline, but they dismiss them being too inaccurate. We show that with a different approach finited differences can be made accurate and effective for rasterisation.

Cubic Splines

Of all twice differentiable curves, cubic splines have been found to be the most versatile and the most economical. A cubic spline $S(x)$ is defined as that curve passing through a set of points ($P_k : (x_k, y_k)$, $0 \leq k \leq n$) commonly known as knots, such that

(1) $S_k(x)$ is a cubic polynomial in the interval $[x_k, x_{k+1}]$, and

(2) $S'(x)$ and $S''(x)$ are continuous at x_k, $k = 1, \ldots, n-1$, and

(3) If the curve is closed, the continuity conditions are extended to include $k = 0, n$.

The accuracy of a spline fit is illustrated by an example. We have modelled the function $y = \sin x$ over the interval $[0, 2\pi]$ with a spline passing through 8 points on the curve and find that the deviation between the curve $\sin x$ and the spline is never greater than half the distance between pixels; so the difference is not visible on the screen. In general, Cubic Splines are smooth curves which minimise curvature. This is proved in Holladay's theorem: that natural cubic splines minimise the integral

$$\int_a^b f''(x)dx$$

where $x_0 = a$ and $x_n = b$. So cubic splines are accurate and smooth. We must now discuss how they can be constructed quickly in integer arithmetic.

Single-valued Functions

If we assume that the second derivatives of the cubic polynomials $S_k(x)$ are known at x_0, x_n, then each cubic polynomial in $S(x)$ is uniquely determined so that the spline can be represented by a tridiagonal matrix equation which is diagonally dominant. Recurrence relations are used to derive a numerically stable solution efficiently. The coefficients of each cubic polynomial are stored in a vector of four real numbers.

We now suppose that the screen is imposed on a fine mesh whose resolution is dependent on the characteristics of the computer being used: the vertical resolution h_Y is given by

$$h_Y = \frac{L}{M}$$

where L is the largest integer allowed by the computer and M is the number of pixels on the graphics screen in the vertical direction. h_Y equals 256 for an Apple microcomputer, and 2097152 for the ICL Perq.

Screen pixels may not coincide with mesh points but the inaccuracy is small. Then each real point (x, y) on the curve is approximated by the nearest mesh integer pair (X, Y) such that

$$X = \frac{1}{W_X}(x - x_{\min}), \qquad Y = \frac{1}{W_Y}(y - y_{\min})$$

and

$$W_X = \frac{x_{\max} - x_{\min}}{Nh_X}, \qquad W_Y = \frac{y_{\max} - y_{\min}}{Mh_Y},$$

where $x_{\min}$, $x_{\max}$, $y_{\min}$ and $y_{\max}$ are the minimum and maximum values of the given graph. Points on the curve now satisfy the equation

$$Y = A_3 X^3 + A_2 X^2 + A_1 X + A_0$$

where the coefficients $A_3, \ldots, A_0$ can be easily derived. Although X and Y are integers, the coefficients are real numbers, but finite differences can be used to compute intermediate points of the mesh curve. In our paper [5], we show that the maximum number of points which can be plotted using this method depends on the degree of the approximating spline, and the value of h_Y. For the values of h_Y quoted above, g is 10 and 186 respectively. In practice, g is made slightly less than this to minimise the accumulative errors. It should be noted here that our algorithm is of limited value for 8-bit microcomputers, such as the Apple, although it can be improved by using parabolic splines ($g = 22$) and backward differences. Since the screen resolution is so low, the difference between order 2 and order 3 splines will not be noticed.

Thus, after the initial forward (or backward) differences have been calculated, intermediate points on the mesh curve can be calculated using integer addition only. For our Perq 2 computer, g was so large that the whole interval between knots can normally be drawn without using backward differences.

Rasterisation

Computation of the next pixel to display depends on the distance of the mesh curve from neighbouring pixel points.

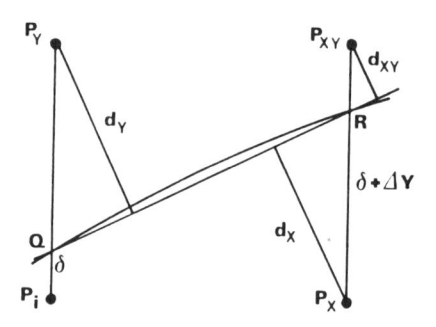

Figure 1. Relationship of the spline to pixel points.

In the diagram, the mesh curve passes through the mesh points Q and R, and the nearest pixel points are P_i, which has just been displayed, P_x, P_y and P_{xy}, d_x and d_y are distances of the mesh curve from P_x and P_y respectively. Using similar triangles, it can be shown that the criterion which determines the next displayable pixel is dependent on δ, h_y and the previously computed forward difference ΔY. This algorithm uses an average of 5.5 integer arithmetic operations per pixel. We show in our paper [5], that our algorithm reduces to Bresenham's for a straight line.

Multi-valued Functions

When the function being plotted turns back on itself and so is multi-valued as in a circle or the letter 'S', the algorithm we have described must be modified because in some intervals the curve may have a high (or indeed an infinite) slope.

Consider our ordered set of points P_0 to P_n. Our first aim is to divide the graph into sections each of which is a single-valued function of Y against X (or for vertical parts of the graph, X against Y). To do this we first compute the slope of the straight line between each two points on the graph and find when it moves from one octant to another.

For example, in the figure the first four points have a slope $\frac{dy}{dx}$ less than 1, so they occur in a section in the first octant. A change then takes place at point P_3, with $P_2 P_3$ occurring in the second octant. We make P_2 the point of separation between the two sections of the graph and in the second section $P_2P_3P_4$, we treat the graph as a function of X against Y, rotating our coordinates through 90°. The process is repeated breaking the graph at P_6 and P_8. Normally an artist drawing the graph will put in more points than this. At least three or four points are needed in each section or the resulting curve is likely to be incorrect. This will then be visually obvious and the artist can insert further points to make the graph follow the shape she requires.

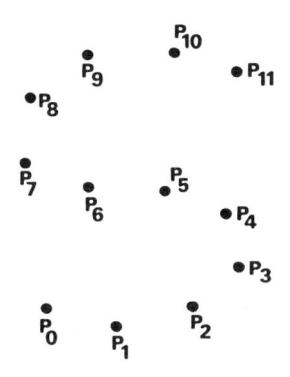

Figure 2. Points illustrating the method used for breaking a multi-value curve into single-valued sections of Y against X or X against Y; the sections are P_0P_2, P_2P_4, P_4P_6, P_6P_8, and P_8P_{11}.

Within each of these sections we can generate a cubic spline graph by the methods we have discussed in the last two sections provided we know the second derivative at the ends of the sections. To find these derivatives we must use a parametrised spline. We write:

$$X = S(t)$$

$$Y = S(t)$$

In these two equations we have expressed both X and Y in terms of a spline function in the parameter t. The parameter t can be set equal to any increasing set of values at the set of points P_0 to P_n. However, to avoid unnecessary oscillations and curvature discontiniuities, it is best to choose the spacing in the t values equal to the lengths of the chords joining the points [3]. We can take $t=0$ at P_0, $t=|P_0P_1|$ at P_1, $t=|P_0P_1| + |P_1P_2|$ at P_2, etc. Splines are then fitted to these two parametrised curves and the second derivative at the end of each section can be determined from the following formula:

$$\frac{d^2y}{dx^2} = \frac{\dot{x}\ddot{y} - \ddot{x}\dot{y}}{x^3}$$

$$\frac{d^2x}{dy^2} = \frac{\ddot{x}\dot{y} - \dot{x}\ddot{y}}{y^3}$$

where the dots denote derivatives with respect to the parameter t. These values of the second derivative can then be used to determine the cubic spline of Y against X or X against Y in each of the sections, ensuring the continuity of the spline and its first and second derivative at each point. In this form, our pixel algorithm described in the previous section can be used over the whole interval.

Conclusion

We have described how our single-valued algorithm for drawing smooth curves through a set of points on a raster screen can be extended to cope with multi-valued graphs. Since the algorithm uses mostly integer arithmetic, and yet gives smooth accurate curves, we expect it to be significantly faster than existing algorithms.

Some of the work for this paper was supported by a research grant from ICL.

References

[1] Barsky, B.A. and Fournier, A., *Computational techniques for parametric curves and surfaces,* Proc. Gr. Interface '82, (1982), 57–71.

[2] Bresenham, J.E., *Algorithm for computer control of a digital plotter,* IBM Systems J. 4, 1 (1965), 25–30.

[3] Epstein, M.P., *On the influence of parametrization in parametric interpolation,* SIAM J. Numer Anal., 13, (1976), 261–268.

[4] Ferguson, J.C., *Multivariable Curve Interpolation,* JACM, 11(2), (April 1964), 221–228.

[5] Leitch, S.L. and Smith, F.J., *The Incremental Display of a Single-Valued Curve,* (to be published).

Generation of Some Chinese Characters with Metafont

Jiarong Li
Department of Numerical Analysis and Computing Science,
Royal Institute of Technology, Stockholm, Sweden

Abstract

An experiment has been made to generate Chinese characters by using the font creation system **METAFONT**. *The method is descriptive in the sense that the character forms and their attributes are described in* **METAFONT** *programs and expressed in mathematical terms. Fonts in different styles and sizes can easily be generated from the same programs by changing a few font parameters. The problem is that a great amount of work is required for measuring and modifying characters since the number of Chinese characters is very large. A group of properties of Chinese characters were observed in the experiment and proved to be useful for reducing the amount of the design work. Thus, these properties are discussed in the paper and some design methods are proposed for the creation of high quality character images.*

Keywords: *character generation, Chinese character, character composition, radical, interim character, stroke, character property, font,* **METAFONT**

Introduction

The traditional Chinese typefaces which are still in use, have been developed in a period of more than one thousand years. New characters have been continually created, and some old characters have disappeared. The number of characters which can be used today is 8000-10000. Among them there are about 2000 characters that appear very frequently [Zhu et al, 78]. Although the basic shape of characters and their strokes remain the same, the characters have been simplified and modified with respect to typographic convenience, legibility and aesthetical aspects. The number of strokes constituting a character has been reduced.

There are slightly more than ten common typefaces, e.g. the Song typeface, the Imitation-Song typeface, the Boldface, the Regular-script, etc. [Wang el al, 84]. Font sizes may vary between 6 picapoints and 56 picapoints, among them the 10.5 picapoint fonts are most common for usual texts. Characters in different typefaces share exactly the same structure so that a horizontal in a certain character in one typeface is also a horizontal stroke in another typeface, a vertical stroke in one typeface is also a vertical stroke in another typeface and so forth. The main differences are actually between the shape of strokes, the width of strokes and the size of strokes.

The numerous Chinese characters are composed of only few kinds of elementary components, called strokes, which normally take vertical straight, horizontal straight, left-curved, right-curved, hooked and dot-like forms. Although Chinese characters have mainly quadratic structure, the characters differ significantly from each other with respect to the positions of strokes, the kinds of strokes, the sizes of strokes, the numbers of strokes that constitute the characters.

Since the strokes are the basic elements constituting a character, one needs to write some general program for stroke generation [*Hobby et al, 82, 84*]. This work involves the description of many details about the strokes, e.g. the description of the general property of serifs, curved stroke, hook, etc. A program for stroke generation should be so general that it is able to generate strokes in many different styles.

Once the shapes of the elementary strokes are defined, one could design the characters. A common method to do it is to copy some existing characters. Since the shapes of strokes could be designed in the same way, one hopes that the overall shape of a character looks like the original one. The advantage is that this method is very simple, since the location of stroke is clearly defined in the Cartesian coordinate system. The relative position of strokes can easily be expressed and algorithms for transformation of coordinates are relatively easy. The problem is that the work needed for measurement is too much when thousands of characters are going to be designed. A normal character is composed of seven to eight strokes. In case of designing the entire set of Chinese characters the total work means to measure tens of thousands of strokes, not mentioning the work to correct and modify the characters. Since this is impractical to carry out, more efficient methods should be worked out. In our case three principles have been applied:

1) Common parts of characters should be designed only once.
2) The number of parameters to define a stroke should be as small as possible.
3) More time is spent on study of frequently used character components.

Hierarchical composition

Most Chinese characters may be regarded as being composed of two components, a *radical* and a simpler character. This division is well-known and is usually used for searching characters in a dictionary. The set of radicals is quite well-defined, and their number is about 200. In the same way, the character after first division can be further divided into two parts, again a radical and a character. This kind of division can be performed until a non-divisible character is obtained. 90% of the Chinese characters have this kind of structure, while the other characters can not be divided directly into radicals and simpler characters. The latter characters can instead be regarded as being composed of radicals and *interim characters* [Sheng et al, 84]. Interim characters are not real characters, rather components of characters. Unlike the radicals, the interim characters have no names and the set of interim characters is relatively poorly defined. Their number is 500 – 600 according to Sheng's estimate. An example of interim character is given in figure 1. Because most non-divisible characters, radicals and interim characters repeatedly occur in many different characters, the total amount of the non-divisible characters, radicals and interim characters is far less than the amount of the characters.

锡 飑 汤 旸 扬 觞 殇 杨 场 炀 疡

Figure 1. Characters composed of the interim character 㐆 and radicals.

The structure of a program for generation of Chinese characters should have the same hierarchy as the character structure, see figure 2. A program for generating one character calls some subroutines which generate the character components. Components are thus copied into different characters.

The copying process is a transformation of the shape of components. The transformation is not always linear, that means the size of strokes is not always scaled up or down proportionally. Instead, the lengths of strokes in most cases are proportionally changed, while the widths of strokes and the serifs remain unchanged. Moreover, some strokes may be replaced with other kinds of strokes, so the structure of components may be changed. The latter form is called the *variant* of the component. A natural way to handle variants is to design them separately.

An investigation shows that the transformation is closely related to the location of components. The Chinese characters can be grouped according to the location of their components into thirteen categories [Su et al]. Copied components in characters of the same category, differ only in length. Thus a subroutine for a component should describe how to calculate the correct lengths of the strokes. This can be easily done in a **METAFONT** program by using the relative position of the endpoints of strokes. The

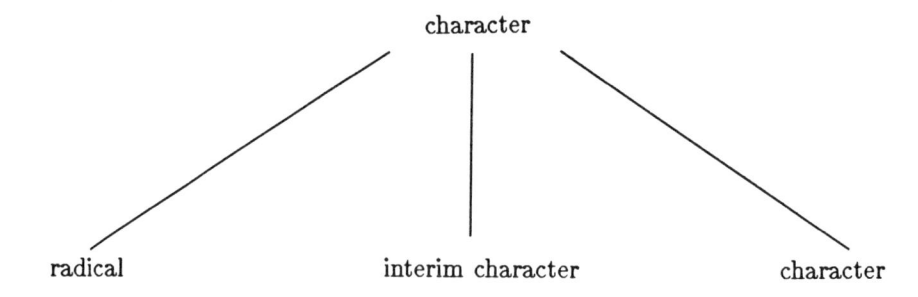

Figure a. Generally a character can be composed of three types of components.

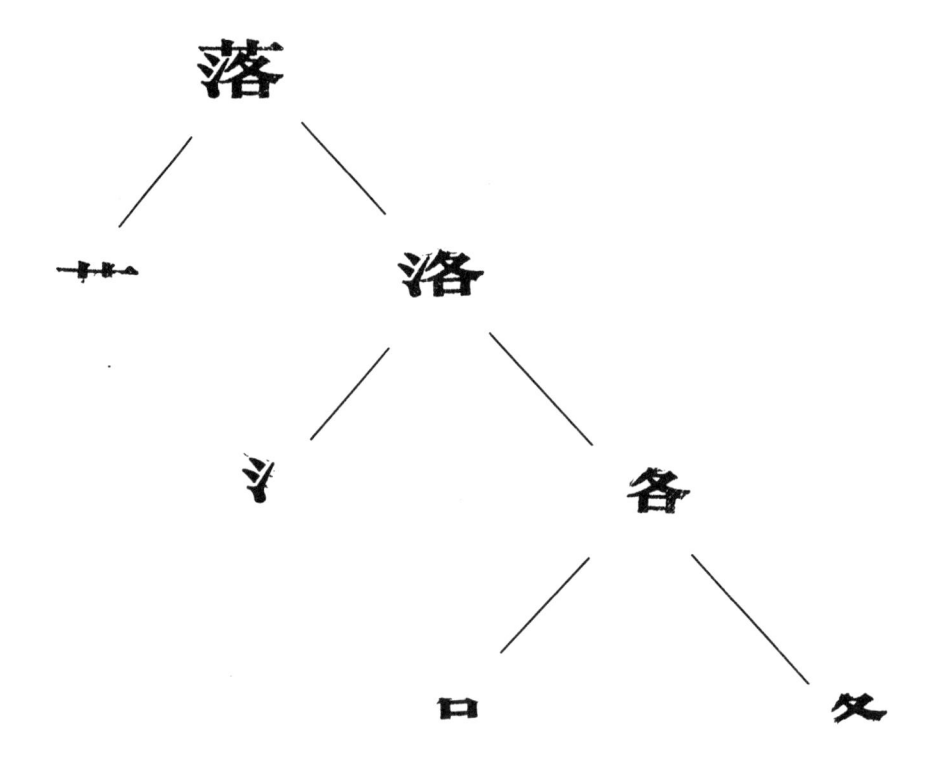

Figure b. The components "艹", "氵", "口", "夂" are all radicals.

Figure 2. Chinese characters have hierarchical structure.

stroke lengths are thus extended or shrinked according to the extent of the particular character.

A subroutine usually has four parameters determining the location and the extent of the component in the character coordinate system. Strokes are defined relatively to each other except the stroke widths and the size of serifs which are controlled by a few global variables. For some components additional parameters are necessary in order to control more complicated parts, e.g. the curvature of a curved stroke or the position of a hook.

For each variant of a component one writes a subroutine. Because the variants normally share the structure more or less, parts of the subroutines can be repeated in several subroutines. The one-to-one correspondence between variants and subroutines does therefore not necessarily mean more programming work. A component normally has only few variants if any variant at all, typically two or three variants.

Because the variants are related to the locations of components, a subroutine call implies the current location of the component. This information can be used to make programming work more easily.

Composition of character components

Non-divisible character, radical and interim character are the three types of components which constitute a Chinese character. Although the different components may have some parts in common, they are regarded as being composed only of strokes. There are a few different types of strokes. Among them *the horizontal stroke, the vertical stroke, the left-falling stroke, the right-falling stroke, the dot-stroke* and *the hook-stroke* are the most common types. Other strokes can be composed with these strokes, if they are not designed separately. All these strokes have about seven or eight parameters to specify the shape. Thus much time must be spent on determining the parameters in order to obtain a correct shape. For example, for a horizontal stroke one needs three parameters to specify the position and the length of the stroke, one parameter to specify the width, a few other parameters to specify the serifs and possible connection to another stroke. However, some of the parameters are related to each other. For horizontal strokes and vertical strokes the serif size depends on the stroke width. A few other parameters may be related to the surroundings, e.g. the serif of a vertical stroke is determined by its connection to another stroke. Another interesting property of vertical strokes is that many vertical strokes terminate at the lower boundary of character components. Because the lower boundary is always first known when copying a component into characters, the length of a vertical stroke can be calculated if the position of the stroke is specified, thus it is unnecessary to specify the length explicitly.

Stroke Symmetry

Symmetry appears in many situations, mostly together with the horizontal strokes and the vertical strokes. Even symmetry between separate points is quite common. Its appearance very much affects the entire shape of the characters, deviations from symmetry would be unacceptable. Therefore one should give special attention to this property in the design work.

(a). The radical *"enclosure"*   (b). Some characters with the radical enclosure

Figure 3. The radical *"enclosure"* and characters containing the radical

The radical *"enclosure"* is a typical example showing symmetric strokes, see figure 3. The whole radical is symmetric with respect to the vertical symmetric axis.

The symmetries can be expressed in following equations

$$\frac{(x_1 + x_2)}{2} = a$$

$$|x_1 - x_2| = l$$

where x_1, x_2 are the x-coordinates of two symmetric points, and are to be calculated, the y-coordinates are known and assumed to be equal. l is the distance between these points and a is the x-coordinate of the middle point.

These equations are easily solved in the **METAFONT** program, since **METAFONT** is able to solve linear equations [*Knuth, 79*]

We shall note that symmetry often occurs together with those straight strokes which extend across the entire character. Characters with radicals seldom have any symmetry with respect to the symmetric axis of the bounding box because the radical and the other components in a character are usually not the same.

Conclusion

The generation of Chinese characters is a computer scientific problem as well as a typographical problem. Knowledge is required from both fields. The hierarchical composition, the reduction of stroke parameters and the utilization of symmetrical properties are methods based on the properties of Chinese characters. Through the experiment one has realized that the measurement and the modification of the characters are two main problems, and the problems can be better solved by using the properties of Chinese character. It is also proved that several **METAFONT** features are useful for designing Chinese characters.

Acknowledgement

The paper is based on my graduation thesis performed at the Royal Institute of Technology in Sweden. I would gracefully thank Yngve Sundblad and Staffan Romberger at The Department of Numerical Analysis and Computer Science for their advice during the work and their careful proof reading of this paper.

Appendix 1

METAFONT subroutine for the radical "*his*".

```
Subroutine his(Var lp,Var rp,Var tp,Var bp):
x1 = 0.08[lp,rp]; y1 = 0.81[bp,tp];
x2 = 0.29[lp,rp]; y2 = tp;
x3 = 0.69[lp,rp]; y3 = y2;
x4 = x2; y4 = 0.63[bp,tp];
x5 = x4; y5 = 0.5[bp,tp];
x6 = lp; y6 = tp - 0.65 * (tp - bp);
x7 = 0.3[lp,rp]; y7 = 0.3[bp,tp];
x8 = 0.04[lp,rp]; y8 = bp;
x9 = 0.63[lp,rp]; y9 = 0.3[bp,tp];
x10 = 0.82[lp,rp]; y10 = 0.15[bp,tp];
Call subbox(lp, rp, tp, bp);
Call nlhs(1, 4, 1, 0);
Call nlvs(2, 8, 1, 0);
Call nlvs(3, 8, 1, 0);
```

```
Call hxstka(x4, y4, x3);
Call hxstka(x5, y5, x3);
Call nlhs(6, 1, 1, 0);
Call piexstk(x7, y7, x8, y8, 0.5[x8,x7],
              0.5[y8,y7], vnlwd, 0.4, 0);
Call dotxstk(x9, y9, x10, y10, x10 + 4 * h).
```

其

Appendix 2

An **METAFONT** program putting two radicals together.

```
charcode 2;
Cpen; Chardw psize; Charwd ptsize; Chardp 0;
            Charic 0; Charht ptsize;
Call his(8 h, 61 h, 95 h, 9 h);
Call moon(43 h, 92 h, 87 h, 5 h, 60 h).
```

期

Appendix 3

The **METAFONT** program for the character "*lai*", using stroke symmetry.

```
charcode 12;
Cpen;Chardw psize; Charwd ptsize; Chardp 0;
```

Charic 0; Charht ptsize;
x12 - x1 = 0.8 * (rb - lb);
0.5[x1,x12]= x7;
y1 = 0.17[ub,db];
x7 - x2 = 0.29 * (rb - lb);
y2 = y1 - 0.5 * vnlwd - 0.02 * (rb - lb);
x7 - x3 = 0.15 * (rb - lb);
y3 = y6 + 0.5 * hnlwd;
x4 - x7 = 0.31 * (rb - lb); y4 = y2;
x5 = x7 + 0.08 * (rb - lb); y5 = y3;
x6 = 0.05[lb,rb];
y6 = y1 - 0.32 * (ub-db);
x7 = 0.5[lb,rb];
y7 = ub;
x8 = x7; y8 = y6; x9 = lb;
y9 = 0.92[ub,db];
x10 = x7 + 0.5 * vnlwd; y10 = y6;
x11 = rb; y11 = 0.15[db,ub];
Call nlhs(1, 5, 0, 0);
Call dotxstk(x2, y2, x3, y3, x3 + 4 * h);
Call piexstk(x4, y4, x5, y5, 0.5[x4,x5],
             0.5[y4,y5], vnlwd, 0.6, 0);
Call nlhs(6, 2, 0, 0);
Call nlvsbb(7, 1, 0, 0);
Call piexstk(x8, y8, x9, y9, 0.36[lb,rb],
             0.27[db,ub], vnlwd, 0.1, 2);
Call naxstk(x10, y10, x11, y11, 0.65[lb,rb],
             0.19[db,ub]).

References

[*Hobby et al, 82*]   John D. Hobby, Gu Guoan: *Using* **METAFONT** *to Design Chinese Characters*, Proceedings of 1982 International Conference of the Chinese-Language Computer Society, Washington D. C., Sept. 1982.

[*Hobby et al, 84*]   John D. Hobby, Gu Guoan: *A Chinese Meta-Font*, TUGbout, The TEX Users Group Newsletter, Vol.5, p 119–136, Nov. 1984.

[*Knuth, 79*]   Donald E. Knuth: TEX and **METAFONT**, *New Directions in Typesetting*, Digital Press, 1979.

[*Li, 84*]   Jiarong Li: *Generation of Some Chinese Characters with* **METAFONT**, Computer Science Report TRITA-NA-8412, The Royal Institute of Technology, 1984.

[*Sheng et al, 84*]   Huanye Sheng, Houchuen He: *A Nesting-Structured Chinese Pattern Dictionary*, Chinese Journal of Computer, Vol.7, p 146–149, Mar. 1984.

[*Su et al*]   Kaigen Su, Chuangao Yi, Re Pen: *The Design of A Analysis System For Chinese Character Components*, Wuhan University.

[*Wang et al, 84*]   Xuan Wang, Zhimin Lu, Zhumei Chen, Yuhai Tang, Yang Xiang: *Augmentation and Reduction for Chinese Character Images with High Resolution*, Chinese Journal of Computer, Vol.7, p 418–426, Nov. 1984.

[*Zhu et al, 78*]   Qiugang Zhu, Guangxian Ni, Congyin Chen: *The Input of Chinese Characters and Man-Machine Interaction*, Chinese Journal of Computers, Vol.1, p 33–54, Jul. 1978.

IMPLEMENTING METAFONT ON AN ICL PERQ

S. Leitch

Department of Computer Science
The Queen's University of Belfast
N. Ireland

Introduction

Metafont was originally written in SAIL, an Algol-like language, but the new Metafont was designed to be portable between many machines which support Pascal. In practice, this means that internal computations and algorithms can be transported, but almost anything which involves interaction between the program and the real world cannot. However, Prof. Knuth and his co-workers have mainly used those parts of Pascal which are not peculiar to Pascal, thereby facilitating translation of the program into similar high-level languages.

This was not the problem on the ICL Perq. The main problem was not only conforming to conventions determined by the operating system, but also to facilities or lack of facilities provided by the Pascal compiler and those aspects of the Perq which are foreign to the operating system. Metafont, being a program with graphical facilities, works best with a high-resolution graphics screen, and that is just what the Perq has.

Some of the restrictions involved considerable work, but most were overcome as minor annoyances. The changes can be conveniently divided into the following classes:

    A) File operations.
    B) Accessing the command line.
    C) Graphics operations.
    D) Pascal variants.
    E) Miscellaneous.

Of the 53 changes, 37 are in classes A and D. This figures support the conjecture that portability is mainly affected by variations between different Pascals, and communication between a Pascal program and the operating system.

Two operating systems run on the ICL Perq: POS and PNX. We are implementing Metafont on Version 3.0 of PNX which is ICL's implementation of UNIX on the Perq.

File operations

Operations on files divide neatly into defining file names, opening or creating files, closing files, and reading from, or writing to files.

1. File names.

Computer scientists appear to have given little consideration to the dirty end of programming, by which is meant interaction between the program and the real computer. There does not seem much point in designing a beautiful high-level language which succeedies in insulating programmers from the computer if the whole effect is marred by providing no mechanisms by which they can connect a program to named files. Standard ISO Pascal provides no means of accessing a named file at run-time, never mind being able to read the name of a file at run-time, and then opening it. Even COBOL, which has been around rather longer than Pascal has difficulties with run-time defined files, so this difficulty is not peculiar to more recent high-level languages.

Metafont needs for files: a text file containing the definition of a font which it uses as input, a binary output file which will contain the salient characteristics of a font (the font-metric data), a binary output file containing the generic font data, and a binary file which is used to load or dump a pre-defined format. Prof. Knuth, in common with many other computer scientists, regards input/output as a necessary evil (see module 24 in MF.WEB) and so does not declare the program's requirements at the outset. Anyone working in industry knows that the file requirements of program are always stated near the beginning of a program specification: after all, computer operation managers need to know the program's requirements so that disc changes can be scheduled, disc drives allocated and so forth.

How those one allocate files whose names are not known until run-time? ISO Pascal assumes that this is handled by the operating system, and only asks that the file variables be stated in the program heading.

Thus a strict program heading of METAFONT would look like this:

program METAFONT(input,output,font _ data,tfm _ file,gf _ file,base _ file);

In practice, it looks like this:

program MF;

This is true for version -40. Later versions may have changed. File variables are defined, using the WEB system, somewhere in the heart of the program. For example, *gf _ file,* to contain generic font data, is defined in module 735.

In practice, file names can be any length up to the maximum allowed by the system, so METAFONT allocates a packed array of 40 characters. Although file names in PNX can only be up to 14 characters long, the hierarchical directory system could mean having any number of directories prepended to the file name. Thus, the METAFONT PLAIN.base file is stored on our system in "/usr/bin/MF" so that its complete name is:

/usr/bin/MF/PLAIN.base

However, 40 characters seem enough. Another minor annoyance is that UNIX constants always terminate with a null character (ASCII zero) so that file names which contain trailing spaces in Pascal must have a null character at the end, otherwise the operating system will look for a file name ending with several spaces: it wont find it, but if some mischance the file is created, it is instructive trying to delete it. Thus the above file name should be declared as follows (the spaces are represented by @ symbols):

/usr/bin/MF/PLAIN.base0@@@@@@@@@@@@@@@@

Note that the '0' takes up one byte only.

One difference between PNX and Knuth's local operating system is that the former uses the slash '/' as a directory delimiter instead of the colon. Other minor changes relate to the whereabouts of default system files.

2. Opening and/or creating files

ICL Pascal on the Perq provides extended versions of the "reset" and "rewrite" procedures, as follows:

reset(file_var,file_name,boolean_var);

rewrite(file_var,file_name,boolean_var);

where "file_var" is a file variable, "file_name" is a literal (such as 'PLAIN.base'), or a constant, or a variable with type *packed array*[1..n] *of char*, where n can take any positive value, and boolean_var is a boolean variable. The idea behind the latter, is that if the file reset cannot be found, or the rewrite fails because there is no space left on the disc, then the boolean variable is set false, otherwise it is set true. Unfortunately, at the time of writing, there is a bug in the compiler, so that the boolean variable is never set false. In a change file for TEX, sent to me from UKC, this was ignored, and the implementor "hoped for the best" (module 27). In a practical implementation, "hoping for the best" is not good enough, so I had to find a way around this. One solution is to use the operating system function *system* which will issue an operating system command and return its result to the program. Thus three packed arrays of characters which start with the characters 'test -f 0', 'test -r 0' and 'test -w 0' are defined, with sufficient space to accommodate any METAFONT file name. The METAFONT file name is concatenated to the first two if it is an input file, and the first and the last if an output file.

The first command determines whether the file exists (and is not a directory), the second determines whether it can be read, and the third whether it can be written to. The results of these tests are incorporated into the WEB definitons *reset_ OK* and *rewrite_ OK* in module 26.

One of the features of the ICL PNX Pascal compiler is that it can neither read nor write packed files of bytes, where a byte is defined by

$$byte = 0..255;$$

To get around this, one has to open the file (*possibly as a packed file of bytes*), get a number, called, in UNIX parlance, a stream number associated with file, and then call a special system routine using this number to access individual bytes. Module 26 contains all the altered functions and procedures. Where stream numbers are used, the file access procedures also need changing (see section 4. below). Fortunately, this only applies to the byte files, *tfm_ file* and *gf_ file*. The word file, which is a *file of integer* can be accessed using standard Pascal routines.

Numerous changes arise from the definitions of terminal input and output in Knuth's local operating system. Defining

$$alpha\_file \quad \text{as} \quad t@\&e@\&x@\&t$$

is a useful WEB trick which prevents the word "text" from being treated specially. The terminal is connected to the UNIX *stdin* and *stdout* channels so that METAFONT could have its input and output redirected.

3. Closing files.

ICL PNX Pascal provides the procedure close to close file, whether input or output. This is adequate for the text and base files, but not for the byte files. The UNIX procedure *fclose* must be used for the latter: since they will have been accessed using a stream number, *fclose* will ensure that the buffer is written to disc before updating the relevant directory.

4. Accessing files.

Reading and writing text files is standard on PNX Pascal. The same applies to the word file. With the byte files, as mentioned in the previous section, system procedures have to be called: *fputc* for output, which requires a stream number. Thus the file variables *tfm_file* and *gf_file* have associated streams *tfm_stream* and *gf_stream* which must be declared globally. These definitions have been added just after the definitions of their corresponding file variables (modules 735 and 1014 respectively).

An alternative method of reading packed byte files is to read them as files of integers, and use Pascal aliasing to unpack them. This would certainly be more efficient then the method used in METAFONT, although Knuth does admit that the METAFONT code for accessing files is designed to specify rather than perform the required actions. The same applies to writing packed byte files. Prof. Knuth used aliasing to unpack word and half_words in the definition of *memory_word*. Thus *tfm_two* can be defined as:

> **var** m : *memory_word*;
> **begin** $m.int := x$;
> $tfm\_out(m.qqqq.b2)$; $tfm\_out(m.qqqq.b3)$;
> **end** ;

saving two integer division. *tfm_four* can be similarly redefined saving six integer divisions.

Accessing the command line

Some operating systems allow a program to be executed with run-time parameters, CP/M and Vax/VMS, for example. UNIX also permits this. In C, the number of parameters is held in the integer variable *argc*, and each parameter in an array of string pointers which is pointed to by the variable *argv*. Both these variables are assigned their values by the operating systems program *shell*. PNX Pascal has a similar mechanism using the variables *pargc* and *vargv* respectively. As Knuth points out, it would be convenient if a user can input font definitions into a file using a text editor, and then run METAFONT by keying:

$$mf < file >$$

where <file> is the name of the input file with type .*mf* (that is, its local name would be <*file*>.*mf*). The following definitions of *pargc* and *pargv* make this possible:

```
type
    par   = packed array [1..80] of char ;
    parp  = ^par;
    pars  = array [0..20] of parp;
    parsp = ^pars;

var
    pargc : integer; extern;
    pargv : parsp;    extern;
```

Graphics Operations

METAFONT confines graphics operations to four primitives of which only three are needed on the Perq: *init_ screen, update_ screen, blank_ rectangle* and *paint_ row*.

1. Windows

This is an opportune place to describe how the screen is handled on PNX. Whereas the screen as a whole can be treated as the terminal, it is more useful to run METAFONT under the Window Management System, which allows one to have up to 31 windows open simultaneously. The user can then multitask, with one or more processes in each window. In fact, each window, with its own keyboard buffer, can be regarded as a virtual UNIX system since PNX has a paged virtual memory of 8M bytes. Theoretically, there is no reason why both TEX and METAFONT should not be run simultaneously. In practice, there is only one disc, so both processes would exhibit considerable degradation.

However, there are good reasons for using several windows for one process, and in this implementation, we have arranged for text and graphical work to appear in two separate windows.

The graphics primitives access a window 750 pixels square (with a resolution of 90 dots to the inch). Although METAFONT allows the user to define up to 16 windows, these are not the windows handled by the Window Management System: rather, they are subsets of the METAFONT graphics windows and exist notionally.

Rectangular areas of a window are most conveniently accessed by the system primitive *wrasop* (window raster operator) which can handle rectangular areas of store as well as, or instead of, windows. It took me nearly a year, on and off, to understand this function, so I think it worthwhile to explain its parameters in detail.

wrasop takes three parameters. The first is the number of the window accessed: this is a UNIX file descriptor and is supplied when a window is opened, of which more anon. If *wrasop* is used between areas of memory, this number is irrelevant. The third parameter is a pointer to a structure which controls clipping. Since clipping is not required on METAFONT, this parameter is defined as an integer in the definition of *wrasop*, and given the value 0 in each call. The second parameter is a pointer to the following structure:

> ROPCtl = **record**
> > ROPDstBase   : ptr_pixel_row;
> > ROPSrcBase   : ptr_pixel_row;
> > ROPHeight   : short;
> > ROPWidth   : short;
> > ROPDstInc   : short;
> > ROPSrcInc   : short;
> > ROPSrcX   : short;
> > ROPSrcY   : short;
> > ROPDstX   : short;
> > ROPDstY   : short;
> > ROPFunc   : short
> **end** ;

where *short* is defined as:

$$short = 0..65535;$$

and *ptr_pixel_row* is defined as:

> ptr_pixel_row = ^pixel_row;
> pixel_row = **packed array** [screen_col] **of** pixel_color;

Both *pixel_color* and *screen_col* are defined in MF.WEB. In practice, *pixel_row* is not necessary since a window-to-window operation can be defined for *paint_row*.

The simplest way of explaining the meaning of these parameters is to give an example of a memory-to-memory raster operation. *wrasop* acts on memory as though it where a **packed array of boolean** , that is, as an array of bits. Whereas Pascal would use array subscripting and would be rather slow, *wrasop* is performed by a "microcode" routine, and so is very fast.

Consider two rectanguler arrays, the source of size 64 * 64 bits, and the destination 128 * 8. We wish to transfer a rectangular area 2 * 3 bits from the source to the destination, as shown in the diagram.

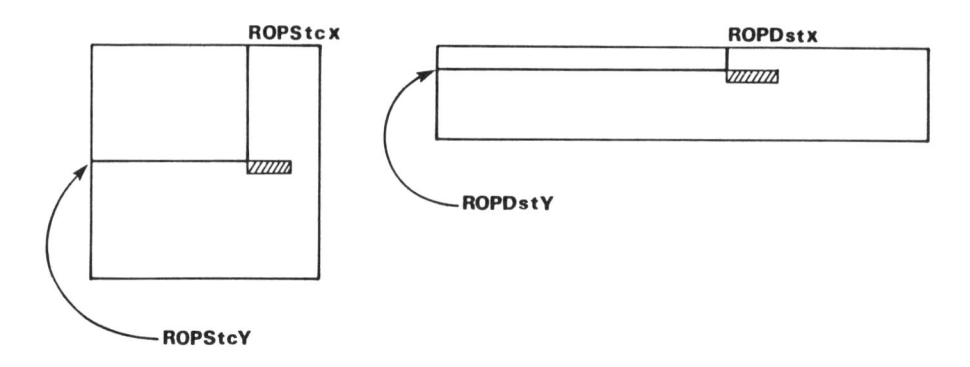

Diagram illustrating parameters for raster operations.

The ROPDstBase and ROPSrcBase fields are pointers to the origin of the arrays (bit(.0..0.)), and must be aligned to a 4-word address. The Pascal procedure *new* ensures this. ROPHeight is 2 and ROPWidth is 3 (note that the hateched areas in the diagram must be the same size). The coordinates of the top left-hand corner of the source and destination rectangles are shown in the diagram. ROPDstInc is the increment which has to be added to the address of a bit to get the address of the corresponding bit in the next row. This increment is given in units of 16-bit words, and must be a multiple of 4. This implies that the lenght of an array must be a multiple of 64 bits, as in the example. This is not really a limitation, since the actual area to be operated on is determined by ROPHeight and ROPWidth, and may have any value, even 1 × 1. In the documentation, ROPDstInc is called the raster scan length, or alternatively, the line length. Here, ROPDstInc is 8 and ROPSrcInc is 4. The function is this case isRRpl which is defined to mean:

Definition area := Source area

For a window-to-window operation, ROPDstBase and ROPSrcBase should be null pointers, when ROPSrcInc and ROPSrcInc are irrilevant, being taken as 48 by default (48×16-bit words = 768 bits).

2. Opening and closing windows.

A window is defined by special file which contains its coded characteristics, including its size, position, whether it has a border, any title, and the background colour. This file has a file name and the *window* can be opened, that is, created and made available as a pseudo-terminal, using the standard Pascal procedure *reset*. However, since subsequent use of *wrasop* needs a file descriptor, it is more convenient to open the window using the system function *open*. Rather than change the many occurrences of *open* in METAFONT, it seemed easier to write the following C routine:

```
copen(s)
char * s;
{
        return(open(s));
}
```

and then define *copen* as an external function in METAFONT. Similarly, *cclose* replaces *close* for the window file. This procedure also deletes the window from the screen.

3. The graphics primitives.

init_screen is redefined as follows:

> **function** init_screen : boolean;
> **begin** new(rop);   null_window:=nil;
>   fdwgr:=copen('/usr/bin/MF/mfGRAPHICS0');
>   init_screen:=true;
> **end** ;

update_screen is not needed because the Window Management System automatically updates a window unless specifically asked not to. Definitions of *ptr_pixel_row*, *pixel_row, short, ptrROPCtl* and *ROPCtl are added to module 519. Module 520, has declarations of rop, null_window,* and *fdwgr* (file descriptor for window graphics) added. *wrasop* is used in the procedures *blank_rectangle* and *paint_row*. The value of *ROPFunc* in *blank_rectangle* is *RXor* which is defined as

$$D := D \; xor \; S$$

where S and D are pixels in the source and destination areas respectively. *paint_row* uses the functions *RXor* and *RXNor*. The latter is defined as

$$D := not(D \; xor \; S)$$

which guarantees that D will be in the foreground colour. In *paint_row*, ROPHeight is 1 (one row is painted at a time), and ROPSrcY and ROPDstY are both r (the row number) since this is a window-to-window operation and the area being operated on is mapped onto itself. The code at the heart of *paint_row* is as follows:

> **for** $k := 0$ **to** $n-1$ **do begin**
>   *with* **rop ^ do begin**
> $ROPWidth := a[k+1] - a[k];$
> $ROPSrcX := a[k];$
> $ROPDstX := ROPSrcX;$
>   **if** $b = white$
>   **then** $ROPFunc := RXor$
>   **else** $ROPFunc := RXnor;$
>   **end** ;
> $wrasop(fdwgr, rop, 0);$
> $b := black - b;$
> **end** ;

Note that by defining *pixel_color* as *white . . black,* and *white* and *black* as 0 and 1 respectively, Knuth as avoided the problems arising from the deceptively simple definition

$$pixel\_color = (white, black);$$

even though *white* and *black* apparently have the same values.

This completes the changes for handling on-line graphics.

Pascal Variants

Several small alterations are required under this heading. Compiler directives in the code are with one exception unnecessary since they are issued with the compilation command. The exception is the include command which is used to read definitions of string functions.

$$^{***}read(/usr/include/pascal.h)$$

This command is added to the system dependencies section. The case clause in PNX Pascal allows otherwise, necessitating a small change to module 10. As in most UNIX systems, the backslash '\' is used as an escape character. ICL PNX Pascal reflects this, and so the initialisation of the *xchr* array in module 21 needs a double backslash:

$$xchr[\texttt{@}'134] := `\backslash\backslash`;$$

ISO Pascal does not permit non-local jumps. One would like to have used the system function *exit,* but this is used extensively in METAFONT as a label, so the C function *cexit* was written and declared in the external procedures module added to the and of the change file.

There are no standard ways in which a Pascal program can get the date or the time. PNX Pascal uses the procedures *date* and *time* to get the date and time respectively as packed arrays of 8 characters. This necessitated a rash of alterations of *time* in METAFONT to some other meaningful identifier: *ttime* was chosen. Module 188 needed altering to extract the values needed.

Finally, all external procedures used by the program must be defined. An extra module was referred to in module 4, and defined in the modules following module 1136.

Miscellaneous

The only changes worth mentioning here are the character set and interrupts. It is possible to create one's own fonts on the Perq (not using METAFONT!) and so an extended character set can be very useful when inputting mathematical text. A special font was designed called *tex.kst* and is available to all users of TeX and METAFONT on our Perq. Extension of the basic ASCII character set involves changing only modules 22 and 49.

Standardised interrupts cannot really be expected. Nevertheless, UNIX provides a variety of interrupts which should be available on any standard UNIX implementation, including keying ctrl-C. PNX adds a few more of which the most useful, as far as METAFONT is concerned, is that caused by tapping the HELP key. Definitions of these interrupts, *sigint* and *sighelp* are added to module 89. The interrupts are caught by the system procedure *psignal* which transfers control to a specified procedure, in this case, *alter_interrupt*. Calls to *psignal* are added to module 90. *alter_interrupt* itself is defined at the end of METAFONT in module 1136 *et seq*.

Implementing METAFONT on the Perq involves three distinct phases:

    1) *Creating the change file.*
    2) *Tangling METAFONT.*
    3) *Compiling METAFONT.*

The changes are fairly simple although the complete change file comes to nearly 680 lines. Tangling METAFONT takes about ten minutes producing a 5300 line Pascal program. Of course, these 5300 lines are equivalent to a normal Pascal program of 11000 lines since tangle outputs as near to 72 characters in each line without regard to layout conventions.

PNX Pascal has a six-pass compiler with object code optimisation which compiles METAFONT in about 1hr 30 min.

Conclusion

Since less than 1%of the METAFONT WEB file is changed, it seems fair to say that Pascal is a suitable language for writing portable programs. Most changes, as expected, were concerned with file handling, and in using facilities peculiar to the Perq, such as high-resolution graphics.

The author would like to acknowledge the support of ICL for the work described in this paper.

The Rôle of Device Independent Output

Ian Utting
University of Kent at Canterbury, UK

TEX's dvi output claims by its very name to be device independent. This paper evaluates the rôle of dvi in attaining that goal, considering the current state of imaging device technologies and page description languages.

Introduction

Device independence is that quality of a document preparation system which allows the same input to the system to be delivered, after formatting, to the largest possible range of output devices (strictly, to *all* output devices). This goal is a worthy one in that it maximises the utility of the system across a broad spectrum of environments and minimises the software effort necessary to provide access to new devices as they become available.

Traditionally, high quality document preparation systems have been limited in the type of devices that they can drive, although some have provided device independence at the level of input to the system by effectively existing in multiple versions with the same input syntax but with various device-specific output formats. A well known example of this approach is the UNIX* Nroff/Troff system, where the nroff variant generates output for a range of low- to medium-quality devices from line-printers and simple VDUs through letter and near-letter quality (NLQ) printers, with troff being used to compile the same source for output on phototypesetters and laser printers. This description of troff represents not the original conception, which generated output only for the Wang/GSI CAT-8 typesetter, but the recent modification known as Device Independent Troff [KER82], in which the system reads in pre-compiled tables describing the capabilities of a specified output device and details of the font set available, which are then used to generate output with a standard syntax, but with the characteristics of the particular output device bound in. Ditroff is now used to drive a variety of devices from the most capable of those usually driven by nroff, such as NLQ matrix printers, to traditional phototypesetters like the Linotron 202 and the Monotype Lasercomp. One result of this binding of the output device characteristics into the formatting process is that the entire lengthy formatting operation, including the device independent parts, must be performed again to generate output for a

---

* UNIX is a Trademark of AT&T Bell Laboratories.

TEX for Scientific Documentation   D. Lucarella, Editor
Copyright ©1985 Addison-Wesley Publishing Company, Inc.

different device.

TEX's approach to device independence appears at first sight to be somewhat different. It aims to produce a device independent output file (the dvi file), the contents of which are "capable of being printed on almost any kind of typographic output device" [KNU84, p. 23]. By analogy with troff, this implies that TEX supports only one device, that is the virtual device specified by the definition of the dvi file, and the quote above expresses the hope that there is a simple (or at least possible) mapping between this device and a large class of devices in the real world.

The dvi virtual device

In order to examine the problems involved in translating from the dvi virtual device to devices in the real world, it is first necessary to characterise the type of device which dvi represents.

A dvi file consists of fixed discrete page images each expressed as a series of binary commands and associated parameters of three major types:

1. **Positioning.** The page images contained in the dvi file are specified in a fourth-quadrant Cartesian coordinate system; that is they are addressed by an (x,y) pair with the $(0,0)$ point at the top left hand corner and with x and y increasing to the right and downwards respectively. The resolution of the device is defined as the *scaled point*, 2^{-16} printers' points or about 5.4×10^{-9} metres, although there may also be a global magnification imposed either by TEX or by the dvi interpreter. The entire resolution is available to dvi, that is objects may be positioned at any point on the page. As in the rest of dvi, many commands have variants with different parameter sizes in order to compress the dvi file as much as possible. In the case of positioning commands, there is also a set of four displacement registers and a stack of their values to optimise recurrent short relative motions.

2. **Font definition and selection.** Fonts are referred to in the body of the dvi file by a number which is associated for the entire document with a given typeface and size. Each font (roman, bold, typewriter etc.) and each size are represented as separate instances, ie. ten-point roman is entirely separate from eight-point roman or ten-point roman displayed at twelve-point. Each font is identified by name, intended size when designed, and magnification. In order to facilitate the global magnification alluded to above, and because fonts are expected to exist only at a limited set of magnifications, both the fonts and the entire document are expected to be magnified on the same scale, known as the *magstep,* this is a geometric scale based on factors of 1.2, thus a ten-point font magnified by a factor of \magstep2 appears at 14.4 point, and at \magstep3 appears at 17.28

point.

3. **Imaging.** Two sorts of marks are made on pages by `dvi`: character shapes selected from a notional current font, and rules (black boxes specified by their width and height). Marks are always made at the notional current position on the page, and may have associated with them an implicit movement in the x-direction by the "width" of the object. In the case of rules, this is simply the width of the rule itself, but for character shapes the value to be used is not directly available in the `dvi` file, but is obtained by TEX when fixing the page image from a "font metrics" (TFM) file specific to the font. Thus, the `dvi` file *in vacuo* does not contain all the information necessary to produce the page images it contains, and a complete definition of the virtual device must include the TFM files. This is equivalent to saying that the `dvi` virtual device has all the fonts for which TFM files exist in the local environment "pre-loaded".

As well as these three basic sets of commands there is a set of uncommitted commands (corresponding to the TEX `\special` control sequence) whose contents and functions are not defined by `dvi`. They are typically used to implement unstructured local additions to the `dvi` virtual device such as graphics primitives or functions specific to a particular real output device.

Real output devices

Devices in the real world can be broadly divided into two groups:

1. **Bit-addressable page imagers.** These are the devices which are most often used to produce output from TEX and typically have an interface very close in style to that defined by the `dvi` virtual device, although of course with very much less available resolution (usually a few hundred pixels per inch). Font bitmaps can be down-loaded to the device (with varying degrees of ease), allowing the use of the Computer Modern font family and its associated TFM files, and characters selected from these fonts can be positioned at any point on the page down to the full resolution of the device. Although some such devices support minimal formatting operations, and some examples will emulate other devices (most commonly Diablo daisy-wheel printers and Tektronix 4000-series vector display terminals), `dvi` interpreters will drive them at their simplest level in order to gain the fine control necessary to do full justice to the care that went in to generating the `dvi` file. Examples of devices in this group include the first generation of xerographic (laser) printers such as the Canon LBP-10 and Xerox 2700 (in all their various guises), phototypesetters like the Autologic APS-5 and some graphics-capable matrix or raster printers like the Epson FX-80 and Versatec devices.

Also included in this group are a new generation of interfaces known as Page Description Languages (PDLs), exemplified by Xerox's Interpress [XER84] and Adobe's PostScript [ADO84]. These systems replace the *ad hoc* collection of control codes and parameters characterising the simple page imagers with interpreters for general purpose programming languages having extensive graphics and imaging facilities. They are included here because, at base, they support the simple page imaging model characteristic of the rest of the group, although because of their inherent flexibility they are capable of performing in the printer itself many of the operations such as co-ordinate scaling and conversion which are normally performed by the dvi-to-device program. These are the devices which are most nearly capable of emulating the dvi environment, to the extent that it is possible to consider implementing a dvi interpreter directly in such languages by creating a file with the syntax of the PDL but the semantics of dvi, that is by writing PDL procedures to perform the functions of the dvi commands. In this context, it is interesting to note that although neither system requires downloaded fonts to take a particular form, the fonts bound in to Adobe's PostScript system are stored in terms of outlines based on Bezier curves, opening up the possibility of a close relationship with the new version of Metafont which internally uses a similar system.

2. **"Higher-level" devices.** In this context, the phrase "higher-level" is used to indicate that the device itself re-makes formatting decisions which have already been made by TEX and which are not derivable from dvi. Such devices often view the world in a way which is alien to the expectations of dvi, a typical example might be a line-based device which is given a 'measure' in which to set a line of text containing identified word spaces whose widths it can then compute to correct the total length of the line. Approaches to diacritics and superior and inferior characters may also be significantly different from the dvi model. For instance, TEX assumes that accents are separate characters which must be floated (possibly horizontally as well as vertically) to fit the character to which they are applied, whereas other devices may perform this function themselves or treat the character/accent pair as a ligature. As Knuth points out [KNU84, p. 54] it is possible to make TEX treat accent characters as ligatures, preventing it from taking it's usual actions, but this is at the expense of changing the input syntax as defined in the TEXbook, leading not only to a dvi file but also to a TEX source file which is output device dependent. To produce superiors and inferiors, TEX uses normal characters from a smaller font as opposed to having a special font for them (possibly with the characters already raised or lowered). Apart

from anything else, typographers might claim that a seven point character and a superior ten point character may be notionally the same size, but have no other traits in common.

This group covers a wide variety of commonly used devices, from multi-font matrix printers (typically designed for use with personal computers and word processing packages) to commercial phototypesetters designed to be driven from their manufacturers' proprietary software. In the latter case, there is often an un-advertised lower-level interface closer in flavour to the page imager devices, but manufacturers may be loathe to reveal details, and as the interface will rarely have been used by any but the manufacturers' higher level software, portions of it may be effectively untested (experience at UKC has shown this to be the case even with the relatively mature 'Slave' interface to the Monotype Lasercomp).

The outcome of this more intelligent approach to driving devices is either that an attempt must be made to circumvent formatting operations which the device wishes to perform, or that dvi must be partially re-parsed to identify the output corresponding to the original TEX expression of operations such as line and word breaking, superscripting and accenting. This is possible in the case of simple text where the predictability of the layout allows these elements to be identified, but there will inevitably be pathological cases, particularly in equations and tabular material, where TEXs 'intention' is unclear.

Fonts

It is impossible to discuss device independence in document formatters without facing the problems of font independence and as such a more useful taxonomy of possible output devices might limit itself to the two groups:

a) Those devices which support the Computer Modern fonts.

b) Those which don't.

In the first case, the possibility of mapping between dvi and the real device depends only on the ability of the device to explicitly position characters at a resolution high enough to satisfy the requirements of the dvi imaging model.

In the second case, there are two possible approaches. If fonts are available whose character sets and widths (metrics) are sufficiently similar to the Computer Modern family, then a dvi file can be produced for Computer Modern and translated to refer to the available fonts, but this will inevitably compromise the quality of layout produced at great expense by TEX and all the fine positioning of characters for kerning and diacritics must be either abandoned or performed anew. This leaves the problem of font sizing; if the source document uses the \magstep system, the fonts used must be available at small point-size increments (14.4 point and 17.28 point are preferred \magstep values), although the Allied Linotype 'Stempel-Haas' font library is available at 0.1 point increments, steps of 0.25 or even 1 point might be considered more usual.

Alternatively, TFM files can be produced for the fonts which are available, but the dvi produced will then only be printable on devices which support those fonts, requiring the costly re-formatting process to be repeated for output to all others. Furthermore, although TFM files contain more information about a font than can usually be extracted from the manufacturer of a device, a large amount of extra information on font names and detailed characteristics is bound in to the standard (and possibly local) TeX macro packages in the form of \mathchar control sequences etc. These too must be changed, and the position becomes one of device independence at the TeX source level only.

The availability of Metafont, the TeX font design package, further complicates this issue as fonts can be designed for local devices and existing fonts altered to satisfy local requirements. The generation by Metafont of TeX-compatible TFM files as well as the requisite character shapes (PXL files) makes this an attractive proposition in isolation, but again the dvi files produced are printable only on devices supporting the newly generated or modified fonts.

Conclusions

The virtual device which dvi implements restricts the set of real-world devices to which it can be mapped to those with which it largely shares an imaging model and a font set. As the technologies and capabilities of real imaging devices move to meet these requirements, under pressure from systems such as TeX and other computer-based composition and graphics systems, this set will inevitably expand (for instance with the announcement of dvi-capable PostScript interfaces for phototypesetting equipment by Allied Linotype). It is useful, however, to consider the elements within the TeX system which impose these restrictions.

Although the imaging model is largely a consequence of a choice within dvi, conditioned perhaps by the model used by the original output devices, it is also related to the attributes of the font set which is assumed to be supported. It is this font set information, distributed throughout the system, which makes the most assumptions about the real output device.

In most cases, TeX parameterises these assumptions into character and accent definitions, but because most users and sites will treat TeX as consisting not only of the program itself but also of its standard macro packages (where most of these assumptions are codified) the information is effectively hidden, and implementing a dvi interpreter for a device which does not support the Computer Modern font family involves not only generating the appropriate TFM files but also modifying the macro packages to reflect the new fonts. In some cases assumptions about the use of characters are made by TEX itself, and to work around these forces the use of syntax which differs from that defined in the TEXbook, restricting the device independence of both the dvi and also the TEX source used to produce it.

Some of these problems, especially accenting and setting lines to a measure, can be alleviated by incorporating more semantic information into the dvi file. Identifying word spaces, line breaks and character/accent pairs explicitly would relax the constraints on their treatment currently imposed by TEX and dvi at the expense of making more decisions in the dvi interpreter; going further and identifying individual *boxes* in dvi would allow this approach to be extended to the setting of equations and tabular material. It must be borne in mind however, that each such decision delayed until the device interpreter increases its complexity and hence the effort required to provide output to a new device.

The general problem of font independence is less tractable and little work has been done in this area. Much of the quality of the output from TEX derives from the extent of its knowledge of the fonts which it uses and because this knowledge permeates the entire system (for instance, the effect of character widths and ligature values on line and page break decisions) its replacement is not a task to be undertaken lightly, notwithstanding the effect which this has on the device independence of both TEX and dvi.

References

ADO84 *PostScript Language Manual*, Adobe Systems Incorporated, Palo Alto Ca., September 1984.

KER82 *A Typesetter-independent TROFF*, Computer Science Technical Report No. 97, B. W. Kernighan, Bell Laboratories, Murray Hill NJ., March 1982.

KNU84 *The TEXbook*, D. E. Knuth, Addison-Wesley, Reading Mass., 1984.

XER84 *Interpress Electronic Printing Standard*, Xerox Corporation, Stamford Conn., April 1984.

A LOW COST LASER BEAM PRINTER CONTROLLER

Luigi Cerofolini

Departement of Mathematics

University of Bologna

A very low cost laser beam printer controller to be plugged into an IBM-PC or compatibles is described and an outline of the driving software living under the DOS operating system is also given. We hope this design will be of some utility to the TEX community in order to provide the growing number of personal computer users with high quality outputs for TEX under the PC.

Introduction

Recent announcement from several manufacturers about the availability of very low cost laser printers make this kind of technology a very real solution for users looking for high quality printing at low price. In fact these printers can have up to 400 dpi (dots per inch) resolution, 8 or 12 pages/min printing speed and a very reasonable price (one manufacturer announced a US$ 1,200 price for the OEMs).

These kind of printers usually need a special controller in order to be connected to a computer through a standard interface. In fact a laser printer receives printing information in the form of bit serial signals carried by a VIDEO line.

The vertical syncronous signal VSYNC is sent from the controller to the printer, while the horizontal syncronous signal HSYNC goes the opposite way. Further communication between the printer and the controller is carried over low speed handshacking signals (PRINT, PREADY,...) and additional serial lines are used for status and diagnostic [1].

There are several laser printer based products on the market available from different manufacturers, but some of them have limited graphic capabilities (their controllers usually emulate daisy-wheel printer commands) while others, with full graphic capabilities, have a relatively high price (in the US$ 10,000 range). The final result is that many TEX users still live with the dilemma: *very* high quality outputs vs *very* low prices. TEX is now available on the IBM-PC, so we decided to add the minimum amount of hardware in order that the the same PC used for TeX could also be used to drive the video interface of the laser printer. Our laser beam printer controller can be plugged into any IBM-PC I/O expansion slot, it is very low cost (it has around 40 standard TTL chips), and has full graphic capabilties. All the fonts and DVI drivers live as ordinary files under the DOS operating system [2].

The PC-BUS interface

This is the only part seen by the driving software and, in addition to the usual logic (buffers, select, DMA and INT stuff) can be seen as a four 8-bits register set, whose components are:

LP_CSR	- laser printer control/status register
VD_CR	- video interface control register
VD_COL	- video column address register
VD_DATA	- video line buffer data register

Bits in these regiters will be commented later while describing the main parts of the controller.

THE PRINTER INTERFACE. This part of the system handles low speed and serial signals for handshaking and controlling the laser printer, and essentially can be identified with LP_CSR, the printer control/status register, whose main signals are as follows:

RDY*	- (R) printer is ready for printing or commands
PRINT*	- (W) start printing operations (nor yet real printing)
VSYNC_RQ*	- (R) vertical sync request from printer
VSYNC*	- (W) vertical sync to the printer (for real printing)
SCLOCK*	- (R/W) bidirectional serial data clock line
SDATA*	- (R/W) bidirectional serial data line for status/commands

All signals with * are active low and the R/W flag is as seen by the controller. More bits are available here, but to be short, we will omit their description.

THE VIDEO INTERFACE. This is the core of the whole system and its main parts are: two line buffers, two 12-bit column counters and the bit-clock. The function of the video interface is to buffer one scanline into one of the two buffers and every time HSYNC* becomes active, that is the printer needs data, the content of the buffer is shifted out into the VIDEO* line clocked by the bit-clock (VIDEO* active means a black dot on the paper). While one buffer is being empied by the bit-clock, the other one is being filled by the driving software. The falling edge of the HSYNC* signal flip-flops buffers selection and also generates an interrupt used by the software to fill one scanline with new data.

The double scanline buffer approach makes the whole time between two edges of HSYNC* available to the software to fill the line buffer with new data. The scanline size, bit-clock and HSYNC* frequencies all depend on the print resolution. For example at 240 dpi resolution we have:

bits/scanline = 2048

bit-clock   = 1,192,840 Hz

HSYNC*   = one every 2,246 us

The double line buffer approach thus gives us more than 2 ms to fill one line buffer: this time is much more than the one needed to fill the 256 bytes long buffer, thus the remaining time can be used to *decompress* the page bit-map data previously set into the PC RAM. The PC has a limited amount of RAM available for the page bit-map, so compression and decompression algorithms are crucial for the controller.

Higher resolution can also be handled by the controller up to the limit the HSYNC* frequency permits the driving software to fill one scanline buffer. Hardware assistance for the compression-decompression algorithms could be very useful in this context, and probably it will be available in a future version of the controller.

In order to control the video interface operations the local CPU writes on VD_CR, the video control register, whose content is as follows:

VD_LDCOL*   - load column select

VD_EN*   - video data enable

VD_IEN*   - video interrupt enable

VD_RST*   - reset the whole interface.

The VD_DATA register is used to load both the scanline buffers and the column counter inside the buffer: the VD_LDCOL* is used to select where written data go. The use of the other bits is quite clear and their comment will be omitted.

INTERFACE CIRCUITRY. The printer is connected to the controller through a cable terminated with a standard 37 pins D-connector. All signals are TTL compatible (outputs are open collector) and use normal 74LS38 buffers and 74LS14 receivers with the exception of VIDEO* and HSYNC* which use differential line drivers and receivers (SN75113 and SN75115 or equivalent).

The driving software

In order to print one page, whose raster image is stored in the local RAM, the driving software executes the following steps:

>   Initialize Printer;
>   Fill Scanline Buffer;
>   if PREADY then begin (* if printer is ready *)
>   End Of Page := false;
>   Scanline # := 1;
>   Assert PRINT;
>   Wait For VSYNC_RQ;
>   Toggle VSYNC;
>   Negate PRINT; (* one page only *)
>   Delay For Upper Margin; (* around 220 ms *)
>   Assert VD_EN and VD_IEN;
>   while (not End Of Page) do Halt; (* interrupts work *)
>   Negate VD_EN and VD_IEN
>   end
>   else begin (* if printer not ready *)
>   Request Printer Status;
>   Message To Operator
>   end;

The HSYNC* interrupt procedure essentially fills one scanline buffer with decompressed bit-map data and can be shortly described as follows: (this also comments the function of some VD_CR bits):

>   Assert VD_LDCOL;
>   Load Column Counter; (* this also negate INTRQ *)
>   Negate VD_COL;
>   Write 256 bytes into VD_DATA; (* DMA channel used *)
>   Assert VD_LDCOL;
>   Load Column Counter;
>   Negate VD_LDCOL
>   Increment scanline #;
>   If(Scanline # > MAXSCAN) then
>   End Of Page := true;

Even a very crude compression algorithm (skipping blank or black lines and using run-lenght encoding) reduces considerably the amount of RAM needed to store one page bit-map, but more work has to be done in this context.

Conclusion

Because of the I/O register based structure of the controller and the quite common (even if no standard exists for now) video interface for laser printers we can say that porting the hardware and software design to different bus structures and/or printers will require very few minor modifications only.

Bibliography

[1] Canon Corp., *LBP-CX laser printer interface reference manual.*, Rev.3. (1984).

[2] IBM Corp., *PC/XT Technical Reference Manual.*, Ref. No.: 6025005. (1984).

gendriv
a driver generator for low cost devices
using built-in fonts

Klaus Guntermann
Institut für Theoretische Informatik
Fachbereich Informatik
Technische Hochschule Darmstadt

Abstract

gendriv *is a program which generates from specifications a device driver program for a low cost (dot matrix or spinning wheel) printer to process output of a text formatter using the built-in fonts of the printer. Specifications must include descriptions of the fonts to use, the printer's command language and the interface to the formatter. The produced output cannot compete with a high resolution device, but for a lot of applications (e.g. WEB program documentation) the built-in fonts of a dot matrix printer with near letter quality fonts provide useful means to get a faster output than plotting the computer modern fonts on the same device. gendriv and the driver program generated by it are written in WEB and have now been implemented on a Siemens 7.551 computer at Technische Hochschule Darmstadt. Up to now driver programs for NDK S-7700 and Santec S700 have been generated.*

1. Introduction

When we obtained our first copy of TEX in 1981, we had no access to a raster output device to print our output using the computer modern fonts. So we started building our own TFM files [1] and wrote a special driver program for a very low resolution dot matrix printer (about 50 dots per inch) using it's built in fonts. The output was of rather low quality, but we could gather experiences using the TEX system and soon decided to buy a dot matrix printer with a higher resolution and fonts with near letter quality. But all the work building TFM files and implementing a driver program had to be redone.

TEX for Scientific Documentation   D. Lucarella, Editor
Copyright ©1985 Addison-Wesley Publishing Company, Inc.

Extending the available character set was difficult and error prone. In using the dot matrix plot mode for each new character the device specific encoding had to be provided and the dots had to be counted to compute the measures for the TFM file.

Another drawback of our first approach was the fact that – from time to time – after a change of our driver program the width information of some modified characters in the TFM file did not match the width used by the driver program so that the right margin was not straight. So we searched a simpler and safer way to get a driver program from specifications by automatic generation.

The two step formatting process using a device independent intermediate form of the output is similar to the use of an intermediate language in a compiler. Some concepts from compiler compiler design can be adapted to generate a driver program from specifications. This is due to the fact that the driver program corresponds to the code generator produced from machine descriptions in a compiler compiler system. But things are simpler in this case than for a compiler compiler.

We started to design a driver generator, called **gendriv** [2], which would accept a complete description of a printer's commands, it's fonts and as an extension to the built-in fonts some additional characters that must be composed either from existing characters, but appearing as a single character to the formatting program, or can be composed from a dot matrix raster.

In addition the interface to the formatting program had to be flexible (not only accounting for another change in the format of TeX's DVI files [3],[4]) to allow processing of a broad range of intermediate languages. The syntax and semantics of formatter output had to be specified. From these a DVI interpreting program segment is generated.

The input language of **gendriv** has a free format and the use of upper and lower case characters is not significant (with the exception of character and string constants). Comments may be introduced freely (as in TeX). Character and string constants are converted to binary values using the **ASCII** coding scheme (even on our Siemens computer using the **EBCDIC** set). All character constants can also be denoted decimal or hexadecimal.

The next chapter gives an overview of the specifications needed to drive an output device and to generate the font descriptions. Chapter 3 covers the interface to a text formatter, in this case TeX. The error handling and performance of **gendriv** and it's generated driver program is the topic of chapter 4. In the last chapter 5 a conclusion is given.

2. The Output Device

First we consider the description of basic operations, like switching of fonts, selection of bold or elongated printing modes, application of programmed character spacing, encoding of move operations and some special purpose commands such as page eject or initialization command sequences. In the second part we cover font descriptions and the third part surveys extensions by additional characters.

2.1 Basic Device Commands

All operations provided by a printing device are usually accessed via so called **escape sequences**. The name stems from the fact that most commands start with the ASCII control character ESC(escape=X'1B').

But neither the generator program nor the generated driver program insist on usage of this special character code. It is absolutely legal to define control ("escape") sequences starting with a device control code as DC1(device control 1=X'11') for example.

In the device definition section of the specifications the following information must be provided:

1. How can we move the printing head across the paper? For TEX we must supply move commands for all directions (up, down, left and right). Moving up on the page can be avoided only if the characters for a page are sorted from top to down before printing anything, because the DVI file contains the output for a single page in any order. Sorting the output avoids problems with mechanical inaccuracies and thus gives more precise positioning. The distances to skip are automatically encoded into a command character sequence when a move has to be done. To allow this the distance for a one unit move has to be specified.

2. For any **font** you want to use you must supply a command sequence to switch to this font. This command sequence is associated with a name, which can be used to designate the proper font when the character widths are specified.

3. If the font can be printed in a different fashion, e.g. bold, elongated or slanted, or if you can switch some font positions to get characters from a national variant of the character set (this is common in Germany for the umlaut characters), you can define a **mode**, associated with the whole set of characters or some subset.

4. At least for one kind of character **spacing** a specification has to be given. In the simplest case the print head moves automatically by the width of the character after printing. However a program mode spacing is supported also allowing the driver program to encode the amount to move before or after each character. For

each font a character spacing has to be specified. Any description of a character spacing includes a name for use in the specifications of built-in fonts.
5. To implement TEX's horizontal and vertical rules we need a feature to paint a given rectangle. This can be done if the device allows access to the dots of the print head to plot any dot raster. The encoding for one column of dots and the covered area must be specified.
6. At the beginning and at the end of a print job and any time a single page starts or is finished some special action has to be done. It is good practice to do a software reset for the printer at the beginning and at the end so that no selections from the previous or for the next print job can mix things up. On a printer that can use single sheets of paper a sheet must be inserted first and dropped after all characters for the page have been printed. For all these actions a special command sequence can be specified which is sent to the device at the appropriate moments.

2.2 The Built-in Fonts

Even a generator program cannot avoid describing each character's dimensions. But if a character is used several times, e.g. to build special symbols as a combination of simple characters, we can make do with entering each character's values just once.

The names of the different dimensions of a character that are going to be used in the description must be declared. For all character sets that TEX is supposed to use we generate a list of character attributes in a PL file. This file, after adding some information about the kind of font (for the wizards: these are the fontdimen parameters etc.), can be transformed into a TFM file by the standard program **PLtoTF** [5] that comes with TEX. For any other formatter an equivalent program would have to be supplied, but this is quite a simple task.

For each character a list of dimensions can be given. These usually include width, height and depth. If the PL-processing program and the formatter allow it, any of these dimensions can be left out. To ease data entry characters sharing the same dimensions can be combined (even using character ranges), so that a font with fixed widths for all characters can be specified giving the first and last character of the font and their three dimension values.

Unfortunately most people do not like fonts with fixed character spacing very much. That means entering a little more information to use a font with proportional character spacing.

Some devices are able to emphasize a character by enlarging the width (or even the height) e.g. by doubling each column (or row) of the stored character raster. Since this is common we allow copying a character set description thereby modifying any (or all) of its character parameters with a single instruction. It is possible to do any constant multiplication (division), or addition (subtraction) of a constant amount to a parameter for all characters in a font. This saves a lot of time in entering a slightly modified character set.

2.3 Defining Additional Characters

Although additional scientific character sets are available for some printing devices now and again a special character that does not belong to any given font is needed for a document.

In this case we can probably construct the needed character in one of two ways:
1. The character can be built from several given characters using overstriking and moving characters, e.g. a symbol for the empty set is often constructed from a slash and a zero at the same printing position. The resulting dimensions can be calculated automatically.
2. On a dot matrix printer it is easy to supply a new character by giving its raster description, that is for the area to be used by the character we specify which parts should stay white and which should be made black (assuming we print black dots on white paper). Knowing the size of a single black dot we can compute the size of the character automatically again.

Both kinds allow specifications of new named "synthetic" fonts consisting of composed or plotted characters respectively. Characters in these fonts can be accessed like any character of a built-in font that has been described, using the name of the font and the character position.

3. The Formatter: TEX

To be able to use a formatter's output the syntax and semantics of the output must be given. But if we want to use our printer as if the computer modern roman fonts were available, we have to do a little more. If we can map the computer modern fonts to our fonts, this allows us to work with very few modifications of the **plain** or any other format. We just have to change the (preloaded) fonts and supply others that masquerade as equivalents.

Anyway it is not possible to achieve the same layout as with the computer modern fonts since we use the character dimensions of the fonts in our output device.

3.1 Font Mapping

To build a font for use by TEX involving as few modifications as possible we must map the positions of any computer modern font to the equivalent characters in any of our fonts described before. The mapping can be done by means of a table. To each position of the TEX font a character is associated. Ranges of characters can be mapped with a single assignment.

For most printers the textfont, scriptfont and scriptscriptfont assignments will be the same because no smaller characters are available. This reduces the amount of work, but there are still the bold, a typewriter style, the italic, the symbol and the extension fonts.

3.2 DVI Processing

The DVI commands have to be interpreted to produce the desired output on a device. This interpretation is generated from the syntactic rules of the DVI language, extended by semantic actions in PASCAL.

The rules may assign scanned values to variables that can be used in the semantic actions. These values include records and arrays for structured and repeated values, respectively. The maximum number of repetitions must be finite, the actual maximum value is an implementation dependent constant of the generator program.

The grammar of the DVI language must not use recursion. This is assured by the fact that no rule may use a forward reference. For the current version of TEX's DVI files this is no restriction.

To simplify the semantic actions several standard routines are used in all generated driver programs and are implemented in a common kernel:

1. The function **setchar(character,fontnumber)** sets a character of the given fontnumber at the current position on the page and returns the width of the character. This width can be used to update the current position.

2. **fontdef(fontnumber,fontname)** links a **fontnumber** to a font with the name **fontname**. The **fontnumber** is used by **setch** to select the desired font. It is impossible to link to a font that was not part of the same run of **gendriv**.

3. The routines **pagestart(pageno)** and **pageend** keep track of the page structure and send the special sequences for entering and leaving a page to the device. The parameter **pageno** can be used to select pages if only parts of a formatted document have to be printed. The ten counters used in **DVItype** [6] are not supported for selection, but one of them can be mapped to **pageno** by the semantic actions.

4. To set horizontal or vertical rules we provide the kernel procedure **rule(height, width)**. It generates a black rectangle of the desired height and width. The dimensions correspond to the dimensions of the current position.

The current position is held in global variables **xpos** and **ypos**. Their dimension is determined by the generator program and cannot be modified by the DVI file. This is no restriction for a stable version of TEX.

4. Use of gendriv

gendriv is implemented on a Siemens 7.551 computer under the operating system BS2000. It has been ported successfully to a MC68000 based PCS CADMUS 9230 computer under the MUNIX operating system.

A driver has been generated for a NDK S-7700 dot matrix printer and a driver for a Santec dot matrix printer is under development. First outputs have been produced already.

4.1 Error Handling

Syntactical errors in the description language are detected and reported by the generator program.

TEX may detect missing characters during the formatting of a text, that have been omitted from the map. These characters should be added to the description and then **gendriv** must be run again. If the fonts lack enough font parameters for math formulas, the font parameter section of the PL files has to be checked. Since these are not produced by **gendriv**, there is no need to rerun the generator program.

If the generated driver program cannot find a font, check your document and/or formats, where the unknown font is (probably a computer modern font has survived). A look at the font list at the end of the DVI file with DVItype may give you a hint.

In case you get other characters than you wanted, you will have to check the font maps of your computer-modern-look-alikes. To help you, you can get a font table from the driver program that corresponds to the tables in appendix F in The TEXbook [7].

4.2 Performance

To generate the driver and the PL files for the NDK S-7700 takes about 20 seconds on our Siemens 7.551.

To run the driver on about 70 pages of WEB program listing takes about 120 seconds. This is less than TEX took to format these pages (about 280 seconds), but about twice as long as our hand-made driver program takes (about 50 seconds). The additional runtime for the generated driver is due to the fact that it uses a lot of tables (with calculation of addresses for the indices), where the hand-tailored program can use a constant, because it knows the device it uses.

However both programs are fast compared to the printing speed on the device.

5. Conclusion

gendriv reduces the effort needed to produce a driver using built-in fonts. Modifications and additions of characters are made easy and safe.

This makes the use of low cost devices even more attractive for output that needs not be portable to other sites. Especially WEB programmers will find helpful that their program listings are printed faster than by using the computer modern fonts when plotted on the same device. Furthermore space requirements for the driver are much less than for a raster device driver, where the raster must be completely set up on the host machine. This even allows use of a personal computer to drive the output device.

References

1. *D. Fuchs:* TeX font metric files. TUGboat, No. 1, Vol. 2 (1981), pp. 12–16
2. *K. Guntermann:* Ein Ansatz zur automatischen Erzeugung von Ausgabetreibern für die Ansteuerung von Zeichendruckern durch Textformatierer. Dissertation, Technische Hochschule Darmstadt, Fachbereich Informatik, 1984 (in German).
3. *D. Fuchs:* The format of TeX's DVI files, version 1. TUGboat, No. 1, Vol. 1 (1980), pp. 17–19
4. *D. Fuchs:* Device-independent File Format. TUGboat, No. 2, Vol. 3 (1982), pp. 14–19
5. *D. E. Knuth:* PLtoTF, in TeXware, Version 2, July 1983, pp. 301–353
6. *D. E. Knuth:* DVItype, in TeXware, Version 2, July 1983, pp. 401–451
7. *D. E. Knuth:* The TeXbook. Addison-Wesley, Reading, Massachussets, 1984

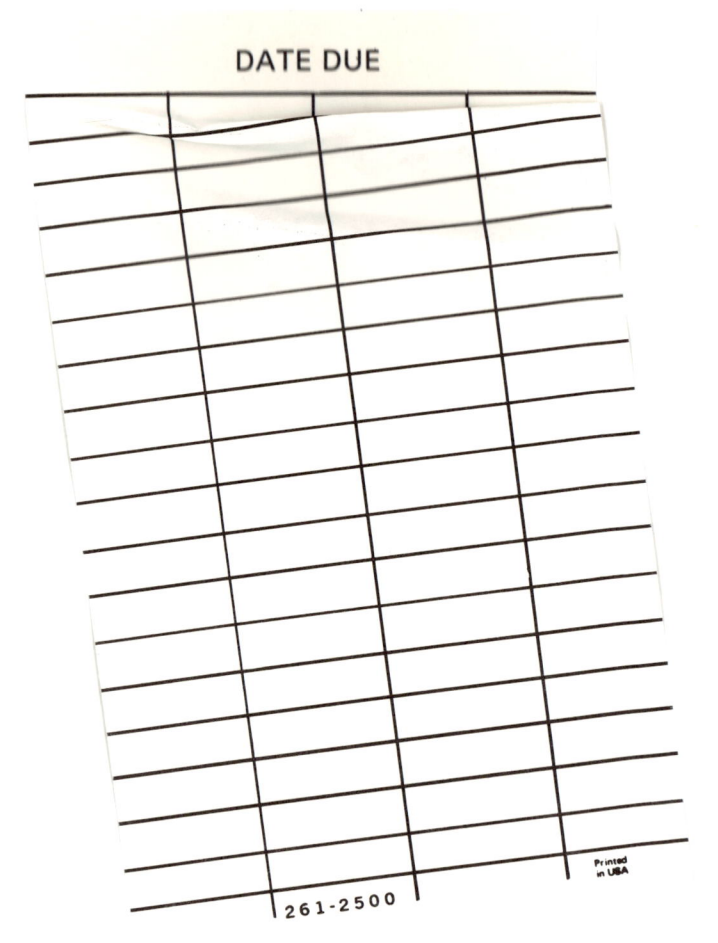

DATE DUE

261-2500

Printed in USA

277636

Other Publications Of Interest From Addison-Wesley

MicroTEX   David Fuchs' full implementation of the TEX language for the IBM PC/XT, AT, PC with a hard disk, and compatible machines, and including a driver for dot matrix printers. MicroTEX gives results that are "indistinguishable from those obtained on mainframe computers." (D. E. Knuth)

The TEXbook   Donald E. Knuth's definitive user's guide and reference manual for TEX.

TEX: The Program   The "almost final" source code listings for the TEX program.

LATEX: A Document Preparation System   Leslie Lamport's complete and most current user's guide and reference manual for his LATEX macros.

I AM INTERESTED.

To receive more information about any of these, or to hear about Addison-Wesley's future books and software for computerized typesetting, simply fill in and mail this reply card.

Name_____   Title_____

Company/School_____

Street Address_____

City_____   State___ Zip_____

Country_____

Specific Interest_____

_____

_____

_____

Or call Addison-Wesley at (617) 944-3700, extension 2677

SOUTHEASTERN MASSACHUSETTS UNIVERSITY
Z253.4.T47 E95 1985
Proceedings of the First European Confer

3 2922 00017 151 9

DATE DUE

MAY 3 1 2007		
MAY 3 1 2007		

Demco, Inc. 38-293

BUSINE
FIRST CLASS

Postage Will Be P

NO POSTAGE
NECESSARY
IF MAILED
IN THE
UNITED STATES

ADDISON-WESLEY
PUBLISHING COMPANY, INC.
Reading, Massachusetts U.S.A. 01867

Dept. CM